AN IMPRINT OF WHAT BOOKS PRESS | LOS ANGELES

ALSO BY CHUCK ROSENTHAL

HOW THE ANIMALS AROUND YOU THINK

THE SEMIOTICS OF ANIMAL COGNITION

Publisher's Cataloging-In-Publication Data
Names: Rosenthal, Chuck, 1951- author.
Title: How the animals around you think : the semiotics of animal cognition / C.P. Rosenthal.
Description: Topanga, CA : Giant Claw, an imprint of What Books Press, [2019] | Includes
    bibliographical references.
Identifiers: ISBN 9781532341427
Subjects: LCSH: Cognition in animals. | Biology--Semiotics.
Classification: LCC QL785 .R67 2019 | DDC 591.5/13--dc23

Cover art: Gronk, *untitled*, 2018
Book design by Ash Good, www.ashgood.design

Giant Claw
363 South Topanga Canyon Boulevard
Topanga, CA 90290

HOW THE ANIMALS AROUND YOU THINK
THE SEMIOTICS OF ANIMAL COGNITION

C.P. Rosenthal

For the animals

CONTENTS

"Though sentience is doomed, we vow to save all of it."

—Shunryu Suzuki

INTRODUCTION

THE THEOLOGICAL ARGUMENT against animal consciousness has long been based on the belief that the other animals do not have immortal, spiritual souls in which thought, virtue, emotion, and sin can adhere. For the philosopher the dividing line is language. Thought is language and language is thought. We have it, they don't. For the scientist, as long as animal behavior (and for some, even human behavior) can be explained without adding on speculations about consciousness, then further speculation about animal consciousness is superfluous. It is the law of science (Ockham's Razor) that the simplest explanation is the best. The theological, philosophical, and scientific arguments are all rigid boundaries protected by sturdy walls, but history has taught us that all walls, be they ideological or actual, will eventually fall. I hope to put some chinks in those walls by exposing some of their paradigms or building blocks.

In the realm of science, the line between people who are willing to talk about animal consciousness and people who are not is often drawn between the kinds of evidence a person is willing to consider. Hard science, behaviorist reductionism, relies on controlled, laboratory experimentation where the experimenter can look at one specific behavior in one, isolated circumstance and repeat the experiment over and over. Soft science, in terms of animals, now called animal anthropology or cognitive ethology, studies animals in context and makes inferences based on those observations. For the hard scientist, those inferences are speculative and those observations suspect to too many uncontrolled contingencies, including the motives and biases of the observer. The "facts" derived from these kinds of studies are not considered experimental, but *anecdotal*, and anecdotes are more like stories than they are science.

Rather than list dozens of circumstances where it *looks* like the animals around me are thinking, I want to talk about common animal behavior that we have all observed over and over and show that in the same way that language demonstrates that I am thinking, these animals are using signs in order to negotiate their worlds, sometimes even to communicate. Much of my analysis will be phenomenological and the behavior, because it will be behavior anyone can observe, will be paradigmatic, not anecdotal, though anyone who has lived with animals for decades has dozens of amusing stories and I won't refrain from telling some of those, as well. I will use examples from the lives of the domestic animals I have known to demonstrate what I'm talking about. I hope to show that understanding this signing behavior, and explaining animal behavior with it, is often simpler than reducing that behavior to thoughtless reactions.

The following essay is a phenomenological analysis of non-human animal behavior using semiotics, social psychology, and Kantian epistemology to construct a cognitive-emotional model of sentient behavior that includes human behavior, as well.

It isn't science. It's a philosophy. Of animals.

PET ME WHILE I EAT

THE CHEESE IS A BIG, SILVER CAT with vertical black stripes. He has leapt from our upper deck through the second story window and now sits on the sill. He looks across the room at me and says, "Meow. Meow-meow." Most cats, in fact, do not say *meow*, but that's one way in which the Cheese is unusual. He wants to eat, but he will not go downstairs to check the food bowls; I must accompany him.

I get up from my chair and he sprints down the stairwell, waiting for me at the bottom of the stairs. When I get there, we walk through the laundry room to the cat room, a small area between the sauna and shower where we keep the cat bowls on a three foot high bench, because if we don't keep the cat food in the air, then dogs will eat it.

He jumps up on the bench. The cat bowls are full. If you own cats you might venture to say, loosely, as I do, that they like rituals. This is an important one. So I reach in the plastic cat food container, grab a bit of dry food and pretend to feed him, putting a little bit in each bowl as the Cheese purrs and arches his back, rubbing against my forearm. And though I wouldn't hold to this beyond my own conjecture, I'll point out that it's evening and the Cheese comes now, when everybody, particularly the other cats, have settled into their evening patterns, because the Cheese prefers to eat without the other cats around him, though there are contextual exceptions.

But he's not eating just yet. First I have to begin to pet him, then he'll settle against my hand, arching into it and purring as he eats. Unlike dogs, who might even be surly or defensive while they devour their food, cats like to be petted while they eat. And often enough, at breakfast most often, I've got all of them in there, four or five or however many, purring and rubbing against my hands.

There's another cat food area in the kitchen where another cat, Romeo, often prefers to eat. Here in the cat room, if the faire is merely dry food, the Cheese will try to wait out the others and eat by himself with me, though if I'm opening a small can of moist food, as I do in the morning, he usually can't wait because the others will eat it all, though sometimes he just gets pissed off and leaves or doesn't show up at all; some things, some times, are more important than food.

But let's go back. It's night time. I've petted the Cheese while he ate and gone back upstairs. Then, from the bottom of the stairs I hear a call. "Meow." He's not done. Well, I could say the hell with him. Surely, if he were hungry enough, he'd just go eat, but I like him and like petting him. I put my book down, get up and walk to the top of the stairway. There he is at the bottom, looking at me, "Meow-meow. Meow-meow-meow."

Let's take a moment and look at what's going on here. The Cheese is meowing at the bottom of the stairs. He began by meowing up the stairway to someone he couldn't see to ask for something that wasn't in front of him. Loosely, because I'll have to talk about what it means to use the word *know*, I might say that the Cheese knew I was upstairs. More so, I'd venture that he isn't even calling for food. He knows perfectly well that there is food in the bowls; we were just in there. Needless to say, he knows, as well, where the food bowls are. He's calling so I will come downstairs and then *do* something that is now not being done, pet him while he eats.

This behavior is more complicated than a simple gesture. For example, let's say a new kitten, Italo, shows up. In the morning, when I'm dividing up that single can of wet food into bowls, the goal is greater than the risk of the Cheese getting miffed and batting somebody around, in fact, as I've said, it might be the Cheese who gets so pissed off that he leaves after a few bites and comes back later. At night, when their bellies are full, everybody is more likely to leave him alone or try to use the food bowls in the kitchen, unless Romeo is guarding them. There might be a pile of abstract behavior in all that, but for now let's not try to read into it. It might simply be reduced to in-the-moment impulses ruled by how badly they want to eat versus how much they want to avoid a fight.

But Italo, who is young, doesn't seem to know or care if his presence pisses the Cheese off, and jumps up onto the cat bench. He might even butt his head into the same bowl the Cheese is using. The Cheese hisses and bats him on the head. Italo backs up and blinks. Though he's much bigger than Italo and could knock him silly, the Cheese jumps down and leaves; runs up the stairs and jumps out the window. The young knucklehead Italo follows him.

In this behavior there is a simple exchange of gestures. Italo appears. The Cheese reacts. Someone might venture to translate the Cheese's swat as saying, "Get out of here!" or "Leave me alone!" but those would be pretty liberal translations. The Cheese cannot say either of those things. He's irritated; he swats. Yet even that is an interpretation, a translation, which very much changes the actual character of what happened in front of me, because I can say that's what happened and the Cheese can't. So does it mean something? Did the Cheese *mean* anything? What do we mean by *mean*? Possibly, in the future, when Italo gets bigger, he might swat back and then the Cheese will swat back again. In fact, outside the house, the Cheese might very well get into a full-fledged fight (I'd venture territorial) with a cat near his size. That's a different behavior in a different context, so let's not go there yet. For now, a swat is a swat, a behavior.

In 1934 a social psychologist named George Herbert Mead wrote a book entitled *Mind, Self, & Society*. The prevailing behaviorist back then was a man named John B. Watson and he believed what all behaviorists yet believe, that all behavior, both animal and human, is determined by genetics and environment and if we knew all the factors we could predict any behavior. The paradigm was Pavlov and his dogs that salivated at the ringing of a bell after being fed when a bell was rung. We didn't need to know whether or not the dogs felt hunger, only that the dogs, over time, associated the ringing bell with being fed, so when they heard the bell they salivated. That association was seen as mechanical as the heat button on your toaster. More so, the dogs didn't choose to salivate, nor could they choose not to salivate, they simply did. Much of human behavior, if not all of it, was seen this way, too. Science didn't need to speculate about the soul or mind, or feelings, things we couldn't observe or prove, because a person's thoughts or intentions (let alone an animal's) were irrelevant to the scientific study of their observable behavior.

Critically, there are already problems here. In humans, at least, feelings are observed, thoughts, feeling, and intentions are expressed in language, however relevant or irrelevant they might be to behavior. Of course, animals can't report on their feelings or intentions. Though more crucial to my argument here, is the comparison of Pavlov's dogs' *association* of the bell with being fed, whether the mechanical metaphor is adequate, regardless of whether or not their salivation was immediate, un-self-conscious, or even determined, i.e. there can be describable cognitive behavior even granting those constraints once we examine the act of association.

Mead regarded himself as a scientist, too. He was, as well, a Darwinist and very influenced by a late 19th century American school of philosophy called Pragmatism. He didn't want to talk about the mind or the soul either, not in any spiritual or ontological way, though at the time, the early 20th century, in terms of behavior, the battle lines were yet continually drawn between the trenches of behavior/determinism and mind/free will (in fact this battle was fought along these lines well into the late 20th century when the philosophical choice was between B.F. Skinner and Jean Paul Sartre). But Mead didn't like the ontological paradigm of behavior determined strictly by genetics and stimulus-response.

Mead was willing to concede that animal behavior was very much determined by genetics and environment, but he didn't like that kind of mechanical, determinist model of the world (let's avoid quantum physics, indeterminacy, and discoherence in discussing animal and human behavior; let's just stay in the phenomenal world in front of us). Mead preferred an organic model. If Watson saw the world like a machine, a complex, sophisticated clock, then Mead preferred the metaphor of a plant. His approach to behavior was not simply "this causes this." He saw behavior, plant, animal, and human, as a dialogue of attitudes and gestures that mutually conditioned each other, which, for him, explained the growth and spontaneity we see all around us.

This was not an argument for animal consciousness. Mead was on his way to explaining the development of language, of symbolic consciousness, by means of what he called the *significant symbol*. Use of significant symbols distinguished the human animal from all the others and permitted us to become self-conscious, to develop a self concept through reflective social interaction.

---

* One might want to take a look at Cheney and Seyfarth's *Baboon Metaphysics, The Evolution of a Social Mind* for a cognitive ethological approach to baboon social behavior in the wild. The book catalogues countless experiments that imply sophisticated social interaction by baboons—intention, memory, communication—and speculates that baboons demonstrate cognition, alluding to Temple Grandin's work with domestic animals and autism, but Cheney and Seyfarth admit that they cannot prove that baboons operate under the recent criteria for cognition, i.e. Theory of Mind, something I will discuss later.

For Mead, mind was the human mind, an *emergent characteristic*, i.e. a phenomenon that emerges from the combination of separate elements, like water emerges from the combination of hydrogen and oxygen. This quality of emergence in our universe accounts for the novelty and spontaneity that promotes change and evolution.

Mind is constituted by our symbolic consciousness, that is, language, an emergent characteristic of our evolving brains and social interaction. Selfhood, or our self concept, arises when our mind, which emerges from our language and culture, encounters other beings and we reflect on our self as a version of other selves. This can only be done in a society of other symbolically conscious human selves. All of this is part of our human evolution.

So, when humans interacted with their environment, they did it reflectively; unlike animals, they could separate themselves from a given stimulus; they could consider, contemplate, predict, and decide using significant symbols, therefore their behavior couldn't be reduced to the behavioral model. But where did this leave animal consciousness? Back where we started. Animals were organic machines, like sophisticated, mobile plants with adaptive central nervous systems, and that was the case whether you believed, like Watson, that humans were organic machines too, or like the 16th century philosopher Rene Descartes who invented the Mind-Body distinction, that humans had souls or minds with thoughts, emotions, intentions and free will.

For Mead, humans evolved into language-using, self-conscious social beings. Animals did not. But on his way to doing what he did, Mead had to compare animal behavior to human behavior and show the difference. This is where he came upon the concept of *the conversation of gestures* (a phrase borrowed from a psychologist named Wundt), which is what Italo and the Cheese just did up there on the cat shelf. Cheese swats Italo. Italo backs up or swats back. The swat is a gesture and we see this kind of thing throughout the animal world: rams fighting, birds doing a mating dance, cats cleaning each other, dogs sniffing butts. It's not that the Cheese didn't *intend* to swat Italo, it's that it's impossible for the Cheese to be aware of his intentions. That would require symbolic consciousness or language and, according to Mead, among many others, animals simply don't have it.

For Mead, if I were to threaten to swat you by raising my hand, I would be communicating to you that I might strike you and simultaneously I would be aware that you understood it. As well, I would be anticipating your response based on our mutual understanding of my threat. For a human, the raised hand is a symbol, an abstract sign from someone to someone about something. If I say, "Let's take a walk" to you, you can understand and visualize the two of us walking together and decide whether you want to or not. My dog, says Mead, simply jumps up excitedly in conditioned reflex; she does not consider, she does not decide. I'll return to this, because this is a distinction that isn't as simple or distinct as Mead might have it.

Of course, we're all aware of the counter examples: dolphins who seem to name their children, the songs of gray whales and birds, seal catching education among the orcas, the signing capabilities of laboratory gorillas, chimps, and bonobos, as well as their apparent ability to recognize themselves in mirrors; it would seem that elephants and cetaceans have exhibited that ability, too. But so far, though it might seem apparent to some of us that these animals are exhibiting the ability to think abstractly, no one has theorized how they might do it. We don't, or barely, understand dolphins, whales, or birds, and likely their songs are not languages, not symbolic communication with a syntax that can adapt or change according to different contexts. The interactions of primates in the wild can be explained, if you're determined enough, as mere conversations of gestures. The signing skills of apes raised by humans do not really demonstrate language, but the ability to respond to and manipulate tactile-visual cues from and to their owners, a little more complex than your dog who grabs your sneakers when you say *walk*.

I must take a moment to digress. I have many friends, animal advocates like me, who talk about the language of animals: talking crows, singing whales, squealing dolphins, warning screams of monkeys and baboons. They say that there are sounds that are used repeatedly in the same contexts to communicate things: predators, the location of food, social hierarchies, etc. But whether or not these are acts of communication might be disputed by those who say we can't establish whether the behavior was intended to do what it apparently accomplishes because animals can't talk to us. Those "signals" well may be rote, un-self-conscious acts; they are not part of a symbolic system that can be adapted to *different* contexts. For example, a monkey might use one sound to warn her group that a terrestrial predator like a lion or snake is approaching, another to indicate the approach of an airborne predator like a hawk, but that is no more language than is jumping up and down when I'm excited. They're just cues. They can't be combined to create new meanings. If dolphins, in fact, have sounds they use for each other, they are no more than that, just sounds applicable in one way to one context, they don't implicate thought. Whether it's dancing bees or predator deceiving birds, the same critique applies. It's all very much like the Cheese swatting Italo. For my part, I'm willing to accept this strict definition of language, but I will argue that we don't need to prove self-conscious intention to demonstrate communication, nor language to demonstrate cognition.

Are we humans the only thinking, feeling beings on earth? Well, signing primates aside, and some of their vocabularies are impressive, it's probably at least as difficult to teach an animal to talk to us as it would be for a dog to teach us how to smell. Let's go back to the Cheese at the bottom of my stairs, apparently meowing to me, whom he cannot see, to come down and do something for him in a place where he isn't. By any definition, the ability to think of something that isn't right in front of you is the ability to hold an abstraction, to think abstractly. Is the Cheese doing that? And if so, how does he do it?

BARKING UP THE
WRONG TREE

HAVE YOU EVER GONE FOR A WALK in the woods with your dog? They like to chase stuff, particularly squirrels. Back in the days when I was studying to become a young philosopher, in a class called epistemology or the theory of knowledge, we talked about this once. (If you've never studied philosophy you might be surprised to find out how often philosophers talk about squirrels). The problem is this: My dog spots a squirrel and lights out after him. In this case it would be my old dog, H.D., who was a squirrel chaser. The squirrel runs up a tree. My dog hops around at the trunk, bouncing off of it, spinning, barking up at the squirrel. From my angle I can see the squirrel hopping from branch to branch above. My dog continues to bark upward. The question is: Does my dog *know* that the squirrel is in the tree?

Common sense might say, well, there's the squirrel and there's my dog barking at him. And from my angle I can confirm that my dog is barking at something that looks like a squirrel. So she knows he's up there. But not so fast. Because my dog cannot confirm that she is aware that she thinks the squirrel is in the tree. She might be correct, but she doesn't *know* it, because knowledge requires self-conscious affirmation. My dog is simply barking at something she sees, a stimulus right above her; there's no thinking involved at all.

Well, even if my dog can't say, "I think there's a squirrel in that tree," can she in fact think there is a squirrel in the tree? Not if she can't think. She's just down there barking up at a squirrel without thinking or knowing that there's a squirrel up there. Certainly, she doesn't know the word *squirrel*. She's just a bunch of bouncing and barking behavior concentrated on a small animal she instinctively chased. I say *instinctively* because I assume no one taught my dog to chase squirrels, though the use of the concept *instinct* to explain behavior isn't without its own problems.

Now what if the squirrel jumps to another tree and my dog doesn't observe that? Now she's barking up the wrong tree. Is my dog mistaken about the squirrel? Can she be correct or mistaken without knowing or thinking anything? Well, I can realize that she is mistaken, but she can't. I could yell, "You're making a mistake old girl!" which would mean nothing to her.

Let's look at my behavior. Let's say that I still think that the squirrel is in the tree and I'm gazing into it with my binoculars assuming I'm going to spot that squirrel any second now. I've haven't said to myself, "I think there's a squirrel in the tree," or "I know there's a squirrel in the tree." I simply lifted my binoculars and spotted the squirrel. What's the difference? The difference is that if you asked me I might say, "I think there's a squirrel up the tree that my dog is barking at." But wait. Let's put the squirrel back in the tree for a moment. H.D. was barking at something. Right now, I know my bookcases are standing behind me even before you ask me. Even before I articulate it, do I not? I turn for a book and there it is. If knowledge is the confirmation of an assumed fact, then it can precede my self-conscious confirmation of that fact. Then H.D. might, as well, know that there is a squirrel in the tree.

Back then, being young philosophers, both our youth and our philosophical natures prevented us from coming to any resolutions to these kinds of problems, but I'm a little older now and I've decided to rethink it.

So my dog chased a squirrel into a tree. She's barking up at him and I raise my binoculars and spot him. Except for the fact that I'm not barking, we're both watching the squirrel. Strictly speaking it is impossible to say whether either of us is more or less conscious of what we're doing except that if you were to ask me if I was aware that I was watching a squirrel I could respond, "Why yes, of course," and my dog could not. If that's how I define *intention, thinking,* and *knowledge,* then I can do those things and my dog cannot. In fact, thus defined, I would have to say that if the squirrel for some reason fell from the tree and I had no intentions toward it at all, I'd just let it run away. Yet my dog on the other hand, though she would likely grab the little fellow and shake him to death, has no intentions whatsoever. I have the potential to have intentions toward the squirrel and my dog, like a robot, would grab it and kill it without any realization, intention, or emotion.

But I don't believe that. Why not? What happens when the squirrel changes trees and my dog observes its escape? My dog stops barking. I scan the tree and can't find the squirrel and then I lower my binoculars. In that case, my dog's behavior cues mine. My dog stopped barking and I realized that the squirrel was gone. But what change occurred in the behavior of my dog? What caused the change in my dog's behavior? Why did she stop barking?

Let's say I'm first to stop scanning the tree because I observed that the squirrel left. My dog is barking at what I conclude to be nothing. Though in these matters animals are more often correct than I am, even if they don't know anything, for the sake of this argument we'll say that my dog is wrong and there is no squirrel in the tree. My thoughtless dog is barking at nothing at all. Yet though one might argue that my dog can be correct or mistaken without knowing it, that is, I can observe that she is correct or mistaken, but she cannot realize either, we must now face the fact that my dog who once barked at a stimulus, the squirrel, is now just barking. She's just continuing her nutty behavior without a stimulus and will eventually wind down like a clock.

But a clock just winds down and a dog changes her behavior. She barks, barks, looks up into the tree, hesitates, barks a few more times, sits, then gets up and comes to me. However rigidly determined that behavior might be, I surmise that for a while she was barking at something she *thought* was in the tree and stopped when she noticed there was nothing there. More reductively, at some point, without the stimulus in front of her, she stopped barking. But however much I might wish to argue that there is no difference between barking at a squirrel and barking at an absent squirrel, there is a difference in behavior that occurs *in the transition* from barking and not barking and it is dependent on noticing there is no longer a squirrel in the tree. More so, to say that there is no difference in my dog's behavior when she is barking at the squirrel and barking at nothing at all is to imply that the behavior is somehow *in* my dog. For however long she was barking at all, she was barking at a removed stimulus and, once again, however simply or mechanically I wish to interpret it, it requires behavior toward a stimulus that is not present, i.e. abstract behavior.

One alternative is to say that when the squirrel left the tree my dog simply continued barking because she was all riled up like that wound clock. But a mechanical clock isn't prodded to behavior by a stimulus, it's wound up, and my dog, however thoughtlessly she might have pursued the squirrel, was barking at the stimulus, the squirrel, while it was in the tree and after it departed. If you ever watched a dog bark you probably noticed that dogs don't bark at nothing at all; they see something, smell something, or hear a sound. If it's a sound they stop, listen, and if they hear it again they bark again, they might even advance toward it. So if my dog is barking up at nothing, where is the stimulus? In the dog. And when she *notices* that the squirrel is no longer there, her behavior changes. If certain mental acts, however rote or miniscule, do not accompany her behavior, then there is no way to describe how or why she would ever behave at all.

During this brief encounter with the squirrel I seem to have observed several different behaviors and attitudes in my dog. In this next example, about going for a walk, I'll use our new dog, Nadine, a Ridgeback-Catahoula mix. After going bananas when I looked at her and said, "Want to go for a walk?" including running to the closet and grabbing my shoes, biting my feet as I put on my socks and sneakers, nuzzling her leash, and then running back and forth from me to the door, in my truck she is less excited. She places her left paw on my right arm as I drive. Often she puts her head on my shoulder. When she does that her eyes get dreamy and her tongue falls out of her mouth sideways. She might lick my neck and right ear, as well.

I know that she recognizes the trailheads, because she removes her paw and lunges when we reach them; if I were to drive beyond the trailhead, she grows agitated and looks out the back window. In fact, her lunging behavior begins when I turn up the road that leads to the trailhead. Something about the road that leads to the trailhead, the trailhead that she cannot yet see, triggers the same behavior as seeing the trailhead. I assume she is anticipating our arrival at the trailhead. When we arrive, she sits very still and does so until I turn off the engine, then she lurches forward again.

Once out of the truck I unleash her and she runs ahead, sniffing the ground, marking spots where I assume other dogs have left their marks. If I stop to urinate, she returns and urinates on top of that. She'll move out ahead of me, return and touch her nose to my knee, than move off again. She displays curiosity. Sounds make her lift her head and tilt it, listening. She pokes her nose into crannies, under logs; she might circle a bush or tree. If she comes to a fork in the path, she'll hesitate. She might wait there or she might choose one, stopping when I reach the fork, moving ahead again if I follow her, following me if I choose the other way and then once again running ahead. We are now in the rhythm of the walk and these behaviors are performed without effort, in a kind of fluidity of pleasure. If I call to her, "Nadine," she'll pause and look at me, eyes wide, tongue slightly out, an expression of active pleasure, in fact I needn't say her name at all. She listens very closely and will return to look at me if I make the slightest of sounds. If she has simply moved out of my sight, she will return to look at me and be off again. Aside from her enthusiasm and apparent pleasure, she seems capable of displaying other expressions, too.

Interestingly, if someone else is parked at the trailhead, Nadine will circle their vehicle, sniffing, mostly at the wheels. Because dogs urinate at the wheels of cars, I assume this is what she's smelling. But as we proceed down the trail, Nadine will often depart from the main trail and begin moving down a tributary. If I follow her, she'll lead me to the people who came in the other car. Just following a scent, you might say, the way I'd follow something I could see. But not quite. If I see people and follow them, then I am following precisely what I see. For Nadine, the smell is present, but not the people. Reductively, one would have to say that she simply follows the smell without anticipating anything else. She's not following the people and their dogs, she's just following the scent and that she's following the scent without expecting to find anything; that would imply that she could hunt without actually hunting *for* anything, dispositions such as hunger aside.

Now we're back on the main trail and a squirrel pops out. For a moment my dog comes to complete attention, stiff, head up, and then lights out after the squirrel. Suddenly her behavior is much more singularly concentrated. When the squirrel climbs the tree my dog hits the trunk with her front paws and springs upward as if she might climb the tree herself if she could. Now the barking. Her behavior is aggressive, almost angry; the barks are not like the sounds she uses to beg or wake me up, yips and whines, not the inquisitive growls offered when she is in my house and hears a sound outside, not the warning yaps toward a stranger who's entered my yard, not the yips when she plays with my kitten or the rumbles she uses to get my attention while I'm reading. I don't translate barks into English, but I know that one is different from another and used at different times in different contexts, not language, admittedly, but as I shall argue, signs.

When she seems to notice that the squirrel is gone she hesitates, as I described earlier with H.D. It's interesting that when she abandons the chase, she does not scoot ahead, returning immediately to her walk behavior, but comes to me almost calmly. I pet her, then she springs ahead again. If we were to encounter other situations, people she doesn't recognize, people she does, other dogs, someone on horseback or mountain bike, Nadine would display different behaviors.

I want to talk in more detail about animal emotions later, so I've tried to describe my walk with Nadine as a series of transitions to different behaviors without reading emotions into them. But it's very difficult to describe some of these transitions without apparently describing the transition from one emotional state to the next, as if a dog exhibiting the behavior of excitement was, in fact, not feeling excited, or a calm dog was not feeling calm. How could a calm dog become excited unless it was stimulated into excitement? If not, I'm asked to imagine that non-human animals are the most stunning kind of stoics who can display radically different behaviors while feeling nothing.

If different emotions do not accompany different behaviors, it is impossible to talk about different behaviors or how transitions from one behavior to another could occur at all. In the animate world, change and feeling go hand in hand. But up till now, because animals don't talk, we haven't had a model, a theory, which allows us to explain or even experiment with how animals might think and feel. Without a theory, people who believe in animal consciousness, I'll call them conceptualists, have been reduced to pointing at examples that seem to imply thought, but these examples can't prove thought and, as well, can be explained by behavioral models, even if those models seem to confound common sense.

Let's go back to the Cheese and George Herbert Mead. Mead was not a strict behaviorist but, as he sometimes described himself, a social behaviorist. He believed that *mind* was an emergent characteristic of language and social interaction. And as a number of thinkers of that time began to realize, meaning was not something that found its expression through language, meaning arose *in* language. This position has grown to prevalence in Western epistemology since the middle of the 19th Century and dominates now.

As a Darwinist, and like Darwin, Mead didn't believe that these abilities had no precedent in what he called the "lower forms;" they evolved from the conversation of gestures used by animals in interaction. Mead, as well, believed that the other organisms must possess *attitudes* toward stimuli, and defined an act "as an impulse that maintains the life process by the selection of certain sorts of stimuli it needs. Thus, the organism creates its environment. The stimulus is the occasion for the expression of the impulse" (MS&S, 6).

Animals create their environments by their attitudes toward finding food, procreation, defending territory, finding safety, raising young, etc. and somehow these things are done, without exception, in a kind of blind, or as philosopher Christine M. Korsgaard might say, "wanton" running from one sensation, one stimulus, to the next. Mead was out to save humanity from the behaviorists by handing them the other animals. Once again he found the key to separating us from the lower forms to be symbol use or language.

For my part, the hinge on the door here swings on the word *attitude*. What is an attitude? A predisposition to behave? It's hard to describe it without seeing it as something that accompanies behavior, if not preceding or lying in anticipation of behavior, something a little different from behavior itself, however much one might wish to explain it as something like "instinct" or "hard wiring," some disposition purely biological.

Among the examples of the difference between humans and animals Mead offers is, well, a man on a walk with his dog in the woods. They come to a chasm. The dog runs back and forth trying to find a point where he can cross. The man, who was simply following the path, has had his walk interrupted and suddenly his mind must contemplate a solution.

> The dog and the man would both try to find a point where they could cross. But what the man could do what the dog could not would be to note that the sides of the chasm seem to be approaching each other in one direction. He picks out the best places to try, and that approach which he indicates to himself determines the way in which he is going to go. If the dog saw at a distance a narrow place he would run to it, but probably he would not be affected by the gradual approach which the human individual symbolically could indicate to himself (Mead, *Mind, Self, and Society*, 122-3).

But this explanation does more to obscure than clarify the distinction between the man and the dog. The dog *tries* to find a place to cross and runs to the narrower place *if* he sees it. The man follows the narrowing, which Mead concludes the dog "probably" cannot do. But even if that debatable conclusion is true, how does the dog differentiate between wider and narrower at all? When and how does the dog conclude that it's narrow enough to cross? Why is the dog trying to cross at all? To a mindless creature, what's the difference between crossing and not crossing? How do we explain these cognitive transitions that Mead simply overlooked in his desire to show the difference between the man and the dog?

Back to the squirrel: supposedly, though my behavior and H.D.'s behavior were comparatively the same, the difference lay in that I could examine the choices I made and she could not examine hers; in effect she made no choices at all, despite that fact that she chose, she changed, and we behaved the same. I can account for my cognitive transitions, she, if she has any, cannot account for hers.

A number of cognitive ethologists have tried to argue for animal consciousness by noting the similarities between humans and animals, not the differences, in terms of observable behavior and the structure of our brains (there are a number of books; the most thorough, I think, is Donald R. Griffin's *Animal Minds*, which catalogues hundreds of experiments in the wild that seem to require animal intelligence). The problem being that though it might make sense to infer that certain animal behaviors, migration for example, or deception or warning cries, imply abstract thinking, we can't demonstrate it. *We don't know how they do it.* Well, is there space between the conversation of gestures and the significant symbol that we haven't explored?

A half century before Mead wrote *Mind, Self, and Society* another American thinker was at work theorizing about symbols and consciousness: Charles Sanders Peirce.

Peirce wrote volumes and published almost nothing, though many now consider him the founder of American Pragmatism and America's greatest philosopher. He had a huge influence on William James (who first theorized the social realized self in his *Psychology*), who in turn influenced Mead. Mead's concepts the *I* and the *Me* were borrowed directly from James. Mead's significant symbol is, in fact, the same as Peirce's concept of the symbol, the culmination of Peirce's semiotics or theory of signs.

It's interesting that across the Atlantic, in France, another philosopher, named Ferdinand Sausure, was developing a theory of signs around the same time as Peirce. Sausure's theories of language would go on to have tremendous influence on European thought, spawning semiology, structural anthropology, structuralism, post-structuralism, Lacanian psychoanalysis, and deconstruction. Peirce's semiotics didn't spawn much of anything.

For Sausure, the meaning of a word, a sign, is arbitrary. Any given sound could become a sign by being attached to a signified object or concept (*Langue*). Then, it's usage, that is, how it functions syntactically in a language (*Parole*) establishes its meaning. When a signifier, a word, is attached to a signified, a thing or concept or another word, a sign arise and its meaning develops in its use in a language applied in a context for its use. As influential as this insight was, it's precisely what falls apart under the analysis of Deconstruction and Post-structuralism. But for our purposes, Sausure's theories, like Mead's, meaning is locked into human symbolic communication, i.e. language. On the other hand, Peirce's semiotics fills that gap between gesture and significant symbol.

I'm going to deal with only the very core of Peirce's sign theory, his concepts of the icon, the index, and the symbol. These are the three basic signs. A sign is something that stands for something to someone, in Peirce's terminology, a *sign* stands for some *object* to an *interpretent*. The object needn't be a thing; it can be a concept or another sign and, interestingly, the interpretent needn't be a human mind, it might even be another sign. For Peirce, the world of meaning, what we call reality, is constructed from this web of triads, i.e. signs, so this quickly gets very complex. These three types of signs are also direct expressions of what he calls his *phenomenological categories* and for this reason there are a few things I'm going to leave out when I talk about these signs. Peirce was willing to go there, but we don't have to. The Cheese is still at the bottom of the steps saying, "Meow-meow."

Peirce's first basic sign is the *icon*. An icon is just as you might think it is. It's a sign that looks like the thing it represents. A picture or a photograph of a dog is an iconic sign of a dog. Let's say it's a photo of my dog, Nadine. Then the photo is the icon/sign that stands for Nadine, the object, to me, the interpretent (or my interpreting symbol-using consciousness, yet another sign). For our purposes, that icon is most often visual, but it could be a smell, a sound, a taste, or something I touch or feel. It smells like popcorn in here; that wail sounds like a fire engine; this tastes like the wine I had yesterday; this feels like silk.

For an icon to function as a sign, it must be recognized and, if the object it represents is not standing right in front of me, it requires me to remember that object.

For our purposes it's interesting to note that a memory occurring in iconic signs is likely accompanied by emotions and an explosion of other iconic signs. When I see a picture of my deceased dog, Piccolo, a dozen memories of his big-heartedness flash to me: his apparent joy to get a snack, his frantic barking at strangers, as well as the sequence of putting him down in the middle of the night after his coming to our bed, whining in pain. These memories might include his smell, his bark, the feeling of his fur against my hand. My eyes might water or my chest ache a little, I feel fondness, affection, sorrow. These memories are icons standing for Piccolo to me. I'm going to call this *iconic consciousness* and we'll have to return to it, but let's note here that these icons of memory will flash to me without any act of awareness or will on my part; I can have them without my saying, "I am having memories of Piccolo," in fact without my employing any language at all.

Peirce's second basic sign is the *index*. An index points to its object. I come to a T in the road. On the road sign an arrow points left. Maybe next to it is the name of a town, Wattsburg, and I now know that "Wattsburg is that way." The arrow is the indexical sign, like a pointing index finger, Wattsburg the object, and my consciousness contains the interpretent. An index is a little more abstract than an icon in that it requires its object in order to be anything at all. A picture is a picture, an image, in and of itself whether or not the thing it is a picture of is present or not, though for it to be a sign it must be a picture of something interpreted as that by someone who sees it. An arrow pointing at nothing is not an index. The index needs the existent thing it is pointing at to be an index and needs an interpreter to be a sign.

Once, when I was living in India, I'd just returned from Nepal with a bunch of Nepali rupees. I soon learned that nobody wants Nepali rupees (not even Nepalis), but now, back in India, I sought to exchange them at the National Bank; I was told that no state banks would do it. I entered the National bank in Gangtok, Sikkim, and finding no activity on the first floor, followed some people up the stairs to the second. There were some people sitting on benches, waiting for something, I supposed, and through a window I saw a man in a room, sitting behind a desk, sleeping on his forearms. Then I saw a sign at the corner of a wall. It said, "Cashier," with an arrow pointing left. I walked left until I reached the end of the wall where there was another sign that said, "Cashier" with an arrow pointing right. Between them, nothing at all. You have to love India. But the point is that those arrows weren't indexes because they didn't have an object. An index must point at something. And though an index functions as an index *if it points* and *if it points to something*, for an index to function as a sign it must point at something and someone must make the connection. When that connection is made, the object pointed to is either seen or imagined or remembered, so in that way the index contains a basic element of the icon, it refers to something. Icons represent. Indexes point.

At the top of Peirce's sign hierarchy sits the symbol. The symbol is the emperor of signs. Its nature is completely abstract because it is generally a sound, a word, and its relationship to its object is arbitrary, that is, unlike the icon that looks like its object, or the index that points to its object, the symbol is attached to its object by convention—Peirce uses the terms law, rule, or habit—and that convention is generally language. For example the word *cat* has nothing to do with the animal at my feet; the French use *chat*, the Spanish *gatto*. The sound we use to designate the animal has nothing to do with the animal; any sound could have been assigned within the language, kitty, meesh-meesh, argpurdle, it doesn't matter, because its meaning is derived from its use in a language and use in a sentence in a given context. The meaning of *cat* when I say "The cat is on the mat," is very different from its meaning when I say "He's a real cool cat."

If we were to follow Peirce, we would need to enter a complicated discussion of the nuances of how a symbol acquires its meaning. So far, Peirce is using the word *symbol* much in the way Ferdinand Sausure uses *sign*. But Peirce's understanding of the symbol is distinctly different than Sausure's and they construct their triangles of meaning very differently.

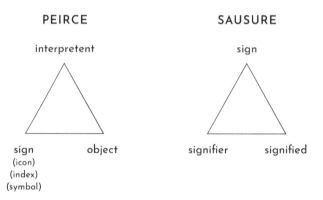

In this schematic comparison, Peirce's symbol functions like Sausure's signifier and his interpretent is equivalent to Sausure's sign. For Sausure, the sign, i.e. meaning, arises *within* the connection between the signifier and the signified. Used in language, it becomes a sign. For Peirce, the connection already exists for the interpretent to connect, though it doesn't become a sign until it arises in the interpretent.

For Sausure, and the Europeans who follow him, meaning only exists at the top of the triangle, in the conventions that govern language signs and in language only. Meaning only occurs in the rules that govern language (*langue*) and its use in a given context (*parole* or speech); the world and the objects of the world do not play a role in how we mean what we say or think. Even apparent icons, like the little man or woman on the bathroom door, function because of the conventions of the connection. For Peirce, the little man is an icon of a man, the little woman an icon of a woman by the picture of the image and what it represents, i.e. the connection, it's meaning, doesn't occur arbitrarily.

For Peirce of the meaning of any sign, be it icon, index, or symbol, contains the thing it indicates. In the case of the symbol, it contains aspects of both the icon and the index. In the sentence *Bill loves Mary*, the symbols *Bill* and *Mary* indicate (point to) Bill and Mary and *love* indicates a kind of affection they feel for each other; within that lies the icon or image we have in our minds of lover and beloved. So though the connection of the sound used in a word (or the written letters) and its relationship to the world is arbitrary, and its meaning constructed by the sentence it's used in, it yet, by virtue of the fact that it contains indexical and iconic elements, points back at the experienced world as a reference. It's meaning isn't completely defined by the language and context, but is defined, as well, by the objects or ideas represented and pointed at.

I've taken a few paragraphs here to discuss ideas that would more properly be treated in several books. These are two very different views of language and consciousness (and they go back as far as the Medieval dispute between Realism and Nominalism, if not Plato and Aristotle). In terms of language theory, that is, how language functions and how it *means*, Peirce's Realism becomes problematic. But in terms of how we *think*, the view that all meaning is in language and language only ignores some fundamental aspects of consciousness that Peirce's semiotics account for, aspects I'll discuss in following chapters. For our purposes, now, if we agree with Sausure, then animals do not employ the conventions of language; they do not mean, they do not think. If we agree with Peirce, then the fundamentals of signing exist in animal behavior.

If the Cheese isn't thinking at the bottom of the stairs, then he's just meowing away for nothing. I'd have to suppose that one day when he was hungry he happened to meow at the bottom of the stairs and I appeared. Then I went down to check the food bowls, which I found empty. I filled them. The Cheese ate, reinforcing his behavior of meowing. I petted the Cheese and that added pleasure became a *contingency* of the reinforcement because genetically, unlike dogs, for some reason or another, cats enjoy being petted while they eat, something that goes back to nursing, something they somehow reiterate without any feeling or memory. In time, the contingency became a part of the reinforcement; the Cheese no longer separated it from being fed; he had to have both. That's the simple answer. The problem is that it's not a simple answer and it doesn't explain much even if it's somewhat correct.

Let me tell you a story, i.e. an anecdote, not evidence. I once lived in a farmhouse in Pennsylvania where I kept a couple dogs and lots of cats. I trained all of them to ring a string of bells that hung outside my back door when they wanted to get in. It was really easy. They came to the door, and in the process of meowing or barking or pawing they eventually struck the bells. Then I let them in. Generally, they learned to strike the bells to get in almost immediately, that is, after the first or second time.

Back then I was a behaviorist and, in fact, for the most part, even in terms of human behavior, I still am. I'm not a mystery to me. Genetics and social conditioning explain most of what I do. But back in Pennsylvania those animals did a couple things that got me thinking. For starters, if I was in the house and didn't come to the door, and then if I didn't come after several rings, they tended to ring the bells *harder*. I was with a friend the first time that happened and he said, "What do you think of that?" and I said, "Well, I guess he really wants to get in."

It was easy to do the follow up experiment. When a cat rang the door bells, I didn't come right away and eventually they rang the bells harder. Off the top, that implied that they might know what they were doing, or at least expected the bell ringing to bring me and when it didn't they got pissed off.

The other thing that I thought I noticed was that despite an experiment I'd read about where cats didn't copy each other's behavior (it's the famous cats-in-a-box experiment where a cat had to press a lever to get out and when one finally did, none of the others imitated it), my new cats seemed to do just that, imitate. One of the veterans rang and got in, then a new cat went up and hit the bells. Since, I've learned that there's a fine line between following and imitating and I don't think the bell behavior was technically imitation. I'll discuss this later.

In a quasi-experiment I pretended to leave the house, then sneaked back to observe the cats. They didn't ring the bells when I wasn't there. They waited for me to come back, which made me think that they connected me being in the house to their getting in, that they saw the bells as an agency for bringing me to open the door, not just a mechanism that caused the door to open, and they remembered whether or not I was inside the house.

These are what a scientist would call anecdotes, and I can't offer them as evidence for animal intelligence or consciousness. There could be a hundred things

I failed to notice. There are no controls. I could just be making stuff up. Each cat could have rung the bells initially by accident. But it was this kind of behavior in the domestic animals around me that got me thinking about animal cognition.

Let's just look at the simple act of ringing the bells. There had to be a *cognitive-emotional transition* between not wanting to get in and then wanting to get in. Those are different things that are related to different behaviors. The bells (and the door, for that matter) had to be *perceived* as a means of entering the house. The cats had to *remember* that ringing the bells got them in. More so, *in* had to be a place they *wanted* to go. And though if you never had a cat or a dog you might argue that they make no connection between the door opening and my opening it to let them out or in, in fact animals request that kind of thing all the time. I'll talk some more about asking behavior later, too. The very least we must notice here is that my coming to the door is inseparable from it being opened and, in the act of ringing the bells, my opening the door must be *anticipated*. However behaviorally reinforced this behavior might be, the behavior is inexplicable without anticipation/cognition. That cognition occurs by means of iconic consciousness, in icon signs.

A behaviorist might point out here that I'm just playing a semantic game; that the difference between sitting under a bush and ringing bells to get indoors is just that, a difference in behavior and there is no animal consciousness experiencing those behaviors or, at the very least, it's superfluous to postulate one. My position is that it is impossible to conceive of behavior without experience, without cognitive-emotional transitions that semiotics explains. I'll examine some examples soon that anyone can observe.

When you start talking about cognition you run into the problem of defining precisely what it is and where it is, that is, though we all seem to be thinking all the time, no one has ever opened a brain and found an idea inside. This falls under a very old philosophical dispute, the mind-body problem. I can't solve that, but as of yet, no one has and maybe nobody can.

But now the Cheese wants me to pet him while he eats. He has an iconic sign of me that he calls to. He expects me to appear. There are smell and taste icons of the food he anticipates, as well as the tactile icons of being petted. He thinks these icons consecutively and repeatedly, like we do. This isn't language. It's not English or French. There's no syntax involved. But it is primitive signing behavior. It explains something else, as well: how animals figure things out.

CROISSANTS ALL DAY LONG!

DOWN THE ROAD FROM OUR HOUSE there's a French café called the Mimosa. Pretty darn convenient. If we wake up and don't feel like making breakfast for ourselves (after feeding everybody else), my partner, Gail, and I can truddle down our steps, go out the tall, wooden gate, down a dozen more steps to reach the road, and then walk to the café for coffee and croissants. On the street we cross behind our carport, then cross an asphalt parking lot that sits in front of a wooden, one-room business structure; it's been a video store, an antique store, now it's a realtors' office. Behind it, stretching steeply up the hill is about a half-acre vacant lot filled with cactuses and wild flowers, oak and fruit trees. The road curves left; we pass a house, a small road, Lookout Trail, heads up the mountain, we cross it and then we're at the café.

Before we had Nadine, we had two other dogs, H.D. and Piccolo. H.D. was a big brown hound mutt, very bright and very stubborn. Piccolo was a big terrier mix, black and white, very hyper, extremely willing to please. We found H.D. as puppy under a trailer at a ranch. Piccolo was older and had been living in a rescue shelter, in a big cage with six other dogs.

One of the things about where we live, Topanga Canyon, is that if there's a place where people gather then there will be dogs there, too, and one day, heading out to the café, Gail said, "Everybody else brings their dogs, let's see if H.D. wants to come."

We couldn't bring Piccolo; he'd be aggressive, nervous, scared, tugging at his leash. No one would enjoy it, not even him, though he likely wouldn't notice if he were enjoying himself or not. But we let H.D. out the gate and she just walked with us down the road (Piccolo whining and barking miserably behind the fence). At the café H.D. immediately went to work, table to table begging for croissants, even pushing other people's dogs out of the way. She barked pretty aggressively at a woman who wouldn't cough up.

"Use your indoor voice!" the woman said.

"Guess this isn't working," said Gail, so we all walked home.

Our property sits on a hillside; I guess technically a small mountain. You have to walk up the steps to our front gate, then another dozen to our ground floor and first decks. Another dozen steps takes you to an intermediate deck, then another twenty to the top deck level with our second floor. Gail's office sits above our house, separately, another flight of ten steps up. A tall, wooden fence, five feet high, lines the property along the vacant lot next door. At the very end of that fence, near the top of the property, we cut a small, square hole; most of the time we covered it with a cement block, but sometimes, when I was home, I opened it and let the dogs do their duty next door in the vacant lot. Piccolo wouldn't go out unless he followed H.D. and because he was raised in a cage for some time he maintained the habit of pooping on the deck and not on grass.

Anyway, the short of it is that the next day we got a call from Claire, the owner of the café. "I think your dog is here. We are trying to close."

I'd been working and not thinking about H.D. but now it was three o'clock and H.D. was sleeping on a couch in the café and wouldn't get off. When Claire tried to move her, H.D. growled. I had to go get her. Once I got her off the couch she followed me home. After that H.D. spent her days, breakfast till three, at the café, begging for croissants and then sleeping on the couch. People I didn't know knew her. I had to go get her at three for a few days, but after that, when Claire closed the place, H.D. got up and came home on her own. Needless to say, there were a lot of very tolerant dog lovers down there.

Potentially there's a lot of complex behavior here, but I only want to talk about one part of it. How did H.D. figure out how to get to the café in the first place? That first day, when I had to go get her, I found that the cement block had been pushed away from the hole in the fence. From there, I could follow a path of pushed down grass diagonally across the vacant lot, behind the Video Store, to the bottom of the lot on the other side where she crossed Lookout Trail and came around a wall where she could then see the café. Soon that became a well-worn path, but how did she do it the first time?

Claire said that the first time she saw H.D. was the morning we brought her with us, so it would seem she hadn't been to the café before that. Because I don't have a sense of smell, I asked people if the café had a smell. People said it smelled a little of coffee, but not of croissants, which weren't baked there, but were trucked in every morning and stored in a glass counter. I would rule out as unlikely that H.D. simply followed the smell of croissants from over a hundred yards away, a smell that people weren't aware of who were sitting in the café, but dogs can really smell. Possibly she associated the coffee smell with croissants and followed that, though that would require her to associate one thing, the smell of coffee, with another, croissants. That kind of association, however mechanical, would require a minimum of abstraction. In any case, it wasn't a smell she'd been responding to previously; she at least had to recognize it, associate it with croissants, then knock the cement block out of the way and head for it on a bee line. That's a possibility. Or she figured out how to get to the café. I want to look at this a bit more closely because it's the kind of "figuring out" behavior we observe in our domestic animals everyday.

Animals are synthetic thinkers. *They put signs together*, they don't analyze them, that is, take ideas apart. The difference between synthetic and analytic thinking was made by Emanuel Kant in the 18th century and since, like most ideas, it's been blown up by, well, analysis, for lack of a better word. But for now, whatever the epistemological arguments for the similarities in how all ideas arise (i.e. Deconstruction), let's just move on with the observation that animals don't analyze ideas, though they do, on occasion, seem to figure things out.

Over twenty-five years ago, when I first moved to Los Angeles, Gail found a late 1940's telephone in an antique store and had it adapted so it could be plugged in the way land lines are today, then she gave it to me. I love that phone. It weighs a ton. It has a hand piece like a big black bone and the sound is the clearest of any phone in our possession, land or cell. It has a big, loud, mechanical ring. The other great thing is that children, raised in the digital, push-button age, can't figure out how to dial it, even after I explain, which should tell us something about the constraints of our experientially acquired conceptual paradigms. But then one day it stopped working. It just went dead.

This could turn into a very long story so I'll just get to the end. I loved that phone so I did something I never do. I opened it up and looked inside. A wire was disconnected. Its end sat near a screw that I unscrewed slightly, placed the end of the wire underneath, and screwed back down. I fixed the phone.

Since, I've fixed a few other things, or tried to, and then reflected on what I did cognitively during the process. One thing I know. I don't use language to do it. I don't narrate to myself what I'm doing. I don't say, "Oh, look, there's a wire disconnected. I wonder where it goes?" I just look. If I do see something disconnected, I try connecting it to the most obvious place. Sometimes, if I don't see the obvious problem, I might be lucky to have a similar situation somewhere else, say if its faucets or pipes or lamps or light switches. I go look at the one that's working and come back and look at the one that isn't, then, remembering the one that works, I might see the difference. Of course, once I do it once, I might remember the next time. Yet however much thinking I might be doing in language while I'm repairing something, I'm not languaging my way through the problem. I'm picturing. I'm moving from one icon sign to the next quite unselfconsciously.

Yesterday, driving to the Valley for groceries, I saw that someone had placed a banner on their fence. It said: "Make Topanga Canyon Blvd. a Toll Road!" As recently as thirty years ago Topanga Canyon was once a refuge for artists, nature lovers and hippies, but our shabby cabins sat on gorgeous, valuable land; increasingly people moved in and built mansions. Worse, as the population of LA expanded, the canyon became a commuter conduit for travel from the west San Fernando Valley to the ocean and the West Side of LA. Over a hundred thousand people a day pour through now at rush hour, driving too fast; there's honking, the roar of engines (in fact, I hear them now, "in my mind" so to speak); there are accidents everyday, sometimes several, often people die.

Even though it was impossible to make the Boulevard a toll road, my sentiments agreed with the banner. Immediately I pictured some kind of toll booth set-up on each end of the canyon, more specifically on the Valley end where the canyon meets Mulholland Drive; traffic bumps to slow the approach, people with Topanga resident stickers passing through, the others stopping to hand over dollars; the line of cars stretching into Woodland Hills. That would be the whole point, to slow people down, to discourage people from passing through.

But more to my point here, the banner caused me to imagine a sequence of images. Aside from how I understood the sentence, *Make Topanga Canyon a Toll Road!* which requires the context that I've just explained as well as the syntactical rules governing the signs in the sentence, I did, in fact, as Peirce suggests, regard the whole sentence as a functioning symbol, pictured the places where the sentence pointed (index), the mouths of the canyon, and then pictured what it would be like to have toll booths (icons), just like thinking about the road during my explanation of it made me *hear* the engines and honking, in fact I'm now calling up the sound of angry men yelling at each other—it happens a lot—

and, if I could smell, I imagine I'd recall the odor of gasoline or carbon monoxide while I picture the cars lined up in front of my house in a traffic jam in the middle of nowhere because somebody wants to take a left.

The question is whether or not any of that is part of the *meaning* of the sentence on the banner. That's a sticky wicket. Certainly it's unlikely I would have imagined those images spontaneously if I hadn't read the banner and my ability to read the banner lies solely in the conventions of the English language. But even if the images that occurred to me, the ones that followed, were not part of the meaning of the sentence, that group of images is not a sequence of utter chaos, meaningless without the sentence. In fact, it was a sequence of images, one following the other, that took off with a sense of its own. It was thinking outside language. Must I be language capable, syntax capable, to do that, to string together a sequence of images? No. Animals do it all the time.

H.D. figured out how to get to the Mimosa Café in much the same way as I fixed my phone. The pieces came together in a series of icons, in iconic consciousness. After her breakfast at home she remembered the café, the smell and taste of the croissants, the pats on her head, the pleasing sounds that people make when a friendly dog comes to them and they think the dog has good taste in people, the warmth of the café when the outside air is wet and cool, bossing other dogs, lying on the couch. She wanted to go there, like I wanted to fix my phone, imagining the old fashioned mechanical ringing, recalling the clarity of voices on the other end.

Likely H.D. had removed the cement block from the fence hole before, had wandered around in the vacant lot previously, possibly she'd crossed it on a diagonal before as well; but she still had to sequence the images toward the goal of arriving at the Mimosa Cafe: remove the block, go out the hole, cross the lot, cross the road, around the building, into the café. She had to connect the wire. She had to imagine where she was going before she went. The sequence of icons fell together for her the way the images came to me when I imagined the toll booths. She had to pass through several cognitive states: desire, memory, recognition. Whether this occurred in some mechanical fashion or fell together organically or spontaneously is irrelevant to me; the fact is that H.D. had to *behave* toward something that was not immediately present to her. That demonstrates abstract thought (see Nick Lund, *Animal Cognition* for "novel short cuts" in animals).

Let's tighten the screws on this. What if the next morning she did, somehow, pick up the peculiar smell of the café a hundred yards down the road and head straight for it? In a similar situation, what would my process be? (I wish I could smell, but I'll have to offer a parallel example using other senses).

Let's say every time I come home from work Nadine and my new kitty, Italo, are waiting for me behind the gate. Tonight I come home and Italo isn't there. The first thing I do is notice his absence and then look around. I might iterate to myself, "Where's Italo?" but that comes pretty late in the sequence, probably after remembering the other times he's been waiting for me. Then I hear a churtling, one of his sounds. I listen. It's coming from the direction of my office and I turn toward my office. I remember Italo sitting in the chair near my desk that morning. At this point I employ the words, "I locked him in," because the concept of locking the door is peculiarly human, abstract and condensed, though the image of my turning the key accompanies it. I put down my books and go to my office. I unlock the door and there he is.

None of this is self-conscious, very little of it is languaged; employing language doesn't figure out the problem for me. I realize Italo's absence, look for him, hear his sound, remember his sitting on my chair in the morning, and then I go to my office. The majority of cognition here is a sequence of icons, mostly visual but some auditory that follow a sequence of cognitive transitions: I notice Italo's absence, I look, I hear, I listen, I recognize, I remember, I go toward the sound, I find and recognize. This sequencing of icon signs is the most basic process of thinking. It's synthetic icon consciousness and it explains a lot of what animals do and how they do it.

Peirce claims that the icon logically and experientially (phenomenologically) precedes the index and symbol. We might add that it precedes it historically as well. In the evolution of human language, first comes picturing, then gesturing, pointing, naming, combining. Cave walls all over the world demonstrate the fact that early cultures painted long before they wrote. As David Abrams points out in *The Spell of the Sensuous*, early writing in China, Mesoamerica and the Middle East consisted of pictographs. Even in the first phonetic writing, developed by Semitic scribes around 1500 B.C.E., the first *aleph-beth*, each letter still symbolized a particular thing: *aleph* meant "ox," *beth* meant "house," *gimmel* meant "camel."

As early as 1966, an American scholar named Robert Scholes was already expressing his fear that written narratives, the short story and the novel, would give way to television and film (*The Nature of Narrative*, Scholes, Kellog). By 1975, William Gass declared that it had already happened. Western culture could no longer produce or appreciate a literary masterpiece. Though literacy is considered to be almost universal in the United States, few people really read anymore. Fewer yet read novels. People don't read the newspaper, they watch the news on TV or on I-pads or phones. If they encounter the written word at all, it's often abbreviated, through text messaging, twittering, or the internet. More likely, they just send each other pictures. The long narrative, as most people encounter it, occurs in the movies, if we can call that long, the short story has been eclipsed by the television sit com and crime, sci-fi, reality TV, and adventure shows, even on PBS. It's a cognitive transition on the societal scale. Sociological change is complex. There are dozens of reasons for this transition, but I only want to talk about one.

Though writing has existed for a few thousand years, reading and writing was dominated by priests and scribes, a small elite, until the invention of the printing press in the 15th century. Afterward came the explosion of literacy, reading, literature. But if reading was ever the dominant form of entertainment and information transmission among large populations, it was only so for a few centuries. The basic means of communicating stories for the majority of human existence has been oral story telling.

Intellectuals like to suggest that reading a story is harder work than watching one on the screen, but reading is not hard work, particularly if the equivalent is a romance or crime novel. Aside from the fact that watching a movie is more like listening to a story than is reading a novel, television and movies communicate to us on a deeper, more ancient level than written narrative. They are sequences of icons and in the human psyche pictures are deeper and more ancient than words. Even more, they're deeper than oral communication, deeper and more stimulating than oral story telling. In humans, sight dominates the other senses.

Most movies that succeed don't even need the dialogue. You need only refuse the earphones on your jet ride across the country to see that even supposedly dialogue heavy movies like romantic comedies can be followed without hearing any of the words at all.

This truth is as unconscious in the psyches of most movie makers and screen writers as it is in psyches of most movie goers. However late film came onto the human scene historically, its medium, moving pictures, is evolutionarily more basic to how all animals think: in sign icons.

The capacity to think abstractly did not spring from homo sapiens like Athena from the head of Zeus. As any number of cognitive ethologists, particularly Mark Bekhoff, but including Darwin himself, have suggested, it evolved, like eyes and tongues and ears and hands and, yes, brains. In fact most animal brains are structured like ours and function like ours in very basic ways; birds are the exception, some ocean animals like octopuses and cuttlefish, as well.

Work by authors like Jane Goodall and Franz De Waal with chimpanzees and bonobos, and Dorothy Cheney and Robert Seyfarth with baboons, find the seeds of human communication and even morality in the social interaction of these primates, arguing, as did Darwin, that the higher intellectual capacities of human beings have evolved from animals, just like our other characteristics have. But how did the intelligence of primates evolve? From what?

Though animals communicate, they do not have languages of their own. And trying to teach them to communicate with us, however noble and interesting, has only set back our understanding them. They communicate to us already in the same way they communicate to each other.

In the attempt to push forward with some speed I've left a number of issues in my wake, suggesting solutions but not thoroughly discussing and defining some key problems. What is cognition? What does it mean to *mean*? What is the mind? What is consciousness? Does it even exist? Does meaning exist only in language? These are philosophical questions that need a different venue for discussion and I think we can "bracket" them, as a phenomenologist might say, and yet continue observing animal behavior that demonstrates the necessity of abstract thinking.

What I'd like to do next is examine some animal behavior that we all see all of the time, behavior that occurs toward something or someone that is not immediately present to the animal. As well, I'd like, once again, to make a phenomenalogical distinction here between anecdotal and essential reference, that is I will bare in mind that some examples are just stories, but more essentially I will try to draw from and analyze examples that anyone who is around domestic animals can observe everyday, even if they are a priest, a scientist, a philosopher, or a linguist. Without arguing about animal language or animal communication, I simply wish to demonstrate that this kind of behavior necessitates abstraction or, more loosely, thought. In fact, behaving toward something that is not present, or behaving in order to achieve a result, is abstract behavior made possible by the use of iconic signs.

YOU CAN'T WAIT
FOR NOTHING

MY HORSE WATCHES CARS. I didn't discover it on my own. A woman at the ranch, Carol, pointed it out to me. "Your horse watches cars," she said.

So what's the big deal? There are several pastures on the road that leads into the stables and she's in one of them. Cars go by all the time. That's what I told Carol.

"Horses don't pay attention to cars," Carol said. "She's looking for you. She loves you."

The back story to that could fill another book (in fact, it has, a fantasy love story I wrote and published called *Ten Thousand Heavens*). As well, I'm deeply sorry to say, that as I was writing this chapter my beloved mare, Jackie O, died of a twisted intestine at the age of 21. I loved her more deeply than I've ever loved an animal, almost as deeply as I've ever loved anyone. I'd known my mare for fifteen years and in that time I saw her almost everyday, though for the first ten years or more I wouldn't really have said she liked me much at all. That's an odd thing to say for a number of reasons, but for starters, what was I doing everyday with an animal that didn't like me? Well, she was gorgeous, smart, athletic, and passionate. Besides, animals don't have thoughts and feelings; they can't like or dislike someone, right? Wouldn't that be an emotional disposition, to like or dislike something or someone?

The problem is that the minute you start talking about an animal that you have a relationship with, you spiral into the hole of *anthropomorphism*, i.e., attributing human characteristics to the non-human. It's the bugbear of cognitive ethology. It's a little bit like trying to talk about how to take apart an engine without being allowed to name the parts. On the other side of it, those of us who live with animals in the day-in-day-out start talking about them like they're our kids. We're not reliable sources of information. I start out by saying my dog is happy to see me when I come home and end up claiming that he called 9-1-1 when I broke my leg.

That aside, whenever I arrived at the ranch I drove past Jackie O's pasture and she looked up. I parked my truck across from the pasture on the other side of the road. I got out of my truck and Jackie O spread her legs, urinated, and then walked to the gate. I went in, gave her a carrot, put her halter on her and took her out. She hadn't always come to me when I arrived, but now she did. In fact, in the last years, I didn't even put the halter on her, I just opened the gate and she walked to a bowl of carrots I placed in front of my tack box. Obviously she recognized me because she came to me. Or would she come to anyone who parked and went to the gate with carrots?

If you have pets you know that some of them will come to almost anyone, dogs more likely than cats, and others won't come to anyone at all, not even you; then there seems to be people they like for no apparent reason. I've watched this first time human-animal greeting/meeting behavior over the years and developed some vague theories about it. Dog people tended to be gregarious; they cooed, had a relaxed posture, and often knelt down to the dog's level; likely they had a familiar smell, even the smell of other dogs, and made friendly, accepting gestures. Cats were often likely to come to people who didn't even like cats because those people sat very still; you can't sit on someone who's chasing you and trying to pet you, in fact that's intimidating, but somebody sitting still is a big, warm lap. If you visit somebody with pets and want them to come to you, just sit down on the floor, on their level. But with cats, sit still.

Thinking of Carol, I recalled that at the last ranch where I kept Jackie O the entry road swept by her pasture, as well, and one day my trainer, Paddy, said to me, "Your horse recognizes your truck. When she sees it, she walks to the gate."

"Is that unusual?" I said.

"Sure is. Some people's horses won't come to them at all."

"Carrots," I said.

"Everybody's got carrots," said my trainer. "She likes you."

There's that word *like* again. And *recognize*, too.

When Paddy used the word *like* she meant it more the way Carol meant *love*, in other words, a strong emotional attachment to me in particular; she didn't mean it the way I do when I say I like chocolate ice cream. Certainly animals have likes and dislikes. Horses like apples and carrots. They don't like celery. Though one could argue, I imagine, that I've already taken things a step too far.

41

Horses eat carrots; they don't eat celery. Why do I need to ascribe an emotion or preference to that behavior?

When I like something I take a certain pleasure when I'm near it or possess it and when I'm without it I might even desire it, that is, want to be near it or want to possess it. For example, I like my friend, Tony, in Philadelphia and, as I think that, I imagine Tony, first his face, now I picture him in a dark, button down shirt with a collar, blue jeans, leather laced shoes; I could go on, but I needn't. Of course, the imagination is an odd place and my picture of Tony is not nearly as vivid to me as, say, my hands in front of me that I'm typing with. As well, I can imagine any number of things that I don't like, clowns for instance, or things that I have little feeling about, like a pencil (though I kind of like pencils), but for our purposes we need only note that if I like something or someone and they are absent, I will think of them, picture them, feel some pleasure in imagining them, perhaps recall a memory of them, and then, likely, feel some longing for their presence.

Liking is different than preferring. I can prefer one thing I don't like over another I don't like, say a crying child over a pushy street clown, or prefer one thing I like over another thing I like; I generally prefer red wine over white wine in the evening, though might prefer white over red on a warm afternoon. But liking what I like is not a preference; I like what I like and dislike what I dislike; I dislike commercials during American football games and though I like football, I'd prefer not to watch it than endure commercials. So first you like or dislike, then you prefer one thing over another.

What I'm trying to figure out here was if my horse liked me, if my horse was capable of having likes and dislikes. Well, generally she preferred an apple to a carrot; if presented with both, she'll first eat the apple, then the carrot. She prefers to graze on fresh grass rather than munch on dry alfalfa. Is she *choosing* one over the other?

You might want to argue that she always chooses the thing she likes more over the thing she likes less and in that way her choices are not choices at all because they are determined. Yet choices like those are no more determined than the choice I make in an ice cream shop when I always choose chocolate, the darker the better. You might point out that now that I've been made aware, I could choose vanilla, while Jackie O could not be made aware that she's choosing and will always pick the fresh grass over the dry.

There are a few problems with that. For one, even Jackie O doesn't *always* choose the same thing. Sometimes, on the riding path, she chooses some alfalfa that has fallen from the feed truck over the grass next to the path, though there might be causes that determine this, as well. And the fact that I choose vanilla in spite of my preference for chocolate could be equally determined. Possibly, my desire to prove I'm undetermined is a greater desire than my preference for chocolate ice cream. As you see, we could go on and on here, and philosophers have, though for my part, whether or not the choice is determined is irrelevant.

If Jackie O chooses an apple over a carrot, she has, in fact, picked one and not the other. And when I order chocolate ice cream, I likely do so without any self-consciousness; my choice is as equally rote as my horse's. We equally have likes and dislikes and have some things that we like more than others. We prefer one thing over another and choose it. This is how we loosely and consistently use the word *choose*, though as philosophers we might stipulate that only self-conscious choices are truly choices and go on to quibble as to whether or not self-conscious choices are free or determined. My point is something different. When Jackie O chooses or when I choose, however unselfconsciously, a cognitive transition has occurred, a disposition accompanied by desire and satisfaction. Jackie O's unselfconscious desires and satisfactions are feelings no different than mine and to make a distinction is to add something to *my* behavior that is unnecessary.

To say that my horse *likes* me is to say, at the very least, that she prefers me over other people, even over other horses, which was, in fact, the case. That preference has to be based on some things she likes that happen when I'm around: apples, carrots, physical attention, things that I had given her everyday for fifteen years that other people had not. Standing in a small herd of horses, she leaves them to join me, my herd of two, as the horse listeners say. To do so, she must *recognize* me.

St. Augustine discussed recognition during his meditation on memory in *The Confessions*, written around 400 C.E. Put simply, he points out that we can't recognize something unless we *re*-cognize, or cognize again what was once in cognition. Without trying to make any point about memory or whether Jackie O thinks about me when I'm absent, recognition marks a cognitive transition accompanied by transitional behavior, from standing motionless, watching, then moving forward to the person recognized. It's not simply that it's equally parsimonious to express this in this way instead of in behavioral contingencies; behavioral contingencies themselves necessarily imply cognitive response. St. Augustine again: "For even beasts and birds have memory; otherwise they would not be able to find their ways back to their dens and nests or do any of the other

43

things they are used to doing; indeed without memory they could not become used to doing anything" (*The Confessions*, Book X, Chapter 20). Sometimes it's just that simple, though what has yet to be discussed is whether or not any memory bridges the gap between cognition and recognition, that is, did Jackie O think about me when I wasn't around.

I decided to conduct some experiments. I parked my truck where Jackie O couldn't see it and I watched the pasture. In fact, when a car went by she lifted her head and watched it. The other horses didn't. So Jackie O looked at vehicles and when she saw mine, recognized it. Given that she recognized my truck, I wanted to know what she recognized. Did she just recognize the truck, or did she recognize me? If I borrowed a car and drove by and parked, though she watched the car, she didn't come to the fence until I got out. Nonetheless, she remembered and recognized that car by the next day. She remembered the new car. As well, if I borrowed yet a different car and stopped by the pasture and looked at her, she recognized me inside the car and came to the fence.

Would she come to the fence if anybody stopped to look at her? She did not. Nor did she come to other people, even if they had carrots. As well, she didn't come to Gail and her mother, even when they drove Gail's car, a car she recognized. When she saw them get out, she walked away. I did not conduct an experiment in which someone else drove my truck. Anyway, if you're a horse owner and have an affectionate relationship with your horse, you can do these experiments yourself, though undoubtedly there might be some differences due to your peculiar relationship with your horse, her personality, and your horse's gender.

Jackie O didn't really seem to like other people or other horses. For the most part she stood by herself, as people at the ranch would say, waiting for me. Though there were exceptions. One was an old, black thoroughbred mare in the pasture named Tasha. Tasha was always at the bottom of any hierarchy and got bullied by everyone, except Jackie O who just kept apart from it all. One day Tasha left the other horses and began following Jackie O around. Jackie O walked away, Tasha followed. Jackie O bit her and walked away. Tasha followed. It went on that way for weeks. Then, when fly season came, the barrier broke. Jackie O permitted Tasha to stand with her, nose to tail, and the two of them brushed flies from each other's faces that way. This began what I might loosely call a companionship and now, when I arrived, Tasha followed Jackie O to greet me at the gate.

I'd always assumed that Jackie O urinated before coming to me because she didn't want to urinate later with me sitting on her kidneys. Of course this is assuming a lot, though I did an experiment with this, too. I wondered whether or not she noticed a difference in how I arrived and whether it would change her urinating behavior. So I asked Gail to come to the ranch with me. When Gail came with me, I never rode, I just cleaned Jackie up. And, in fact, when I came with Gail, Jackie didn't urinate, leading me to surmise that she urinated in anticipation of my riding her and distinguished between the two different situations, my coming alone and my coming with Gail. Actually, in the early days, if I brought Gail to the ranch Jackie O urinated *at* Gail, but that's something else altogether.

Most horse people will tell you that horse herds are organized under strict, linear hierarchies of domination (ethologists call them *linear transitive dominance hierarchies*) but I don't see how anybody who has observed a group of domestic horses on a daily basis could come to that conclusion. Part of the reason, in terms of domestic horses, is that the people most involved with horses are trainers; the horses they work with are isolated in stalls and when they get them out they're looking for results. One on one, the domination model is simple and usually works. But like a lot of animals, not just primates and insects, horses are social creatures and the politics inside a herd are very fluid, comprised of changing alliances and shifts in power, some of which happen very quickly, as when a horse's owner shows up and a horse that might seem lower in the hierarchy is suddenly allied with the most powerful sentience present, the human owner. This is another example where much current cognitive ethology has missed the boat with its concentration on primate societies. In the search for the proto-human in our closest relatives it has failed to take a close look at the social interactions (dare I say social psychology) in packs and herds. I've read some studies with wolves and wild horses, but I've noted that, ironically, our domestic animals, the ones that live around us daily, are for the most part ignored.

There's another problem here in that models or paradigms, as much as they serve heuristically to guide our conjectures about animal behavior, sometimes become lenses through which we perceive animal behavior. For example, for decades the patriarchal values of Western researchers led them to impose those same social structures on animals, many of whom, it turned out, organized their social groups under matriarchies. Horses are a classic example, where it was discovered (by a woman) that wild herds weren't governed by stallions, but guided by lead mares. Now the lead mare model, as valuable as it is, dominates, probably over-dominates, our interpretation of horse herd interaction (in fact, it's slipped into the common parlance referring to female behavior across species).

In Jackie O's pasture, depending on its constituency, alliances and shifts occurred all of the time. Sometimes Jackie dominated the pasture, other times, when a bigger, tougher horse was introduced, that horse, sometimes a gelding and sometimes a mare, dominated, but when it did, Jackie withdrew and kept to herself. Often, when that happened, some of the horses who were being dominated drifted, like Tasha, to Jackie O. The pasture would have two mini-herds and if the new domineering horse attempted to re-integrate the runaways, the new alliance fought him and kept separate. In fact, the ranch hands even learned to feed the two groups separately to dissuade conflict. If in the wild a herd was always led by a lead mare, in the less than natural situation of the domestic pasture, with no stallions around, a gelding sometimes dominated the group.

The details involved in all of this are for a different kind of book, but I would venture to say that this kind of complex social interaction might imply a little bit of anticipation and calculation, as well as some emotion, tons of cognitive/emotional transitions accompanied by iconic semiotics expressed in oral, olfactory, auditory, visual, and tactile gestures, given and received.

I cleaned and tacked Jackie O in a little space between my tack locker and the pasture fence, and now that Tasha had buddied-up with Jackie O, often, not always, she tried to stand near us at the fence while I tacked Jackie. This always pissed Jackie O off and she pinned her ears and hissed at Tasha. If you think animals don't have any emotions then you've never owned a mare, because there's a huge difference between a pissed off mare and a content one. In the past, I'd always chased the other carrot mooching horses away, but my heart went out to old Tasha to whom I sneaked carrots, and even some scratches and eye cleaning. In time, Jackie got used to having her there and only got pissed off once in a while, say, if Tasha dared put her head over the fence.

Horses are extremely tactile animals and in the herd this translates to an acute sense of placement and space, of placement *in* space. When you train a horse "on the ground," space issues are paramount and you must teach your horse not to come into your space unless you request it, to respond to your movements at a distance, and to permit you to enter her space, that is touch her anywhere, without her getting upset. I like to describe this as *spatial tactility*, that is, like fish swimming in a school, it's as if horses *feel through space*, and watching a group of horses in motion invites that comparison, however different the sensory apparatus of fish and herd animals might be. School fish have a sensory device in their spine that senses the movement of the fish near them. I'd venture to say that in mammals that response is more semiotic. Anyway, that space over the fence was the line Tasha couldn't cross when Jackie O was with me.

This began as a simple anecdote about waiting, but just getting out of my truck and getting my horse out of the pasture introduced a lot of complexities. In fact, I wondered whether my horse waited for me. It's something that all of us who spend our lives with animals think about. Do they think about us when we are not there? And it goes to the crux of this question of whether or not they can think about something that's not in front of their faces; given that they think, so to speak, about what is in front of them, we might learn something about the latter by examining the former. My argument here has been that even in immediate situations, the conversation of gestures between animals or between me and an animal, is a semiotic one that requires three elements to explain, rather than a model of action–reaction. And once again, I'm going to work very hard here to make a small point and I don't want to draw extensive conclusions from it. Do animals wait?

This began as a meditation for me and fell into an accidental experiment. My ranch closed on Mondays and on Tuesday when I showed up Jackie O was usually waiting at the gate instead of standing in the field. In common parlance I might say, well, I come six days in a row and when I miss a day Jackie wants me to come and so goes to the gate and waits for me to show up. By now, however much common sense that makes, you know that this simple explanation is loaded with unprovable assumptions: that Jackie O notices a day go by and notices that I did not come that day, that she misses me, that she wants to see me, that she waits for me, all of which necessitates cognition and emotion, as well, my observation is subjective and anecdotal, not experimental.

A few years ago, after seeing Jackie O almost everyday for twelve years, I spent four months traveling in India. Lucky for me, I got to do it with Gail and our daughter, Marlena. Needless to say, I thought about my horse, and my other animals, too, everyday, in fact I had to practice not thinking about them. When I returned home, my ranch manager said that after I left Jackie O stopped eating for a few weeks and, in general, behaved with so much lethargy they once called the vet to make sure she wasn't sick. Okay, change of circumstance and then a change of behavior; no thought required. Though on my first day back at the ranch after returning from India, Jackie O was lying in the middle of the pasture. She hadn't looked for my truck. But when I called to her she looked up with something that I would describe as incredulity, then leapt to her feet and ran to me. I won't describe the emotional reunion, but when your horse runs to you, that's an amazing feeling.

Nonetheless, I can talk about this event non-conceptually. The apparent emotion aside, and given that my ranch manager didn't over-read Jackie O's behavior, that is, assume she'd be depressed if I left, all I can really surmise is that after getting daily attention for twelve years, my sudden absence created a void in Jackie O's behavior patterns.

Besides, we all have these stories about our pets. When I come home from work, Nadine is, well, waiting at the gate it would seem, and bounces and yaps and wriggles ecstatically. The cats drop out of the trees and off nearby buildings, if they aren't already waiting outside the fence, and begin meowing and rubbing until they all follow me into the house like a scene from *Snow White*. They want to be petted and they want to eat, though my animals can get in and out of the house whenever they want and the cat bowls generally have food in them already. I give Nadine a snack and the cats, well, I pet them while they eat.

A strict non-conceptualist would have me believe one of a number of things about this event. One would be that my animals sit brainlessly like toasters while I am gone and, when I arrive, turn on like toasters to the stimulus of my arrival. Another might be that they have gone about their day in their brainless tasks, sleeping, sniffing, barking at sounds, climbing trees, one thing after another until they are interrupted by my arrival and that's just the next brainless bundle of reactions that occurs.

Let's put aside that much of this is learned behavior, on their part as well as mine; there's yet one evident problem with these non-conceptualist explanations: location. Location, location, location. My dog wasn't ruffling around behind my house, burying or unburying bones; the cats weren't hustling the neighbors for food or out hunting, they were all gathered at the gate where I enter. This is paradigmatic; if you have pets, they display this waiting behavior too.

Without ascribing any specific thought or emotion to a waiting animal, waiting requires abstraction, even if it is simply to an inner recreation of a vague, future stimulus, though I doubt that the stimulus is vague even if, as I've noted, any thought is more vague than an actual perception. Likely it requires specific sensory icons of me or Gail or Marlena, because I know if the UPS woman comes to the gate, the dog barks angrily and the cats run away. No, they were waiting for a family member. Our absence was discerned and our presence desired, then they had to go to the place from which we leave and enter, they had to recognize and remember that, and then they had to stay there, and despite any number of possible present distractions, had to behave, by waiting, toward something which was not present. These are semiotic acts. How can you wait without waiting for something, something or someone who isn't there?

If you've ever waited up late with your dog for your lover or child to return home, then you've witnessed waiting behavior, in fact, if your loved one is late and hasn't called, your dog's behavior is probably pretty similar to your own. I will likely be reading in my chair and Nadine will be lying across from me in her favorite corner of the couch. Romeo, Gail's cat, will be outside, likely on the roof of my office where he watches the gate. Nadine's ears will perk at any sound coming from the front of the house: an auto parking next door, a voice, a clatter on the road, and this isn't behavior she'd exhibit if we were all home and she is spurred by an unusual sound or a sound at the gate. When waiting her head jerks up and ears move forward; there is a muffled roofing, and if the approach sounds continue she moves downstairs toward the door. When alarmed she jumps up and barks loudly, moving directly toward the sound, which could be emanating from any number of directions. Of course, she'll hear Gail's car pull into the carport long before I do, straighten up to attention, and race downstairs and out the door when she hears the clatter of the gate handle. That dogs recognize specific engine sounds and foots steps is pretty much common knowledge.

There are words that can key this behavior, too, "Mama" in the case of Gail. Our daughter doesn't live with us anymore, but if we expected her arrival and said "sister," Nadine would go into waiting behavior, listening for her to arrive. She waits as well for our friend, Antonio, who almost always brings meat for an *asado*. The words "Tio Antonio" or "Tio Carne" will arouse her to excitement. And though these specific examples might be called subjective and anecdotal, this waiting behavior is something we have all observed and is paradigmatic. There are probably a million non-conceptualists who came home to a waiting pet today.

Speaking of hunting, which I'll talk about more later, here's a great waiting story. Our house in Topanga is a mountain cabin built into the side of the hill in 1923. Our front deck is also our kitchen roof, its floor over fifteen feet from the ground. When we moved in the railing was just a bunch of plywood sheets nailed to two-by-fours. The deck was drained by three small holes at the bottom of the plywood sheets, three small arches at floor level, one in each front corner of the porch and one in the middle. Drain pipes ran down the front of the house and carried the rainwater to a flowerbed below. That all ended when during an *El Niño* the drain holes plugged with leaves, the porch filled with water and the roof collapsed. But before that happened I noticed that any number of my cats would sit, front legs folded in front of them, staring at those drain holes. Maybe they'd been watching too many Tom and Jerry cartoons. Those "mouse holes" were fifteen feet in the air.

I thought I was nuts, or they were, until one day a mouse popped out of one of the holes. What prompted a mouse to climb fifteen feet up the inside of a vertical drain pipe? I don't even know how it was done, given that the interior of the pipe was smooth and the pipe interior much larger than the mouse. But if you own a house you know that mice want to get in it. Something about mouses and houses. And it must have occurred often enough for my cats to be sitting around waiting for it to happen. That's what they were waiting for. They were waiting for a mouse. Waiting is often how cat's hunt. And they weren't waiting for an elephant. They weren't waiting for Santa Claus. They were waiting for a mouse.

Now I'm back in front of the corral and about to mount Jackie O. I walk her across the road and pace her a little before tightening the cinch; if she keeps her head straight and doesn't act up, I give her a carrot. Then I grab her mane in my left hand, place my foot in the stirrup, and I'm up. Tasha begins to scream. It's not quite a whinny. Nor is it the sound of an animal in pain. It's a shrill scream and comes from her chest. It's a call. It sounds like a complaint. And she does it the whole time I'm gone with Jackie O.

If I ride up above the pasture, around a hill and out of sight, I can still hear her calling. And if I hit the trail, then on my way back, before I'm in sight of the pasture, I hear her. And when we return, she is at the fence, her chest pressed against it, her neck stretched out, screaming still, until Jackie O and I arrive. Then she calms and makes a grumbling sound in her throat, a nicker.

In that forty-five minutes to an hour while we were gone, Tasha passed through a number of cognitive-emotional transitions (and Jackie O did, too, but let's stick with some simple ones). She stopped eating and left a pile of alfalfa to join Jackie and me at the fence. She nickered at my arrival, I assume to get my attention. She became upset when we left and stayed upset until we returned, whereupon she calmed down.

I would prefer to regard these as a series of semiotic transitions, as well. For example, a choice has been made to leave one favorable circumstance, munching on alfalfa, for another circumstance, standing near me and Jackie O. One could argue that the choice was rote and determined by a preference, though most choices, human included, are quite rote and preference determined. Though often enough, in this circumstance, for Tasha, the choice appeared weighed, because she didn't always come, in fact, Jackie didn't always come either, say if the weather was very hot and she was standing comfortably having flies brushed from her face with someone else's tail, or it was extremely inclement, cold and rainy, and the horses were standing together under their awning, shielding each other from the rain and using each other's body heat to warm themselves.

In the first circumstance, brushing away flies, horses must stand next to each other, facing the opposite direction, head to butt, so they can brush flies from each other's faces, in the second, huddling, horses who don't get along and don't generally spend time with each other stand together quietly. However non-conceptually one wishes to explain the behavior, it is difficult to argue that the desire to be comfortable in a certain kind of way, a desire to move from an uncomfortable situation, does not *precede* the action taken to become more comfortable. The cognitive-emotional event precedes the behavior and creates a transition, the desire to move from dissatisfaction to satisfaction.

Fly swishing behavior is a solution that all horses use, likely a combination of herd behavior and learning and the fact that horses swish their tails at a part of their body being irritated, or sometimes when they're just irritated (once again, whether or not horses are *hard wired* to swish their tails is irrelevant), though, as is often the case with horses, these social solutions can require behavior different from what they are normally inclined to do. Horses who stand apart from each other on a cool, fly-less day, when bothered by flies on their face, solve the problem by standing head to tail and swishing their tails. Jackie O's swishing of her tail does not get rid the flies on her own face, but the flies on Tasha's face, and Tasha's tail brushes the flies from Jackie's face.

I'm unconcerned whether or not either of them *realize* what they're doing. I'm simply interested in explaining the movement from one cognitive-emotional disposition, irritation from flies on their faces, to doing something about it more complex than shaking their heads, arguably a reflex. The horse doesn't have to think through the problem to a solution, but must think in consecutive icons to enact it, must desire an end to the irritation and perform the remembered solution. A mechanical metaphor for this behavior fails because a machine doesn't get irritated, nor is it self-motivated to seek a solution. It does not have what Mead would call an *attitude*. Though I'm inclined to speculate that the solution is conceived in advance of the solution behavior, my argument here is only that the movement to relieve irritation, the desire to move from irritation to non-irritation by behaving in a cooperative way requires a semiotic act, a thought. These kinds of acts of social cooperation by animals do not *imply* forethought, they *exhibit* it. In a dialectic of iconic consciousness and behavior, it is an example where the behavior *follows* the thought, and if the animal does not have a cognitive-emotional disposition, then there would never be any reason whatsoever for any change of behavior, let alone a purposeful or cooperative one.

Let's go back to my fixing the telephone. My old telephone doesn't work and I want it to work. That's my cognitive-emotional disposition. I pick up the handle and place it to my ear and I don't hear a dial tone. I want to hear a dial tone and in its absence I hear one in my memory. That's what I want, and that simple, integral moment is what we share with any sentient being that desires to move from an unsatisfactory disposition to a satisfactory one.

I know the land line is good because I've plugged a working phone into the wall and it gave me a dial tone. I plug my old phone in to a different line and don't get a dial tone. So the problem is in my phone. This kind of troubleshooting is pretty cognitive. My brother is an electrical engineer and I've watched him fix things. At this stage I'm thinking in language; I might even be talking out loud to myself, "Try another phone," though that "other phone," upstairs on the cabinet, I picture, gray, sitting on the wooden cabinet, and I picture where it's plugged in, as well. Anyone who contends that we *think only in language* just needs to take a moment and watch herself think. The question is whether language enables us to think in icons or whether it's the other way around, or something else. Again, if we use Peirce's model, icons are logically and phenomenalogically prior to symbols, though this does not mean that they don't co-arise in symbol users, i.e. humans, and not arise at all in non-humans. Again, I'm trying to isolate animal behavior that insists on the use of icons.

Anyway, once I know that the problem is in my phone I turn it over, see the tiny screws holding the bottom cover to the base, think "I need a small screwdriver," but now I'm already picturing one of my small screwdrivers, one with a yellow plastic handle, another with a black rubber one, inside my red tool chest in the laundry room between the sink and the dryer.

I open the bottom of the phone and peer inside. I spot the unconnected wire. The semiotics don't have to be contemplative. In fact the behavior, my seeing the unconnected wire and reaching to reconnect it, follows a series of iconic perceptions; I've called this synthetic icon cognition. The icons occur immediately and my behavior follows soon after I think this non-reflexive synthetic series of icons. I see the unconnected wire. Experience has taught me that unconnected wires lead to machines not working. I see where the wire has likely come loose and envision connecting it. Then I do it. I lift the headphone and there's a dial tone.

This is not an argument that contends we don't think in language. I think in language constantly, but if my contemplations are not entirely abstract, then my thoughts are accompanied by memories and emotions (listening to music is a great example), visual, tactile, auditory, and olfactory icons. I have no sense of smell, but if I've neglected the cat litter, then when I clean it I get a burning feeling in my nose and I'm recalling that feeling right now. But fixing something is an excellent paradigm for iconic primacy. If you have children, then you've spent countless Christmas Eves putting together toys to which there are no language instructions at all, just diagrams and arrows, icons and indexes.

When H.D. figured out how to get to the Mimosa Café for croissants, it came together in a series of icons, and possible indexes, in the way I fixed my phone. Non-conceptualists have argued that animals don't use indexes, but most animals don't have fingers or draw arrows, so pointing with fingers and arrows doesn't mean anything to them. They point with their bodies and their heads and, of course, the context has to mean something. A dog staring at the door is indicating she wants out, out there, where she's pointing.

I have bracketed the fixing of my phone from several issues because I wanted to create a paradigm for iconic problem solving. More complex is how I arrived at choosing the phone as my example (and not, say, the water pump to my outdoor fountain), my memory of fixing the phone, my examination of that memory, the levels of my awareness (when did I become aware that I was fixing my telephone and must I be self-conscious to be aware?). We'll revisit these questions, though it's my position that the relationship between language/syntax, words/symbols, and icons/images and how they function together in consciousness is very entangled and complex. What's important here is the point that *meaningful* cognition can occur on the level of icons, icon memory, and synthetic icon cognition without employing language.

Meanwhile, back at the ranch, I imagine, though I doubt, that some of Tasha's behavior when I arrive can be explained non-conceptually as rote, dyadic responses to immediate stimuli. But not the waiting. Even if you were to argue that Tasha's calling became a substitute for our presence, a self-stimulating act, her self-stimulation must still stand in a triadic relationship to her desire for our return, if not, then our return wouldn't satisfy her; she wouldn't change from being dissatisfied to satisfied. More so, that kind of self-stimulation is the cognitive-emotional component of all waiting, the way I might stimulate my jealousy by continuing to recall the incident that created it.

Let's go back up to my reading chair in the living room where I'm waiting for Gail to come home. The Zen say, "Waiting is war," and I remind myself of that as the hour grows late. It's 11:30 p.m. I expected her home before 10:30 and she hasn't called and it would be a clear intrusion on her privacy to call her in this circumstance. Like Nadine, I'm listening for the front gate (or waiting for the phone to ring). I hear a siren on the road and worry that Gail's been in an accident somewhere on the notorious S curves. If you have children who drive then you've done this a thousand times. I don't say to myself, "I'm worried Gail has had an accident," instead I get a chill from the siren, I picture her in her car, I picture the curves, I see the strobe of the ambulance light. Then I recall what I already know, that she's gone to a speech and a dinner with a Nobel Prize winner. Insanely, I imagine her across the table from him; she's gorgeous and fascinating and he's fascinated; I imagine him, African, charming, intelligent, wealthier and more famous than me. I don't narrate this, but picture it. It's madness, but I'm jealous. My memory leaps to a troubled time early in our relationship when she came home, still flushed from intimacy with another man and I feel the anger and humiliation I felt then. As well, I keep picturing her coming home, parking her car, the carport light goes on, she comes through the gate, comes through the front door. If I use language at all it's to tell myself to stop being an idiot, to stop this sequence of provocative, useless emotions, stop being jealous and mad at her for something she hasn't even done. Calm down. Stop waiting. Anyway, fifteen minutes later Nadine's ears perk, she woofs, looks at me and looks at the stairs, Gail comes through the door and Nadine runs down the stairs to her and I follow.

Waiting is an act of self stimulation. If I were not thinking about Gail, fondly or otherwise, and desiring her return, I wouldn't be waiting at all and without memory and accompanying emotion, I cannot wait. And neither can Tasha or Nadine.

In the process of writing this book it's become increasingly apparent to me how difficult it is to categorize aspects of behavior and thinking and how essential categorizing is to human understanding. Yesterday, I tried to explain to Gail my memory of fixing my phone. How do you explain an experience, the experience of experiencing, the memory of that, the awareness of the memory? And who does it and where is it? Of course, nobody has ever answered those questions. Gail said to me, "Maybe you can't take it apart. To analyze you must categorize and you can't categorize the experience into parts. It doesn't come in separable parts. When you take it apart it disappears." Well, that's a poet for you. I've already talked about paradigmatic behavior that exhibits cognitive-emotional dispositions and transitions. I want to talk about a few more of what I'll call *core dispositions* before talking explicitly about animal emotions.

STOP, I THINK
I'M HUNTING

WE KNOW THAT CHIMPS MAKE AND USE TOOLS and weapons. Even non-conceptualists admit it. And dolphins sure do make a lot of noise and learn tricks. Recent investigations seem to indicate that they name each other using clicks. But there's a little bit of a problem in trying to communicate with our "closest animal relatives" and the other big brained animals like cetaceans and elephants. As smart as they are, they don't possess syntactical, symbolic communication, i.e. language, and their failure to learn it diminishes the arguments for their thoughts and feelings, even more damningly for the animals "lower" than them on the intelligence scale. Anybody who has worked with animals and people, which I have for the last 40 years, knows how worthless those kinds of rating scales are; linear, univocal, mechanistic and reductionist, they are tools, not knowledge. In terms of animal behavior, we must, at the very least, break from the vocabulary and paradigms of the non-conceptualists, if not from their methodology as well.

Where I live, if you don't have cats, then you have rats, and it's that simple. This produces some situations that aren't the most comfortable: carrion left next to your shoes or next to where you're sleeping or, worse, the long killing rituals when the cats bring live rodents inside. When that happens I try to catch the rodent and put it outside my fence; that doesn't mean somebody else, or even the original cat, isn't going to catch it again and bring it back in.

There are other compromises. If you let them out to catch rats, then they will on occasion catch birds. If you've spent much time studying birds, either in nature or in books, then you know they are beautiful and possess almost mysterious capabilities in terms of memory, such as migration and food storage, tool use, diversionary tactics to lure hunters from their young, and even forms of apparent communication through song. But in millions of years they haven't completely solved cats. A few birds die every year, but my cats die, too, as the prey of pumas, coyotes, bobcats, owls, eagles, hawks, and human beings who run over them thoughtlessly on the road (in fact, very recently my new kitten, Italo, was run down and killed by someone who was speeding and who could have avoided him by simply hitting the brakes). Interestingly, the few birds that are killed are newcomers; we have several families of orioles, finches, and wrens who have learned the cats and successfully raise families here every year.

I want to start with another story, though there's the seed of the hunting paradigm inside it. As a young man I spent a lot of time in different graduate schools trying to find my intellectual niche in a range of things from the history of philosophy, to Peirce's semiotics, to sociological theory, Buddhism, critical theory and the theory of language, particularly structuralism and deconstruction, to reading all the work of dozens of literary writers, and I did this around the country in a lot of different places for almost fifteen years, though I was teaching, too, and mowing lawns and tearing down and building houses and collecting garbage and running gyms in Boys and Girls Clubs and, eventually, writing novels.

Through all of this I owned or lived with a lot of different animals in different situations but in the end I moved around a lot and by fate or circumstance ended up with only one animal who I took with me everywhere from 1973 until his death in 1990, a big orange, long-haired cat named, well, in the end named Mr. Puff (because if you live with cats, then you know that they have many, many names). In that amount of time a lot of tales and legends developed around Mr. Puff and his multitudinous episodes from San Francisco to New York City to Washington, D.C. to Los Angeles and everywhere in between. In fact I almost wrote a book about Mr. Puff and maybe someday I will, but for now I offer only this story.

Gail and I met at the University of Utah, the last stop in my graduate school sojourn, and after we got those Ph.D.'s we decided to fly to D.C. where Gail's dad, Div, a GM guy, said he could help us get a deal on a new car that we could drive back to our new jobs in Los Angeles. We bought a cat carrier, put Mr. Puff on the plane and met him at the airport where we drove him to Gail's parents' house in Rockville, a Maryland suburb outside D.C.

Div didn't like cats or, like a lot of people, thought he didn't, and had never had a cat in his house. What he did have was a nest of ground squirrels under his back patio who wreaked havoc with his lawn. He'd tried everything to get rid of them, traps, poisons, the works. He was a dog man and I thought of suggesting a terrier to solve his problem, but he wasn't really the kind of guy who thought animals solved problems; for him it was more like, add an animal and you add a problem.

Now Mr. Puff preferred not to use a cat litter if avoidable, and when possible took his business outside; as well, at Gail's parents' place there was a big tree in the back yard that he liked to climb and sit in. Then he spotted a ground squirrel emerge from under the patio across the way. Worse for the ground squirrels, Mr. Puff could camp on the cement patio above and behind their hole and wait for them to come out. Div noticed this, too. And despite it being so hot and muggy outside that you had to swim through the air, Div opened the sliding door to the patio enough so Mr. Puff could sit inside the air conditioning and wait for squirrels. And this he did. He killed them and he ate them. And it would seem that he preferred to hunt them while sitting in the air conditioned kitchen as opposed to a more advantageous spot, closer to the hole but out in the muggy heat. In two weeks Mr. Puff ended Div's ground squirrel problem.

Here is the anthropological model for how humans and cats came together in the first agricultural communities however many thousands of years ago. With the dawn of agriculture came permanent communities to cultivate it. With that came food storage and with food storage came rodents. So a city was a particularly advantageous place for small cats to move in and live because it offered protection from larger predators and an abundance of small, grain eating game. Small cats don't eat goats or sheep or cows, or domestic birds big enough for people to eat, and unlike big cats they don't eat people. It was a match made in, well, cities, and to this day a cat is a more urban animal than a dog despite being, in many ways, a bit less human friendly. In an urban environment they are more efficient predators. A cat's hunting techniques are more suited to the urban domain and our mutual domestication with them occurred later than our partnership with dogs for precisely that reason. The pack hunting behavior of dogs is more suited to roving hunter-gatherers.

Back when I lived in rural Pennsylvania the farmers made it very clear that we weren't to let our dogs rove at night, because when we did, they gathered in packs and took down goats, sheep, and calves, raided chicken coups. As far as the farmers were concerned it was open season on any dog roving after dusk. Temple Grandin has gone so far as to speculate that it was wolves and wild dogs that taught the first hunter-gatherers the initial aspects of civilization: strategic hunting in teams, communal child care, division of labor, and care for the elderly, reversing the anthropocentric model of domestication. In any case, in general, the predation habits of dogs are much better suited to open terrain and migratory human life styles, hence their earlier domestication.

Aside from these compatibilities of human material culture and animal habits, there are issues of the dialectic of temperament on the part of the human cultures and animal cultures that make domestication possible; for example, why the horse and not the zebra? *Animal culture* is a phrase that raises a lot of scientific hairs and, of course, it has its adherents and detractors, along with extensive debate on how culture is to be defined (see *The Question of Animal Culture*, Kevin N. Laland and Bennet G. Galeg, eds.).

So the story of Div and Mr. Puff is a very, very old one. Mr. Puff answered the age-old cat-hater's question: Why would anybody want a cat? Once you break that barrier you learn that they can be affectionate, demanding, surly, and everything else domestic animals become, in the case of cats add aesthetic athleticism and behavioral idiosyncrasy. But when we left to drive back west to our new jobs in Los Angeles, Div said that well, if we wanted, we could leave Mr. Puff with him, and I imagine if he'd not retired to a condominium in Florida where animals weren't permitted, he'd might have gotten a cat.

There are a number of interesting aspects to that anecdote, but I want to break it down to the paradigm of hunting. Some kinds of hunting require tremendous patience and the cognitive dilemma is the same as waiting. You can't wait for nothing and you can't hunt for nothing. Unlike my cats and the mouse holes in the sky, where the cats could keep the mouse exits in their sight, a kind of reminder of what they were waiting for, Mr. Puff positioned himself above and behind the squirrel hole where he couldn't be seen by an exiting squirrel but neither could he see the hole. I doubt he could smell or hear the squirrels beneath the cement, but even if he could, those would be signs of the absent squirrels to which he was the *interpretant*. Sensory reminders became even less likely when he moved farther away and sat inside the air conditioned kitchen where there were multiple distractions, including noises, people, and food smells. If the mouse hole in the sky was the sign to my cats for the hunted mouse, to which my cats were the interpretants, in the case of Mr. Puff, that sign had to occur in his memory and concentration.

Anyone can observe this hunting/waiting behavior in their cats. When a cat brings a rodent into the house, she'll release it and catch it again and again, at some point letting it run under something. After immediately checking all the exits, she'll back off and place herself somewhere she can see all of them, and then wait.

The semiotics of hunting/waiting explains more complicated kinds of hunting too. In my years with cats I've usually found females to be more efficient and consistent hunters, though not always. I believed this because they hunted for their kittens as well as for themselves and, in fact, I've found that females who I permitted to have a litter were often better hunters than one's who I've had spayed before they have one (I understand that allowing my female to have kittens is controversial; when I did so, then I only permitted it once and when I did it I placed them all and kept the ones I didn't place. Now I no longer let my cats, male or female, breed). My black female cat, Yoko Dodo, for example, is now fifteen and doesn't hunt anymore, though I had her spayed before she had any kittens. In her youth she was quite territorial and pugnacious, but she was never an avid hunter.

But now I have two neutered males, Cheese and Romeo, who are very active hunters. They hunt almost anything that's smaller than them: mice and rats, moles, ground squirrels and tree squirrels, baby and adolescent possums, lizards, birds. The Cheese, who weighs twenty pounds, brings in big urban pigeons (technically doves) and rabbits. Romeo, on occasion, hunts tree squirrels. There seems to be a rule about whether or not they bring them in for the play ritual. Things that are tougher to kill they bring in already dead, but regardless, if they kill it, they place it near the side of our bed or in the bathroom, sometimes on the doorstep, somewhere, it would seem, that we'll be sure to see it. Rodents, including rabbits, they then often eat.

I assume that tougher animals like possum or tree squirrels or adult rabbits are killed on the spot because they must be. They can't just be picked up and carried in alive. When I see them, their throats are opened. Sometimes it's clear that the cat has found a family of something. Cheese, in particular does this with pigeons and possum and baby rabbits; he brings in one a night until, I assume, he's rubbed them out. Of course, this entails remembering where he found them last time.

The kinds of animals the two males tend to kill correlates loosely with their own personalities, their size, and their separate hunting territories, and it's interesting that they hunt in distinctly separate territories. Cheese is quite large and operates in the vacant lot to the south of our property. Like his mother, his behavior is almost coy. When he comes into a room he meows and rubs at a distance, slowly circling toward me and away from me before circling my chair, then finally jumping onto my lap, then jumping down, then finally jumping up again and settling in. In fact, it was six years before he even did that, a different story. The Cheese often hunts in the open field, sometimes sitting on a rock and waiting for the grass to move, though apparently he finds nests out there as well.

Romeo is smaller, dark, with abnormally large forearms. His behavior is always univocal. He comes in and walks up to you and sits down. He works the nooks and crannies of the two houses north of us, the opposite side of the house. He's more likely to bring in mice and rats, more likely to bring them in alive and make a great show of it, leaving the dead animal in the living room or near our bed. Cheese would prefer to leave his carnage on a doorstep or just outside the cat room. Sometimes they leave their prey for us and sometimes they eat them and I don't know why.

Of these two predators, if they were both to spot a bird high in a tree, the Cheese might watch it for a short while and then, as if deciding he couldn't catch it, walk off. Romeo won't take his eyes off of it until it flies away. I can't quite imagine how either of them catch a bird; I haven't seen it, though I've timed Romeo and know he can get twenty feet up our bottle brush tree in under two seconds. Cheese can't get as high in a small tree because he's too big and that's possibly why he loses interest, though in general the Cheese loses interest in things much more quickly than Romeo who will watch the rustling in a tree with intense concentration for long minutes.

I've had a lot of cats and both of these two are relatively bright, but I'm looking for an example of hunting behavior that requires a relatively sophisticated process of synthetic semiotic thinking: Romeo's tree squirrel hunting.

Where I live the tree squirrels don't spend much time on the ground, it's too dangerous. You could argue that squirrels are *hard wired* for that, though I've always found it to be a bad, mechanical metaphor and, in fact, if you go to my college campus or almost any public place you'll find plump tree squirrels all over the lawn, sometimes quite far from any tree, some will even eat out of your hand. Same squirrels, different environments, different behaviors. The squirrels around my house tend to move in the highest limbs of my oak tree, limbs that won't support the weight of a cat, and when they travel from tree to tree they use wires: electric wires, phone wires, cable TV wires. You'll see urban rats and possums use wires like this as well.

Based on the same logic as waiting or hunting, this is semiotic behavior because you can't avoid nothing; you have to be avoiding something. If you travel by wire instead of on the ground, you must be avoiding ground predators. Topanga has a number of aerial predators, though the area where I live, Fernwood, is thick with trees and not compatible with the kind of highflying hunting practiced by the falcons and hawks I see commonly at the ranch where there's a lot of open space. There the squirrels travel quickly from one underground tunnel to another.

How aware the squirrel is that she's avoiding predators is irrelevant; the avoidance behavior occurs toward a potential and absent predator and in place of non-avoidance behavior, that is, traveling on the ground or on top of the fence where, in fact, my cats spend time. The next thing to ask is whether or not each squirrel has to learn this for herself and, if so, how it is learned, or if the behavior is somehow transmitted among squirrels and, if so, how is that done.

Inadvertently, I was witness to parts of Romeo's first squirrel hunt. On the southeast corner of our property there's a telephone pole and from it two wires extend to our house, a cable wire to the second story southeast corner and an electric cable to the second story northeast corner, both at the front of my house. Both go through the thick branches of our big California Oak tree. I never see squirrels on those wires, though a lot of wires also run parallel to the road and squirrels sometimes traveled up and down the boulevard that way. There are, as well, wires that extend over the vacant lot to the houses above us on the hill; a high, thick electric wire and several cable wires about five feet below it. I often saw a squirrel travel across the vacant lot on the high wire, then drop down to the lower wires where they ran to the top of a wooden fence. The squirrel swung down to the fence from there and disappeared.

Sometimes I saw the squirrel coming from the other direction. He ran all the way to the telephone pole and then proceeded down the boulevard on the wire that hung in the open, high above the road, toward the Mimosa Café (I don't think he was going for croissants, I never saw him there); I never saw him go in the other direction where the wires ran in front of my fence and through the thick bows of another tree. I assume that's because a predator like a cat could be waiting in those boughs and, in fact, it had been hunting territory for my female calico, Music Batty, for years. Now she's gone and the territory is Romeo's. As I've noted, I suppose that traveling by open wires would leave a squirrel vulnerable to a bird of prey, but eagles don't come into this human inhabited side of the road and I've only seen hawks pick up rodents and snakes, and this at the ranch where there's much more open field; I haven't seen that near my home. Crows predate on road carrion here, though will pick up living rodents at the ranch. Recently I learned that owls do hunt near my house when one attacked a kitten on my deck.

One day I saw a squirrel running across the wire from the telephone pole, over the lot toward the fence, though the fence itself was not visible from my angle. Romeo, sitting on the floor of my living room, looked out the big window and saw the squirrel, too. That day when Romeo left the house he went over to the vacant lot, rare behavior for him because it was not his hunting territory, and in the morning the squirrel was dead on my living room floor, a Romeo drop spot. A few weeks later I spotted another squirrel crossing the lot by wire and he ended up dead in my living room, too. That ended the squirrel crossing for a couple years, though recently there is a new squirrel using the wires and he has not been hunted.

In general I'd always assumed that a squirrel would be too tough for a cat, but I guess I was wrong. Further, I know that some kind of size evaluation must be made by the cat predator. The Cheese, who is fifty percent bigger than Romeo, generally kills bigger animals than Romeo does. I'm not saying it's a self-conscious choice, but somehow some animals are perceived as too big. Where is that "too big" line? In the case of Romeo, the biggest rats were about a third his size, but the squirrels were bigger than the rats he caught and, as stated earlier, he apparently killed the squirrels immediately; if he'd been roughing up a squirrel in the living room, I'd have heard it. The only other time he killed immediately was when my female, Ichi Bu, had a litter and he went in the closet and started killing the males, he got three of six kittens before I caught him, and he left them on the living room floor as well, another story. Cheese will kill a rabbit half his size. The urban pigeons, though light in weight, looked a big as our female cat, Yoko Dodo, which would imply a different evaluation for birds. However instinctive, these evaluations must occur semiotically. Again, this is paradigmatic, watch your cats hunt.

Back to the first squirrel; Romeo saw what I saw and he had to go to the spot where the lower wire neared the fence, likely waiting on the two-by-four that formed the fence frame, thus hidden by the top eight inches or so of the fence. My cats sit and travel on these frames all the time. It's possible he waited somewhere else, somewhere the squirrel came down to the ground on the other side of the fence. Regardless, Romeo had to perceive that the wire was a means of travel for the squirrel. He had to follow the wire and go and wait at a spot where the wire and the squirrel were both accessible to him.

Possibly he first went there and then observed where the squirrel came down. Still, he had to go to that spot based on his observations of the squirrel traveling on the wire and where the wire went and then wait there, hidden, for the next time. To figure this out required memory and figuring by the use of synthetic icon cognition.

Hiding is another interesting behavior that I'll have to discuss, but this kind of pursuit and wait hunting, this kind of thinking, is a part of certain kinds of basic hunting behavior, in fact that's what H.D. was doing when she figured out how to go to the Mimosa. She was croissant hunting. A sequence of icons occurs consecutively and the animal acts on them. Romeo went to the place where the squirrel became accessible and waited there; he had to go to a place not in front of him at the time and wait for a squirrel that wasn't in front of his face. He had to make an inference about where the squirrel traveled, go there, and wait. He had to wait for the squirrel he remembered, not some other animal. More so, the behavior had to be initiated by icon cognition, however much the start of the behavior ignited a string of hunt icons, possibly occurring simultaneously with the hunt. Regardless, the series of behaviors leading to his waiting behind the fence had to be initiated cognitively.

Moreover, the proclivity to hunt, or think, in a given way isn't behavior ubiquitous in one species nor exclusive to a given species. Like waiting, a good deal of animal learning has a lot to do with intelligence, with kinds of intelligence, with the tendencies of a given personality, and the desire of the animal for the thing hunted or waited for. Jackie O waited for me. Though Tasha did not wait for me, after I arrived the context changed; Jackie O left and she waited for Jackie O and me to return; that is, when her companion left her, her disposition changed from satisfaction to dissatisfaction and she called out and waited. Cheese was as bright as Romeo, and though he seemed capable of waiting abstractly on a rock for something to move, or going to a nest where he'd previously found prey (I don't know how he originally found the nests); he didn't seem to have the desire or concentration to figure out how to hunt a squirrel. Romeo did, even in Cheese's territory.

After H.D. died, Gail and I decided to give an older, somewhat calmer, Piccolo, his crack at the Mimosa Café. It didn't work out so well. He was still too hyper. But after his first visit he'd whine at the fence when we left and kept whining and yipping until we returned, the same kind of self-stimulated waiting as Tasha displayed. And though he was big enough to remove the cement block from the fence hole, he never did. Nonetheless, if we forgot to close the hole, when we left him he scampered up the steps to the top of the property, out the hole, then followed the fence to the bottom of the property where he'd spot us and run to us. Whether it was intelligence or inclination, he never made that triangle across the vacant lot that H.D. did, even though the worn path was there, and he never went to the café without us. Even though the path still existed and he sometimes traveled it, he never used it to follow us or head out for croissants on his own. Once, though, when Gail and I drove with him to the ranch where I first kept Jackie O, about two hundred yards down the road, after Gail drove home Piccolo noticed she was gone and ran home down the road he'd never set foot on previously.

In general, Piccolo wasn't a thinker and I imagine the first time he pursued us to the cafe came somewhat as a coincidence, but even that first time he had to conceive the sequence: that going out the hole would get him outside, he had to remember that, then run from the bottom of the steps to the top of the property, out the hole and down the fence until he saw us. Further, H.D. and Piccolo had very different personalities, inclinations, and desires. H.D. was strong willed, independent, more capable of calculation, and wanted croissants, if not a sphere of domination. Piccolo wanted to be with us.

Like most of our animals, Piccolo was a rescue and in his first couple of years with us he was just a bundle of mania, nervousness, and fear. He had cage habits, like preferring to defecate on a solid surface, our lower deck (yes, the poop deck), instead of on the dirt ground, habits that were never broken. Obviously he'd been abandoned by a household with a doorbell, because though we've never had one, when he heard a doorbell on the television he'd race downstairs to the front door, barking like a fool. It took him a long time to learn to ignore TV doorbells and to move in the specific direction of a sound, though I saw the moment it happened. Something thumped on our top deck. Piccolo jumped up, rampaging toward the stairs that led down to the front door, the opposite direction. Then he paused at the top of the steps, perked his ears, and ran barking through the bedroom to the deck. "Hey" I said to my family. "Piccolo had a thought."

It wasn't his first thought, but it was his first cognitive decision. If Piccolo was a bundle of frantic behaviors, one following another, he was, as well, a bundle of consecutive frantic icons and emotions, often without any meaningful sequence. I believed that he wasn't as stupid as he seemed, that his learning was inhibited by past mistreatment and his nervous disposition, and if we could get him to calm down he might begin to behave in ways that followed iconic sequences, his first learning of new things, his first figuring things out. This proved to be true. The lesson is that cognition is a form of behavior and even in human beings it's seldom separable from visible behavior and seldom contemplative or free of hundreds of behavioral contingencies. Nonetheless, sometimes cognitive behavior precedes visible behavior, initiates it, and that is an emergent characteristic of sentience.

THE GAZE

AT LEAST DOMESTICALLY, the kind of line-of-sight hunting demonstrated by Romeo seems peculiar to cats. As well, cats demonstrate peculiar ways of taking possession. Aside from direct confrontation over territories like the food bowls, there are places in the house perceived as power places: the hassock in front of my chair, spots on either side of Gail, dining room chairs, Marlena's room, the inside of my dresser, and others. In general, Romeo sits on Gail's left on the couch, Nadine on her right. Nadine likes to curl up and sleep on the other end of the couch, too, and when she does Romeo will place himself on Gail's right, between Nadine and Gail, facing Nadine. Often enough, if Nadine wakes up and sees him there, she'll charge at him, but even if she is awake he might taunt her by throwing his tail in her face. This is ritualized now. Her lunges are generally without a show of teeth. Romeo raises a paw, even bats, but doesn't extend his claws, though it can, on occasion, escalate to fangs and claws and Gail steps in and places Romeo back on her left. Nadine settles in on her right.

Anyone who has cats knows that they take possession and special positioning very seriously. Mucha Plata attacked the telephone that I held close to my face, as well as the Rololdex near the phone, the cards of which I "petted" or stroked trying to find a number. She knocked them on the floor. Veronica, who for the most part ignores me, takes exception to my lap top, and will try to sit on my lap if I open the computer when I sit on my chair. Though Veronica and Yoko will share the hassock at my feet, Romeo will not share that space, and though he can intimidate one of them to move, he can't intimidate the two of them. Any cat owner will tell you tales of their cats placing themselves between the book or newspaper that they're trying to read. At this point, Romeo responds to the newspaper immediately; when I bring it in and put it on the kitchen counter while preparing breakfast, he sits on it. He sits on any part of the paper not being read at the time. He sleeps on the laptops in our business office. In the case of Gail, any object to which she gives her attention will be immediately sat on when she puts it down.

Dogs seem less territorial in that way, though they can be emphatically possessive of things they perceive as *theirs*. Avarice for food is not very abstract. When I'm carving the Thanksgiving turkey, Nadine and her three guest cousins are pretty univocal in their greed. Bones are a little more ambiguous. There are usually bones lying around the house and Nadine doesn't want any other animal near them. She'll chase cats away from them, take them away from other dogs. But a bone, no matter how old and flavor bereft, can still be seen as food, iconically if not actually, and the competition for it simply that, maybe. But Nadine will protect her toys, as well. H.D., who did not play with toys, would collect Piccolo's toys under the dining room table and then lie down on them. Later I'll look at Nadine's use of bones and toys to mark territory.

The question is whether or not the act of taking possession of something implies any kind of proto-selfhood, if there is any semiotic progression from identifying an object or a territory as something to protect from others, a progression to some level of body awareness, a progression to recognizing oneself in mirrors as do the higher primates.

Animals look at us, more often than not because they want something. If Nikki, my new horse, wants a carrot she'll face me and pound her hoof, or if I'm not looking at her, rumble and pound her hoof until I look at her. Nadine will come into the kitchen and woof or whine, she might even look at the spot on the counter where her snacks are kept, look at me, then look at the counter, then look at me, at my face, and then the counter again. This is very common behavior in dogs; anyone can observe it. When H.D. wanted to leave somewhere, she put her paw on my knee, looked at me, then looked at the door, or even in the direction of a door that was out of sight. Veronica will cry, take a step toward the cat room, stop and turn, look at my face and cry again, then step again. That animals point with their heads and bodies indicates a primitive use of indexes. To argue that it's too primitive, that is, immediate and not abstract, eradicates the concept of the index entirely; almost all indexes anybody uses point right at something: that cup right there, that food on the counter, that door, or in H.D.'s case, out, let's go home, a home many miles away.

But right now I'm more interested in eye contact. Obviously, in the way a cat will go straight to my hand if she wants to be petted, disregarding the rest of my personhood entirely, animals become very aware that our faces are what they have to relate to if they want something to happen. That's how you get our attention. If Veronica wants to be petted while she eats, she enters the room, looks up at my face and mews. If I stop petting her while she eats, she turns and looks at me, at my face, and mews until I begin petting her again. She doesn't rub on my hand, she looks at my face. This could all be seen as rote and simple enough. She has simply associated my face as the thing that gets her what she wants, my face and my eyes. But there are more immediate and obvious objects she could appeal to, like the food container itself or my hands that reach in and put the food in the bowls.

The other day, Veronica was hiding in the bamboo between the vacant lot and our house because Gail's mom was visiting. Veronica leaves the house when we have any guests at all (Romeo is the opposite, if they don't bring dogs, and crawls all over the guest, ambiguously exploiting the line between domination and affection). Veronica had missed breakfast, but when I got up from reading the paper and walked to the big windows on that side of the house, she sprung from her hiding spot, looked up at me across the patio and through the window into the house, looked at my face, and then scampered around the front of the house, through the downstairs door, and when I turned she was at the bottom of the stairs, looking up at me. Mew. Pet her while she eats.

If you've owned female cats, then you know that they have an uncanny understanding of the interior geography of your house. From the outside, they know where you are inside. Music Batty, who lived outside, would be at my feet the moment I walked out any door. In the early Eighties, when I lived in a huge apartment complex in Davis, California, my female cat, Kih-hen, found and entered our apartment from the second story back balcony. Recently we spotted Romeo sitting on the fence behind the house next door, a good thirty yards away at a forty-five-degree angle, looking toward our corner window from where he could see Gail, and from where, in her seat at the corner of the couch, she could see him. Call it accidental, but I'll return to that.

Any pet owner knows that our animals don't just look at our faces, they look us in the eyes. The eyes may be the window to the soul, but an animal needn't know that they are windows to mine or theirs. If we lead and express with our faces, then the eyes are the action of the face. To get our attention you must get our glance. So I don't believe that Veronica or any other animal knows she is looking me in the eyes, using her eyes to look at my eyes. She's learned that she must get me to look at her to get my attention, though once again, that we meet each other's gaze is uncanny.

Most people, in fact, do not meet my gaze when they speak to me, and I would have to attribute the gaze of an animal as remarkably unselfconscious in direct opposition to the same behavior in humans who must do it very consciously; attributing very different intentions to the same behavior when, upon inspection, the issue of the consciousness or self-consciousness is an arbitrary distinction, behaviorally or otherwise. When battling cats face off, they look each other in the eyes; we face off to request, to beg, to battle, to express our affection; it's part of the body language of the act or gesture, animal or human; as William James pointed out, consciousness is not a process that resides only in the mind or brain but in the whole body of the organism; the source of the icon is in the gesture. Eye contact is eye contact pure and simple and the symbolic meaning of it is something added on, something that comes after; the human request, "look me in the eyes" is the request for that simple gesture first and foremost.

Back to Romeo, staring into the house from thirty yards away, looking at Gail. When Gail and I watch TV, he crosses the room and jumps up onto the cabinet the screen sits on. He sits in front of the screen; he sits in front of the middle of the screen ten feet away. This is a little different than sitting on a laptop or a newspaper. Even if he's simply dominating the object of our attention, like judging where the squirrel traveled, he must take note of where we are looking and place himself between it and us. Further, he cannot get on the flat screen. He must place his body in front of it. He must see where we are looking and place himself between us and the TV.

Because cats don't empathize—I'll discuss that more later—if I go to the television and put Romeo on the floor, he'll jump back up. He's a cat. He can do that over and over. So I said to Gail, "Let's conduct an experiment. Let's stop looking at the screen and start talking to each other." When we did, Romeo got down. And that's how we get him to get down now. But to do so he must notice that we are no longer looking at him and the screen, that we are no longer paying attention *to him*.

When Veronica displays in front of me as I sit in my chair, moving toward me then moving away, back and forth, flicking her tail, then finally rolling on her back and exposing her prodigious stomach, she raises her head and looks at me from between her legs. I've seen this kind of display, i.e rolling head to head, between males and females during mating, though exposing the stomach is mostly done by the female. Loosely I might say that when she looks at me she's looking to see if I'm watching her, yet if that assumes too much awareness on her part, then at least I can say that like waiting or hunting, she can't display to no one for no reason. The display requires a context, an attitude, a desire for my attention and is an icon to me for that. I have a new chubby female, Frida, who now does the same thing.

The act of getting our attention in any context requires that an animal desires the transition from one cognitive emotional state, say being hungry or wanting to be petted, to the state of having us give them food or pet them (or both!). Getting our attention is an action taken to solve that transition. It's cognitive/emotional even if not premeditated. The animal must notice whether or not our attention has been achieved by seeing that our behavior has changed; now we're looking at him. Now he can make his request, point, move toward, bark or mew, or all of those, other transitions. It's absurd to try to explain that behavior without acknowledging those series of cognitive/emotional states, even if we might argue that the animal technically doesn't notice that we *see him*, he only notices the behavior that next leads to getting what he wants, our looking at him.

Romeo's sitting in front of the TV combines cognitive/emotional needs: his desire for attention and his desire to dominate; as I've stated above, these are difficult to separate. But unlike sitting on my lap or rubbing on me, it combines with line-of-sight hunting and the understanding of where we are looking. He doesn't play with the images on the TV screen, as many cats will do, patting at fishes or birds—one of our cats, Ichi Bu, played with Jay Leno's hands during his monologue and even ran to the television screen when she heard the Tonight Show theme—but he must comprehend on some level that we are looking at the screen, or that our attention is toward the screen. Whether or not he understands that we are now looking at him, though in fact we are, and he is looking at us, its roots lie in "getting attention" behavior, in the gaze, in a preternatural understanding of eyes and looking, demonstrated even more explicitly by his getting down when we turn our attention away from him, that being a transition similar to Nadine's when she comprehends that the squirrel is no longer in the tree, though, of course, in this instance, a bit more sophisticated, and in this behavior lies the rudiments of self recognition demonstrated in primates and elephants and dolphins, the *comprehension of being looked at*, the rudiments of the social self in Mead's conversation of gestures, Mead failing to observe the conversation of iconic repertoire involved. Here, in the icons of getting our attention, facial recognition, the rudiments of understanding that they are being looked at, in eye contact, in the gaze, in line-of-sight hunting. Here lies the early soul of selfhood, or in the words of Jacques Lacan paraphrasing Merleau Ponty, " . . . we are beings who are looked at and it is this which makes us conscious." Unfortunately, Lacan is referring only to human consciousness.

WHAT'S UP
IN EUROPE?

SPEAKING OF EUROPEAN THINKERS in this matter, in recent years a number of Post-Structural, European philosophers, including Jean-Christophe Bailly, Giorgio Agamben, and Jacques Derrida, taking the nod from Maurice Merleau-Ponty's *Nature: Course Notes from the College de France* (*La Nature: Notes, cours du College de France*, 1956-60), have begun to discuss animal sentience and cognition. Agamben (*The Open: Man and Animal*) and Bailly (*The Animal Side*) concentrate on Heidegger's interpretation of the breakthrough work of the early 20th Century zoologist Jakob von Uexküll's concept of *umwelt*, a neo-Kantian concept that distinguishes between the world such as it exists in itself and the world as the world known by a living being (approximating Kant's distinction between neumena and phenomena).

Uexküll opposed the Cartesian subject (consciousness)—machine distinction as well as what he regarded as previous scientific notions that anthropomorphized animals. Nonetheless, he describes animal behavior as a kind of melody pre-written in the animal body and played out in the environment in a laborious, if gorgeous, mutual conditioning. The *umwelt* of an animal provokes its milieu and the animal is in return conditioned by its milieu in so far as its *umwelt*, or biological capabilities, can be influenced given the predetermination of its biology. How the animal manipulates its world, e.g., how a spider's web creates a transition between the spider and the world, is a dialectic that is the very beginning of culture. However much this might remind us of Mead's conversation of gestures and lead us toward semiotics, Uexküll insists that the animal, without symbolic awareness, is more like an embodied goal than a cognitive being, a Leibniz-like windowless monad. The animal is not self-consciously aware of the world. In that sense he regards the *umwelt* of the non-human animal as "closed."

This is certainly how Heidegger reads him when he comes to the conclusion, like Descartes—as Derrida points out in *The Animal That Therefore I Am*—that the animal, unlike the human, is incapable of *dasein*, of "being in the world." As Agemban elucidates, for Heidegger, "the stone, lifeless, is worldless (*weltlos*), the animal is poor in the world (*weltarm*), man is world-forming (*weltbilden*)."

If Ponty is more or less an explication of Uexküll, among many others, in his analysis of the history of the concept of *Nature*, Agamben is more or less an analysis of Heidegger's explication, and agreement, with Uexküll.

> Insofar as the animal knows neither beings nor non-beings, neither open nor closed, it is outside of being; it is outside in an exteriority more external than any open, and inside in an intimacy more internal than any closedness. To let the animal would then mean: to let it be *outside of being*. The zone of non-knowledge—or of a-knowledge—that is at issue here is beyond both knowing and not-knowing, beyond both disconcealing and concealing, beyond both being and the nothing (Gamben, *The Open*, p. 91).

This is pretty murky territory, a dance of subtleties and denials but clearly an affirmation of Heidegger that doesn't leave much room for animal cognition.

Deconstructing a moment when during a night time drive down a back road a driver (him?) and a passenger spot a deer in the woods, Jean-Christophe Bailly renounces Heidegger in favor of Rilke, comparing "looking" to "hunting" and the act of being looked at to the act of being hunted, again a recognition of some kind of awareness and unawareness both. There is a Derridian-like reversal in the suggestion of cognition in "being hunted," that the experience of hunting and being hunted is one inseparably shared between human and animal. We gaze, and they gaze.

> My concern is not that we should credit animals with access to thought; it is that we should move beyond human exclusivity, that we should let go of the eternally renewed credo according to which our species is the pinnacle of creation and has a unique future (Bailly, *The Animal Side*, p.15).

This suggestion is not new. Mark Twain said it; Derrida attributes the view to Montaigne; this without referring to non-technological cultures which, ages in the past, granted animal life consciousness, subjectivity, even equality, but Bailly performs a classic Derridian subversion of the human–animal dualism by intimating that the human *umwelt*, enclosed by the categorical narrowness of language, might possibly be less open than the *umwelt* of animal sentience. Reiterating Bentham, he suggests that we should not ask, do they think? but do they suffer?

The Animal Side is less an argument for animal cognition than a plea for humanity to treat animals as sentience to which we owe moral obligations. There is no theory, per se, but poetic presentation, argumentation ala Bachelard, for a re-thinking of our relationship toward animals, and the suggestion that the world would be a better place for having done it, for us as well as them.

Derrida, whose lectures during the 1997 ten-day Cerisy conference became the book *The Animal That Therefore I Am* (2008), pre-dates Bailly by fourteen years. Bailly's method is obviously deconstructive and his essay, like Derrida's, begins with a moment when he is confronted by an animal. In Derrida's case it is when he emerges naked from his bathroom and is confronted by his pet cat. This leads him to a winding deconstruction of the thought of Descartes, Kant, Heidegger, Lacan, and Levinas (he takes his shots at Aristotle, too) under the aegis of critiquing what he calls an ideational epoch of denying animals any subjectivity, to the point of slaughtering them and enslaving them without conscience. He is quick to point out, as well, that the term *animal* makes no reference to any specific animal or animal species we might be talking about. Could it be that apes gaze but ticks do not? As in all Derrida's work, there is a proliferation of qualification and digression, more questioning than stating, but the gist is that in our times, modern times since Descartes, not much has changed in the philosophical approach to animals; it is yet Cartesian. Derrida, in the beginning and the end, is always both nominalist and nihilist, and these critiques and his analysis will not leap to any statement about animal cognition, only suggesting that it might be high time someone, say a philosopher of animals, did.

To my mind, yet under the methodological influence of Hegel (as well as Descartes and Husserl), these discussions are meditative and dialectical, and tend to concentrate on the gaps or *caesurae* both separating human from animal and yet shared by human and animal, attempts to reassert the mystery, but not offer any suggestions or observations that deal with animal behavior and try to explain it; a kind of arm chair animal anthropology of admirable sentiment, at times even poetic sentiment, though they offer little to move the understanding of animal cognition forward.

FOLLOWING
AND HIDING

PART OF THE PROBLEM IN DISPUTING animal cognition with the non-conceptualists is that they have always been able to name the game and the rules, and they always play at home. If meaningful thinking only occurs in language, then conceptualists must show that animals have languages, and they don't. Consequently, in the search for glints of abstract behavior, we're immediately inclined to look for it at the top of the big brain chain: cetaceans, primates, sometimes elephants. Whales and elephants are hard to experiment on. Dolphin sonar communication has been pretty indecipherable, and though they seem to use the same sounds to refer to each other as individuals—some people have referred to that as a naming—it's still a long way from language and more akin to baby seals recognizing their mother's unique call. Dolphins sure can learn a lot of tricks, even follow verbal commands, but that's still easily explained by cuing and reinforcement models.

We have captive primates who demonstrate the use of sign languages—matching symbols to things, asking for things, naming—but they don't demonstrate the use of syntax, that is, the construction of abstract meaning based on context and the rules of how words take on meaning in a sentence. This, syntax, is the dividing line between whether you believe that cognition is an emergent characteristic of the human brain only, or whether it is an emergent characteristic of sentience.

Cheney and Seyfarth's amazing and exhaustive work with baboons in the wild (*Baboon Metaphysics*) leads them to what they call a "Theory of Social Mind." But their problem, methodologically, is that they must infer the possibility of cognition in baboons from what they see as ostensible social behavior. Their experiments in the wild with various call recognitions seem to imply, they argue, that baboons make cognitive distinctions about one caller over another based on social context and troop hierarchy. They speculate, then, that cognition often arises from social contexts, though there are other primates, like orangutans, who seem just as smart and who aren't social, and other animals, like hyenas and wolves, who are quite social but not apparently as smart. (I say "apparently" because the description of intelligence in terms of a linear progression of behavioral abilities is another problem with non-conceptualist, experimental analysis of behavior). Further, Cheney and Seyfarth admit that behavioral contingencies could explain baboon social responses.

In the end, they offer a postulation, not a theory, that baboons demonstrate cognition and do so because they need it to negotiate their complex social environment. They speculate about what this apparent social behavior in baboons might imply, instead of developing a theory that would guide their observations and experiments. The fact is, they're right, but they haven't really got a theory of cognitive behavior to work from. So in spite of what would seem to be repeated and overwhelming evidence of cognitive behavior in the social interactions of baboons, without a theory, they find themselves, once again, floating in the void; baboons do not have syntax and only display behavior, and if we can't find cognition at the top of the non-human brain chain, good luck finding it below.

This problem lies at the center of Donald R. Griffins's copious study, *Animal Minds*, as well. He offers thousands of examples of animal and insect behavior—the warning calls of birds, as well as migration and behavior that distracts predators from their nests, the location dances of bees, squirrels that hide food and mislead others who are watching them—that seem to imply cognition, but he doesn't have a theory.

If I am forced to infer cognitive activity from a given behavior, because cognition is not observable, the game is already lost because observable, physical behavior becomes logically and chronologically primary to any observation, so physical behavior appears to explain itself. Why add cognition? Worse, cognition implies a being who thinks and not wanting to step into an ontological discussion about the nature of cognition, conceptualists must argue from the non-conceptualist premise of monist materialism; the world is physical and there are physical causes and effects from which we try to glean regularities in order to understand them and, if we're lucky, manipulate them. Behavior can be tested in that world, cognition cannot. More so, to distinguish between cognition and behavior is to fall into the black hole of the mind-body problem. This is how animal cognition is crucified on the cross of ontology, syntax and science. The syntax-behavior dualism proves as fatal to animal cognition as the mind-body one; in fact it's just another version of it.

Ontological questions aside, in terms of humans, no one would deny that we think (syntax), the question is whether or not it has any relevance to how we behave. Even in your personal life, if you go around taking people at their word, you're in for a lot of trouble. My personal policy with human beings is that if they do something twice, then that's the behavior I can always expect. If your new acquaintance shows up late for your appointment twice in a row, then that's what you can expect from then on and her reasons don't matter; caught in traffic, babysitter didn't show, lost track of the time. She might even be sincere, but she will always be late unless, possibly, you change your behavior and take off after waiting ten minutes. That student who wants me to over-enroll him in my class because he got to registration late? If I enroll him, he's going to be late for class often and miss a lot of classes and assignments. I had to think to figure that out; I had to have it happen to me again and again over a number of years before I changed my behavior: don't enroll him no matter what the excuses and how congenial he appears.

Though much cognition is irrelevant to an individual's eventual behavior, cognition itself is behavior, too, replete with habits, reinforcement, contingencies and contextual evocations. Take a moment to notice what you think when you enter contexts that you repeat often, say, when you enter a given room or get in the car. Likely, you begin to think about the same stuff every time, sometimes image for image, word for word.

There are times, like when I decide not to wait for my persistently tardy friend, where my cognitive behavior acts to alter the context of my cognitive/emotional disposition from a dissatisfactory one to one that is more satisfactory, in the hope of spurring an unsatisfactory cognitive/emotional disposition in my friend, enough so that it might cause her to reflect upon changing her behavior in order to keep my friendship. In fact, she might not be capable, or she might not desire it enough, or she might change briefly and then backslide, then it's time for me to reflect on my behavior again, though I'll almost guarantee that a long talk with her will change nothing.

Much behavior, both human and animal, does not need cognition to explain it (though Virginia Woolf's *Mrs. Dalloway* might). Much cognition comes after the fact, or after the act. But cognition is behavior, *cognitive behavior*. What I've tried to demonstrate thus far is that though much of human cognition takes place in language, a good deal of human cognition is both non-verbal and meaningful and that semiotic cognition occurs within, without, or along with, language. Further, I wouldn't be the first to point out that much language behavior isn't reflective or self-conscious at all. Language gives us exponential cognitive capacities, among them reflection and creativity, but those capacities don't come automatically. I knew a pretty smart young woman in college who once said to me, "Before I met you, I never reflected on anything. I just moved from one thing to the next."

A further problem in equating syntax with meaning is the problematic conflation of awareness with self-consciousness when, in fact, awareness requires neither language nor self-consciousness. Anyone who has practiced meditation knows that you can be perfectly aware without either. Awareness is a kind of mental watching. I am aware that I am writing now, but that awareness does not manifest itself in a constant verbal self-reminding that "I am writing now." Sometimes I'm not aware that I'm writing, I'm just writing, in language, quite unselfconsciously. So too, with thought.

Much human intelligence finds its roots in the ability to think in language, but awareness does not. The elements that constitute the capacity for awareness are pre-lingual. Awareness requires semiotic capabilities. Its evolutionary routes lie deep in the behaviors of waiting and hunting and watching and those potentials are often developed and honed in social interaction. This is why chimpanzees can learn to recognize themselves in mirrors and make and use primitive tools. As David Bekoff has argued, these capacities are part of the evolution of sentience, they didn't spring miraculously from the head of humanity or Zeus. My dog can be aware that there is a squirrel in the tree. To be aware that she is aware requires language.

Non-human animals, as well as humans, display levels of cognitive/emotional behavior and, using semiotics, act on it. That all meaningful cognition occurs only in language is simply wrong. That cognitive behavior is irrelevant to explaining observable behavior is wrong, too. In fact, as I've tried to demonstrate, if *thoughts* other than our own are not observable, cognitive behavior, cognitive/emotional transitions, are observable. But non-conceptualists have controlled the theories and the vocabulary by which we've analyzed behavior. An alternative model with an alternative vocabulary might offer explanations both more simple and confirmable, as well.

A good example of falling victim to vocabulary is the issue of whether or not animals imitate each other. Asking that question already eliminates the possibility of confirmation, because imitation requires self-consciousness and animals aren't self-conscious. Animals don't imitate (unless we look for possibilities in the highest non-human primates, as in chimpanzee tool use, but even this does not appear self-conscious), but animals do follow, an act which does not require self-consciousness, but does require cognition and awareness.

Let's re-examine the famous cats-in-a-box experiment. A half-dozen cats are placed in a large box with nothing in it but a lever that opens a door. If one cat accidentally hits the lever and the door opens and she goes out, the other cats do not imitate her and hit the lever. Conclusion, cats don't learn by imitation.

There are several contextual problems here. For starters, cats like to sit in boxes or bags. If you have a cat, you've likely found him sitting in a cardboard box for hours. Put an empty paper grocery bag on the floor, your cat will go inside and rumble around. So, next, it's unlikely that any of the cats would want to leave the box, to leave a certain and safe situation for an uncertain one. Further, the cats weren't dropped into the box *tabula rasa*. They have histories and memories in regard to leaving a secure place, including a box, for an unknown one. Possibly, if something that caused a dissatisfactory cognitive/emotional disposition were placed in the box, and some known reward, such as safety and food, were outside the box, one of the other cats would have followed the first one toward that door and pawed at it, likely accidentally hitting the lever and opening it. Like the bells outside my farmhouse door, I guarantee it would only take once or twice for the other cats to learn to hit the lever.

When Italo first began to go outside, he had to remember—as St. Augustine would remind us—how he got out in order to get back in, in his case the back bedroom door. But sitting in the living room one day he observed the Cheese jump to one of our big windows and then jump from there to the railing of our top, back deck. Of course, Italo did not think, "Hey, there's another way to get outside. I'll do what Cheese did." But he made the semiotic distinction between out and in. Had the cognitive/emotional disposition to go out (where the Cheese went), and he followed the icon of Cheese jumping onto the window sill. There, he hesitated in front of the leap, about three feet across and one foot up, the drop, if he missed, about ten feet. The first time, after hesitating for a number of minutes, he jumped back into the living room (How are we to characterize that choice made amidst uncertainty, fear, and desire? How does a cat first decide whether or not he can successfully complete a leap?). But the next time he did it. He jumped. And he came back in that way, too, jumping from the railing to the sill, something he hadn't done before. He had to remember where and how he got out and know that the way out was also the way in, even if that inference was very implicit, because there are other ways out and in and my cats don't always come back in the same way they left. They also recognize a closed window and don't jump into the glass, though they can see through it. I don't know how that is learned, but I know it isn't trial and error. Further, though I've used Italo as the example here, this behavior is paradigmatic; I've seen dozens of cats do this and other kinds of following.

Even if my cats always choose to come in at the most convenient entrance to where they happen to be located when they want to come in, if that access is closed, they'll try another, or if they see me inside, cry at me to open the window or door. Often enough, they'll leave by one way but request to be let in another. How is that decision made? At the very least, how can they want to come in without *wanting*?

In a week Italo knew all the ways to get in and out, the doors and windows, and how to get to the front balcony by coming over the roof or climbing the avocado tree and dropping down. I watched this closely and I observed that in the beginning, the first times he did these things they followed closely on the heels of Cheese or Romeo doing them.

However mechanically and unselfconsciously we might wish to explain this learning behavior, it isn't arbitrary behavior linked by a gratifying stimulus to a given response. He didn't learn to poke a blue square over a yellow one because he was rewarded after accidentally poking the blue square and not rewarded when he poked the yellow one. His disposition preceded the learning. The behavior followed a desire. Italo had to distinguish between in and out and desire a change in his disposition of *in*, that is somehow want to leave *in* and go *out*. That distinction is semiotic. Our animals desire to go in or out all of the time, and to want one to replace the other requires semiotic cognition, wanting *in* is likely to include desires for warmth, affection, food, a favorite place to sleep. *Out* might mean needs for defecation and urination, including territorial marking, desires to hunt, to scratch and climb trees, or visit the neighbor who gives him tuna. In Italo's case, when first learning, he had to cognize that Cheese got *out* by jumping out the window. The learning behavior was self-stimulated by his disposition, a disposition that stimulated his following. Again, this is not simply an anecdote, but paradigmatic behavior that you can observe in your home everyday.

Implicit in my argument here has been the contention that the search for animal cognition often aims too high. Researchers want to see symbolic intelligence and look for it in the animals apparently most capable of demonstrating it. But for the most part, animals don't think in symbols (though sometimes they do). They think in signs. This follows a long spectrum from limited use in predators like fish and spiders, to sophisticated use by animals like chimps and whales. The spectrum has breadth, as well, explaining the kinds of semiotic communication that occur in honey bees and the memory capacities of birds who store food or migrate. Intelligence, like most things, is neither linear nor univocal, not in the progression from less intelligence to more, nor in quality or kind of intelligence, like the differences between the ability of birds to migrate compared to the ability of lions to plan a hunt in a group; in both cases biology, necessity, and context have been at work a long time.

The non-conceptualist failure to make certain distinctions is as nettlesome as their desire to insist on distinctions which are not so distinct. My dog, Nadine, likes to play hide and seek, especially after a walk when I've opened my truck door and I'm waiting for her to jump in; but she's very bad at it. Like a child who thinks she's invisible when her eyes are closed, Nadine will hide behind a bush, peering out from behind it with most of her body quite visible to me. But am I to conclude that Nadine isn't hiding simply because she isn't hidden? What is she doing? I must add here that as she got older she became more sophisticated; when she wanted to hide, she removed herself from my line of vision, though sometimes, when anticipating a walk, she'll run outside and sit behind a bush. I imagine, in this case, her anticipation crosses over into waiting/hunting behavior. These kinds of behavioral crossovers are common in all of us; if I feel nervous or threatened I might yell at my daughter or partner.

My cats are much more effective at hiding. When I crossed the country by auto with Mr. Puff, he could hide all twenty pounds of himself in a hotel room to my complete bewilderment. I could conclude that cats are just smaller, but likely their ability to hide is linked, as well, to their mode of predation. Dogs are chasers, cats are waiters and hiders. In fact while my dogs chased moving prey, lizards, birds, squirrels, by lighting out after them, my cats were much more likely to entrap sighted prey by taking away angles, that is, cutting off where the animal was trying to flee.

Italo loved to play with Nadine. He would roll over, let her place her snout on his stomach, and hug and pat it, claws in. One game they played a lot was for her to chase him behind something long, like a couch or a wide cabinet. Nadine quickly learned that if Italo went in one side, then he came out the other, and she ran there to wait for him. Italo quickly learned she'd be waiting and reversed directions and came out the side he went in, until she learned that and waited for him there, whereupon he went back to his original behavior of running out the other end. That went on and on, but Italo was always a step ahead of Nadine.

Nadine is bright. She has a pretty large vocabulary of single words she recognizes and responds to with specific behaviors: Momma, Dad, Sister (my daughter), boyfriend (my daughter's boyfriend), out, dinner, breakfast, snack, walk, the phrase "take a walk," hot tub, her own name -Nadine, as well as the pronouns she and her, and the word dog, the names of our close friends and their pets, on and on, unlike my cats who seem to care very little about most of my specific sounds; yet in her play with Italo, Nadine never learned, or never chose to learn, to position herself at an angle where she could see both ends of the couch or cabinet. I say "chose to learn" because she is clearly intelligent enough, but the chase, the playing chase, was deeper than her desire to catch Italo. She displays this behavior in reverse when she plays with Gail, running with a toy, dropping it in front of Gail, then grabbing it when Gail reaches for it, or letting Gail pick it up and then chasing Gail.

In terms of Nadine and Italo I wouldn't venture to speculate about who was more intelligent, because like the difference between lions and birds the *kind* of intelligence has everything to do with it. I doubt Piccolo would have ever figured out stage one, that Italo came out the other end. The other cats aren't that fond of play or Nadine and simply take the high ground, though when they hide from her on the floor—I don't know why they choose one and not the other—they place themselves out of site or somewhere inaccessible and stay put. The behavior in between these appears to be a form of taunting—you've seen it—where the cat places herself in sight of the dog, say, on the top of a fence, and sits there watching while the dog barks and jumps below.

What I'm implying here is that hiding, like waiting and hunting, are generically related behaviors. Nadine waits for us at the gate, the cats wait up in the trees. Nadine pursues prey, the cats stalk, using combinations of waiting and hiding, which explains why they hide better. Do cats hide better because they're more aware that they're hiding? Well, there are some peculiar differences in the paradigms of wait/hunt behavior in my cats, depending on the context.

My cats waited in the open while watching the mouse holes in the sky, where the element of surprise was simply that they were waiting there, as if aware that the ascending mice couldn't see them. Mr. Puff waited for the ground squirrels behind the entrance hole where the emerging squirrels couldn't see him, because in front of the hole, they could. Romeo hid behind the top of the fence to wait for the squirrel.

Line-of-sight hunting intelligence harbors, as Romeo demonstrated by sitting in front of the television, a body awareness, a proto-self awareness to hide from the sight of prey. Certainly, in animals like cats, hunting dispositions are deeply biological; cats don't learn to hide from the sight of potential prey by trial and error, anymore than a hawk learns to capture a poisonous snake by grabbing it just behind the head. But to hide, in any case, you must *hide from*, and in hunting, hide from something not present, in some cases anticipating the line of sight of what a potential prey would see when it emerged from its own hiding.

When Nadine hides behind a bush, she certainly acts as if I can't see her. If I look right at her and call her, she doesn't move. I have to pretend to find her before she jumps out and runs to my truck. If I deny that Nadine is hiding because she's not good at it, because she doesn't seem to be aware that she's visible, then do I acknowledge that the hiding behavior of my cats does demonstrate awareness because they are good at it? No. Simply, they hide and hide/hunt in different ways in different contexts. But hiding exhibits implicit intentionality that needn't be self-conscious.

A non-conceptualist model simply doesn't explain the subtle differences in all these kinds of hiding. By insisting on a dualism, self-conscious awareness or none, the subtleties and levels of semiotic awareness in these different kinds of hiding, each responding to context, can't be observed. Nadine aside, whose behavior is playful and with little at stake, the cats, whose behavior determines a successful hunt or not, interpret the necessities and degrees of their hiding, understanding the context by a sequence of signs and adjusting their behavior accordingly. To insist that they learn by trial and error how to hide from prey ignores their interpretation of contexts where they perceive that they don't have to hide. Even so, learning by trial and error requires semiotic cognition at some point, however minimal, and barely accounts for the speed with which they learn or their ability to generalize from one hunting context to another and apply the correct kind of hiding. Once again, when I'm at the ranch I observe hawks swoop to the ground and pick up rattlesnakes by the neck, flying away with the live snake dangling. They land on a fence or branch and kill the poisonous snake by pecking at its head. Where is the trial and error, the learning curve, there? Non-conceptually, I'm forced to fall into that mysterious hole of biological explanation, hard-wired instinct, but upon any reflection at all, the leap from biology to behavior is pretty mystical.

The issue is not whether or not the figuring is mechanical or rote, it's that recognition of the context must occur, the situation must be interpreted, behavior enacted as a prelude to expectations. Self-awareness isn't needed to do these things. Semiotic cognition is needed. Reducing these behaviors under the blinders of behavioral contingencies simply disregards much of the behavior. It's like trying to fit an elephant in a garbage can; if you can do it, it ain't an elephant no more.

THE
COUNTER
CULTURE

THERE WAS A TIME WHEN I didn't feed my animals by hand, didn't feed them any human food, didn't let my cats go up on the table or on the counters, but all things change. For starters, after H.D. and Piccolo died, Gail got our new dog, Nadine, and Gail never followed those rules. In fact, Gail is not very big on rules at all. She has no interest for training animals. She doesn't even teach her dogs to sit, stay, or lie down on command (I do, if reluctantly, but if Gail wants Nadine to stop bugging her and go lie down, I have to make Nadine do it).

When Marlena lived with us and we had H.D. and Piccolo, she taught Piccolo to sit, jump up, and roll over. Though H.D. was considerably brighter, she wanted nothing to do with any of that. If you tried to make her do something to get a reward, she walked away. In fact it's a myth that animals, dogs in particular, value food above everything. There are other things, in context, more or equally important, like affection and ritual or, in H.D.'s case, something else, an attitude, something unfigurable.

When we adopted Nadine from an animal rescue in South Central Los Angeles, she was extremely timid. She'd obviously had a bad experience with a man because she was afraid of me at first, then, when her confidence grew, she barked madly at me every time I entered a room; it didn't matter if I'd only left for ten seconds. She yet does this with friends, men in particular, who visit for the first time or if she hasn't seen them for several months. As well, there are people she accepts much more quickly than others and some friends who she has never quite accepted, even when encouraged by dog snacks. She's a wonderful dog, often acutely aware of what's going on around her. For example, if we're getting ready to leave the house without her, she recognizes the behavioral pattern, hangs her head and goes to her spot on the couch, lying down with her head moping between her paws. Though she prefers to spend time with Gail, if Gail takes a shower, preparing to leave, Nadine will come down to my office and sit with me, anticipating Gail's departure. If I take off my clothes, Nadine runs to the hot tub and runs around it, in fact I only have to say, "hot tub," to get her to do it. If I begin to put other clothes back on, she recognizes immediately whether or not I'm dressing for a run or dressing to ride Nikki. If I grab my running socks she explodes into excited frenzy. And as with her barking at new people, she then seems to fall into an impenetrable behavioral hole. But humans fall into these behavioral holes, too.

Nadine is part Ridgeback and part Catahoula. If you read about them you find that both breeds are notoriously rambunctious and needy. When we went on line to research them, one piece of advice for Ridgebacks was, "Not for first-time dog owners," another for Catahoula, "Difficult to control; great if you like dog training." Well, as I said, Gail doesn't train dogs. Let anarchy reign.

And reign it did. Because as Nadine became accustomed to her new home she turned out to be one hell of a lot of dog. Her energy is boundless. She loves to play. She loves to be chased and bait you with a toy. And she loves to chase. Cats. My cats. They headed for the high ground, counters and tables, and began traveling around the house above Nadine. Because Nadine preferred to be upstairs in the living room with us, the cats inhabited the counters downstairs in the kitchen. And so began the Counter Culture.

I like a room full of cats and I missed having my cats around me. Age had taken Music Batty and Meesh. Mucha Plata was killed on the road. There were only three cats then, Yoko, Cheese, and Romeo, and they were all downstairs on the counters and nowhere else. I felt particularly bad for Romeo who was intensely attached to Gail. She'd adopted him as a kitten from a homeless man who sat across from us at an outdoor café in Malibu, a long-hair mackerel kitten in his lap.

Gail looked at the kitten and the kitten seemed to be looking at Gail. "That's a gorgeous kitten," Gail said to me.

"You don't even like cats," I said. Though we both knew that wasn't precisely true. When we first moved to Los Angeles she rescued a Norwegian Forest Cat and named her Elizabeth Taylor; they had a long and intimate relationship, though a few years after we moved to Topanga a mountain lion showed up in our avocado tree and the next day Liz was gone.

"Is that your kitten?" Gail asked the man.

"I'm waiting to give him to somebody," he said.

"Can I hold him?" said Gail.

The guy gave her the kitten and the kitten clung to her and purred madly.

"How long have you been waiting?" said Gail.

"Couple hours."

"I'll take him," she said.

"He's never been indoors," the man said.

Anyway, Romeo took to the indoors like a sailor to a ship. Piccolo had died, so we didn't have a dog, and Romeo followed Gail everywhere. And though I fed him everyday, but for that I didn't exist. In fact, if I tried to touch him or approached Gail while she was holding him, he hissed at me, which flies in the face of the conventional wisdom that if you want to be the most important person in an animal's life, just feed him. That's contradicted around my house all the time. I not only feed Nadine half the time, I take her for runs everyday. She likes me. She loves Gail. She waits nervously for Gail when Gail is away, always wants to sit next to her, sleep next to her; she competes with Romeo for Gail's attention.

Well so did Romeo until Nadine showed up. Now he spent his time outside or sulked next to the food bowls I set up for him on the far counter in the kitchen. Gail felt bad and went down to console him. He was inconsolable. She couldn't raise a purr from him. That went on for eighteen months. Then I got Italo.

Italo was an irrepressible extrovert. We always isolate kittens when we bring them in, but when I put him in Marlena's old bedroom he came out in an hour. He loved to run and chase with Nadine. She could put her nose under him and toss him in the air or he'd roll on his back and let her rest her head there. He baited her by playing with her toys. When he wasn't doing all that, he sat or slept with me, even at night, Gail and me separating him and Nadine. He followed me doggedly, down to my office, around the house and, unfortunately, even out the gate to my truck. I'd carry him back up to the house and close him in, but often he'd be waiting outside the gate for me when I got home.

Another minor change. Unlike H.D. or Piccolo, Nadine was an aggressive beggar. Gail indulged her, so I began to let Italo sit on the table next to me when I ate.

The original development of the Counter Culture startled me. I knew that cats often chose to remove themselves from situations they found unpleasant, but the Counter Culture went on for a year and a half. Nadine was bothersome and playfully aggressive, but two of these cats, Cheese and Yoko Dodo, had lived with two dogs all their lives.

If you have a cat, then you know that they go through a lot of behavioral transitions over the length of their lives, some lasting longer than others. Mr. Puff always had one room in the house he wouldn't go in, and that room changed every year or so. When he was thirteen he suddenly became fascinated with ribbons; chased and played with them constantly, he even dragged one around with him everywhere he went. That lasted about a year and when he was done with ribbons he was totally done. Dangle a ribbon in front of him and he'd yawn.

So I suppose the cats might have just fallen into the habit of never coming upstairs, and when and if one of them changed his mind, there was Nadine to remind him. But it wasn't so simple. Gail believed that Romeo was aggressively denying her. However I might want to describe the cats' emotions, the choice to never come upstairs seemed willful.

But with the arrival of Italo who spent time upstairs with us and Nadine, a change occurred. One night Romeo appeared upstairs and walked to the edge of the dining table, two leaps away from where Gail sat on the end of the couch. He left, but the next morning, after I fed the cats downstairs, he came upstairs and joined Italo, whom he didn't like at all, on the table for breakfast, the two of them bothering me for my cereal milk. Romeo had never done this before. Yoko appeared the next morning at my feet. The Counter Culture had turned into anarchy.

And so it went. Now Yoko Dodo crossed the living room by a system of furniture tunnels in order to sit on the hassock at my feet, because Italo was on my lap. If Nadine came up to her, Yoko nailed her. Nadine snarled. There was no love there. Romeo made the leap from table to chair to couch and placed himself at Gail's thigh, Nadine's head on the other thigh, the two of them glaring at each other. Sometimes Nadine snipped at him. He didn't budge. Finally, the Cheese came in the window, rubbed on the table legs, danced and meowed around the room, Nadine watching intently, sometimes even lunging slightly in the Cheese's direction, though she was loath to budge because it would give Gail's lap to Romeo. So the Cheese leapt into the chair next to mine. Italo lay next to my thigh. After eighteen months, the cat strike ended in a matter of days. Everybody was back. Though now we were stuck with the Counter Culture.

While Italo was alive, Gail and I talked about the cultural shift. When he came upon the scene, though the other cats weren't coming upstairs, Italo had no problem integrating into the Counter Culture downstairs. He jumped onto the cat bench in the morning and joined the disgruntled strikers for breakfast. Cheese whacked him on the head. Romeo hissed. Yoko growled. Italo ignored them. He was incorrigible (like Nadine). And when he was downstairs or outside, he followed Romeo everywhere, up the trees, over the roof, on top my office. Both were long hair mackerels and we speculated that Italo had other mackerels in his litter; his mother was mackerel, his uncle was mackerel, so he followed another mackerel because it was familiar, he'd been around them for much of his young life.

The strike was broken, I think, when Romeo noticed that Italo was going upstairs and he followed him. Yoko followed Romeo. Cheese followed them. If it wasn't choice, it was certainly change. But of course, implicitly, choice was involved. A disposition to behave one way was replaced by a disposition to behave another way. The Counter Culture didn't like Nadine now any more than they did two days previous. And however much you might want to break down the sequence of events into the behavioral contingencies of each cat's separate behavior, it was a group change; they all left for eighteen months and then they all came back.

The Counter Culture didn't like guests, either, especially if they brought a dog. Within seconds my cats disappeared. When the guests left, even if they'd spent the night, within a minute Yoko came out from under the futon, Romeo dropped out of a tree, the Cheese came through the window. Meow. Time to eat. Though after Italo's arrival, Romeo began to entertain guests if they didn't bring a dog.

In a society of animals, particularly within a species, individuals often fill various roles, though I've yet to really find the formula. Back in my Pennsylvania farmhouse days, the cats dealt with intruders by hiding around the yard behind bushes, then jumping out all at once in attack posture. It always worked, even against big dogs, but it's the only time I've ever observed team behavior in domestic cats.

In the era before the Counter Culture, I had a huge orange male named Littel. Littel was missing his right hind foot because Music Batty left the umbilical cord wrapped around it the night she gave birth. By morning it was too late. Littel did fine, but the stub obviously pained him sometimes and it made him surly. Cats' personalities grow into their bodies and Littel grew into a large and sometimes angry enforcer. But he never rushed out to face an intruder. Any cat intruder was always greeted first by little grey Meesh. Meesh was like one of those journeyman boxers, tough as could be, who lost more fights than he won and never turned down a fight. He had scars on his face, a broken tail, a split ear. The intruder had to get through Meesh to get to Littel. Meesh went out, Littel watched. When Meesh was done, win or lose, Littel went out to face an enemy quite unwilling for another fight. After a knock-down drag-out with Meesh nobody was ever ready to handle a bear hug from twenty pounds of surly Littel.

In that group, Littel's mother, Music Batty, was the mouser. Music Batty moved outside when we got Piccolo and never moved back in; he was too frantic and she avoided him at all cost; you might venture to say she hated him (though I haven't talked about emotions); she lived on the upper porch, plucked rats out of the trees and patrolled the mouse holes in the sky. Yoko Dodo was young then, but when Littel died she took to the decks and roof and fought intruders with Meesh. When Music Batty died Yoko began mousing. When Meesh died she took his place on my lap. When Romeo appeared, she stopped fighting intruders and let him fight; each of these being changes in her behavior in relation to changing social circumstances. When I adopted Mucha Plata, a notorious hunter, Yoko stopped hunting mice, though after Mucha Plata's death, the great division of territorial hunting occurred. Suddenly Romeo and Cheese grew up and became predators.

Littel died at ten from an infected wound on his stub. It was a death I regretted very much because I tried to cure the wound myself, but when it got worse and I got him to the vet, his organs were failing, though there were indications that his organs were already failing and that's why he got the infection. But his appetite had been good. Had he increased his water intake? Was I not watching closely enough? When you care for a lot of animals you make these kinds of judgment calls; it happens often when they get old. Can they survive? How much suffering? When do you put them down? Music died at thirteen while sleeping in a patch of sun on the porch with Meesh. Meesh got cancer at seventeen and we euthanized him when he stopped eating and moving. I realized then, with Meesh, that it didn't get easier. It never got easier.

H.D. had died from cancer the month before. The pain threw her into a rage. When we took her to the emergency clinic in the middle of the night, after the doctor readied her to be euthanized, she got up and walked to the door to leave. You go to the vet, you get better, you go home. That broke my heart, to lead her away from the door back into the room where we put her to sleep. I can still feel her huge death sigh as I held her. We went to India for four months after Meesh died. When we got back, Piccolo died of cancer, too. Gail still mentions him almost everyday.

I took Italo's death very badly. He was hit on the road during rush hour, just after dawn. Had the driver bothered to tap his brakes, he'd have missed him clean. His back legs were motionless, but he was conscious. Gail held him as we rushed into L.A. trying to find an emergency vet. The whole time he kept trying to get out of her arms. We switched drivers and I held him. He calmed down completely. He was my kitty. He'd followed me everywhere; even as I watered the plants he scampered after the hose and played with the spouting water. There, in the truck, he wanted me to hold him.

His spine was broken and we had to put him down. I didn't have much time to grieve for him because two weeks later Jackie O died of a twisted intestine and colic. Putting down your horse might be the hardest thing of all.

Italo's death created another shift in the Counter Culture. Suddenly, my vacant lap became important to everybody. Yoko, Cheese, and even Romeo began sitting on me or around me, someone in my lap, someone on the hassock, someone else on the chair next to me. All of a sudden, after almost two years of being ignored by the Counter Culture, I had cats, cats, cats, not that it stopped Nadine from thrusting her head into the mix.

Unhappy with this kind of peaceful stasis, Gail coaxed me into rescuing two kittens for Father's Day: brother and sister, the Lebowitzes, Jughead and Veronica. Jughead was male, a mackerel, Veronica mostly white with big black patches. Jughead was radically affectionate and decided he was my cat within an hour of his arrival. His sister was the opposite, shy and aloof, she wouldn't even let me touch her, not even while she ate.

These adoptions prompted another behavioral shift, though Yoko, old and wise, barely blinked. Now, if Jughead wanted to sit on my lap, Yoko took the hassock, if not, she took my lap. If the kittens tried to play with her, she was as impassive as a rock. The Cheese became newly enraged by the intruders and sometimes left the house for days, sometimes returning for breakfast or at dusk; he hated the kittens and snarled at them. He came through the window and danced back and forth at the top of the stairs, his eyes glaring across the room. Did he want me to pet him while he ate? Yes. And he didn't want anybody else's company. Romeo, who had disliked Italo, seemed less concerned with these new kittens; he sat next to Gail's thigh across from Nadine. Nadine lunged at him.

He ignored her. Though if Nadine gave up and sat at the other end of the couch, Romeo tried to place himself between her and Gail, sometimes even dancing between them and throwing his butt in Nadine's face until she reacted.

If you've had domestic cats, you're familiar with this kind of taunting. In our early L.A. days, when we lived in a very tough section of Venice, a good friend of ours gave us a German Shepherd, Jazzie, who was a stunning guard dog, loyal and vigilant; she patrolled our fences with such intensity and ferocity that gang members often offered to buy her from us. But at night I'd be awakened by her snapping at growling and leaping against the fence. There, at the top of the fence, one of our cats, Marcoline, lay sprawled, a paw dangling just out of the reach of Jazzie's snapping jaws; he lifted it ever-so-slightly as she lunged, his head tilting back and forth, bemused, as if he were watching the most unusual thing. He did this every night I didn't manage to lock him in.

I've been using the word *culture* rather loosely and I'll have to take some time to explain more precisely what I mean, but the addition of the new kittens changed, well, the politics of the house. Cheese began to assert himself, I thought, finally, because of his size, as the alpha male, though I'd be proven wrong. He spat at the kittens. He made a point to push Romeo away from food bowls, even Romeo's special food bowls on the kitchen counter. If the two encountered each other, they usually squared off. Romeo didn't really back down, but the Cheese was almost twice his size. His domination seemed clear.

Of course, Romeo could always sit on Gail unchallenged. The Cheese didn't cross that line, an act, of what? of what kind of discernment? More interesting, when Gail wasn't around, Romeo began to hang out with Nadine, sleeping near her, walking around the house with her, sometimes, it seemed, almost using her as a shield between himself and the Cheese. Nadine seemed to take to this. What happened to the animosity? Well, if Gail was on the couch, the old brother-sister rivalry was the same. Other than that, Nadine and Romeo were now companions. Contempt had bred familiarity.

More exactly, Romeo and Nadine were in fact more familiar with each other and Romeo, now under the heat from Cheese, placed himself where the Cheese couldn't threaten him, though it's a little more complex than that because Romeo became completely tolerant of Yoko and the kittens, too. Cheese's new aggressiveness brought Romeo more closely into the community. He came to me more often now, crossing from the couch, over the lamp table, over another chair, and sat on the arm of my chair while Jughead curled on my lap and Yoko curled at my feet. He became more friendly with Yoko and much more tolerant with the kittens. He began to bring them mice. Though even Cheese stepped up to the plate and, despite his disdain, began bringing them birds. However you might want to speculate or disregard that behavior, it followed Romeo's, as if in response to it.

If you've seen communities of domestic cats, then you've seen this shift in middle-aged males. Meesh, for example, despite being rather diminutive, was an aggressive fighter. Snakes, big dogs, Tom's, possum, Meesh backed down from nobody and often got beat up. But as Meesh aged he did less and less fighting and became a sort of *pater familias*. Suddenly Meesh was tolerant of everything and everyone; dogs, puppies, kittens. A complete turnaround; now if somebody needed a warm body, they could go to Meesh and, in return, no one ever bothered Meesh; he could walk between snarling jaws and flashing claws, sleep where he wanted, eat from whatever bowl he chose, including the dogs', while they ate. The community shifted. And I don't know if Romeo was ready for that big of a change yet, but the situation around him changed and the *pattern* of his behavior, his *gestalt* toward the other animals changed.

Dogs are pack animals and if Nadine's pack included cats, well, fine, just roll them over and sniff their bellies if they'll let you. She accepted Romeo's companionship; Romeo was her new buddy, unless Gail sat between them. And as Nadine matured, she increasingly adapted her behavior to what she perceived as the family's agendas. She was more aggressive about potential intruders, quicker to accept people we accepted. Thanklessly in terms of the cats, when we built stairs to our roof, she cleared the roof of Tom's, raccoons, possums.

Anyone who has spent time with domestic animals, whether in the house or in the pasture, has seen these kinds of shifting alliances, although sometimes it's hard for people, even people who work with animals, to see beyond their ideas and just watch the behavior. How many decades did it take someone to notice that wild horse herds were led my mares, not stallions? Likewise, now, horse people down the line assume that any group of horses will align itself in a strict, linear hierarchy, that is, one horse will dominate all the others, the second will submit to her (or him, in a pasture it could be a gelding) and dominate the rest, then the third horse on down to the last. To my experience, this is far too simple and general.

When I pastured Jackie O at her last ranch, she joined two middle aged geldings, Bernard, a bay, and Howard, dark dapple gray; then two big, red, saddle bred brood mares, a mother, Pleasant, no longer servicing, and her daughter, Precious, still sexually active. In the tradition of naming horses, Pleasant was nasty and Precious mean. Pleasant was domineering, backed by Precious, and the two geldings were equally cowed and bullied.

When Jackie O entered the scene she fought with Pleasant and Precious constantly, neither dominating nor submitting, though I'd say she was taking the worst of it because I was daily dressing her wounds on her flanks and neck. Finally she did what she often did in pasture, she simply withdrew. She stood off by herself and waited for me to come. The hands threw her a separate pile of alfalfa that she'd fight to defend, so the two mares left her alone. But Bernard and Howard, fed up, it seemed, by the two bully mares, soon began to wander over to Jackie O. With them she shared her food. She stood between them, her face to their tails, and they brushed flies from each other in that way, a distinct advantage for her, two tails on her face and both flanks protected. She didn't bully them, but they followed her everywhere. Sometimes, annoyed at their constant presence, she nipped at them. The pasture, far from being a simple, linear hierarchy, now contained two small, separate herds that didn't interact.

Then Bernard got shipped off, Howard died of colic, and Precious was moved out to breed. The managers moved in an Arabian gelding, Mike, Tasha, the old, black thoroughbred mare, and a big red thoroughbred gelding who I called Dummie. Dummie roared in and took over. Pleasant folded immediately, as did Mike and Tasha. Jackie O fought him. At one point her wounds were so severe I talked to management about removing her. Then one day, when I found a huge gouge in her flank, I stayed on Jackie O's back after our ride, picked up my lasso and went into the pasture. We chased Dummie around for twenty minutes. He bucked and kicked and snarled at us, sometimes facing off and rearing up, but with me on her back, Jackie O was fearless. We chased him around and around. After that he left her alone, and I only had to look at him to chase him away.

Jackie O went off on her own again and stood in the far corner by herself. And Dummie left her alone. And however I'd altered the power politics of the pasture, some of the new behavior had to be in effect when I wasn't present. In other words, even if it was Jackie O's alliance with me (the new "big horse" of the pasture) that made Dummie back off, he had to remember and act according to that alliance even when I wasn't present. On the other hand, maybe he wasn't smart enough to realize that I couldn't hurt him when I wasn't there. Either that or he did realize that if he hurt Jackie O again I'd be back in there after him. But even in the most reductionist behavioral terms, that is, if Jackie O somehow now meant *me and Jackie O*, (a reduction that requires a more convoluted reasoning than the non-conceptual explanation; how and why did Dummie's behavior to Jackie O change? was I an absent contingency?), regardless, when I wasn't present Dummie had to be behaving toward Jackie O as if I were there, an abstract threat.

Then the re-herding happened again. Mike and Tasha, constantly bullied by Dummie and Precious, wandered over to Jackie O. Again, Jackie O stood between them head to tail for fly brushing. Again, the two new "friends" followed her everywhere. Mike was later removed and, as you know, Tasha became extremely attached.

Much of this domestic animal behavior I've talked about here, though not experimentally observed, is paradigmatic, in other words, if you live with and around animals it's the kind of behavior you can observe everyday. You will see individual and group adjustments in adaptation to changing circumstances and these adjustments occur with and toward other animals in the domestic community, as well as toward us, we who are also members. In some ways, we are a family, or a living organism. The animal perceives the change in his environment and moves with or against other animals to preserve or advance his power or increase protection. That's politics, and it's no less on display in my living room than it is at your local university's English Department. If you think consciousness is irrelevant to behavior, then the English department is no different. If you think self-consciousness is the dividing line, then you're clearly unaware how rote the desire to gain power and protect oneself is, even in universities. Just look at the behavior. And to understand the behavior in either case, among cats or English professors, it's necessary to perceive the cognitive emotional state in the organism, an iconic semiotic one in my cats, a progression that perceives a change, desires to redress it, and adjusts behavior.

I have one more story, which is unabashedly anecdotal, but has always stood for me as the paramount example of animal politics. In the previous generation of my household animals there co-existed two of the brightest that I'd ever known, Gail's dog, H.D., and my Maine Coon, Mucha Plata. I'll talk about them both later when I investigate symbolic behavior in animals, something that's not that common in dogs and cats.

H.D. was one tough hound, stubborn and brooding, rigid and clear about household political hierarchies. And in terms of the other animals, at that time two dogs and seven cats (not counting Mucha Plata's kittens), H.D. was top furry quadruped and willing to enforce it. She hated to travel. She wanted to be home, dominating the house. When she encountered other dogs in public, she stood dead still and let them sniff her. If they didn't quickly move along, or if they tried to dominate her by placing their head over her neck, she spun, hitting them with her huge chest, knocking them down and pinning them, jaws on their throat.

She was so domineering that she challenged my daughter for number three in the house, challenged Jackie O at the ranch, and took on any house guest that stayed long enough to imply possible residency. Jackie O took care of herself with a lashing fore hoof that sent H.D. rolling. I had to step in when H.D. challenged people. She's the only dog I ever had to threaten with physical violence.

Mucha Plata was a marvel of subtlety, a silver beauty with fur that cascaded to the floor, legs like Cossack pantaloons, a huge, fluffy dancing tail. When she entered a room, she pranced and gurgled for forty-five minutes before settling down next to my thigh. She exhibited some of the most remarkable and inexplicable behavior. For example, when Gail and Marlena did each other's nails on the couch, she jumped between them and put her paw in the air at Gail. Gail ran the emery board lightly over Mucha Plata's claws. She did it every time. Of course, cats groom themselves, and Mucha Plata, a mother, had groomed her kittens, but this was a leap in the iconography of grooming, perceiving the females giving each other attention and joining in. If it were not so peculiarly anecdotal, I'd unpack and analyze the inferences.

I've seen a number of females raise litters, but when it came to motherhood, Mucha Plata was a totalitarian. The night she birthed she screamed in pain. I tried to set her up in our closet with towels and drinking water, but she couldn't stay still. She ran out of the closet, and it was then that I spotted the open second story window. She flew out of the house, across to the deck, fleeing, I assumed, from her pain.

We spent a worried night. And a worried breakfast before Mucha Plata appeared at my feet. She walked to the center of the room and stopped and turned and gurgled. Clearly I was to follow, and I did. She led me to the closet where there on the towels five huge kittens were lined up in a row, dry and clean, not a bit of afterbirth in sight.

There was always one she favored. He wasn't the biggest, nor the most aggressive. He was just her favorite. That was the Cheese. She bathed him first and fed him first, hunted most predominantly for him, played with him more. He was clearly her pick of the litter, but the Cheese wasn't domineering, in fact he was furtive. But she picked him, so we kept him. He's still furtive. But nature or nurture, he is now one big, bad ass, who yet battles Romeo for number one cat in our house.

Motherhood is complex because the biological burden of mothering: birthing, cleaning, protecting, feeding, the teaching of hunting, are all complex, and however biologically determined much of that behavior is—I tend to see them as biological dispositions, not determined behavior—it's still complex. Mechanical, univocal explanations leave too many gaps. During motherhood Mucha Plata displayed a number of behavioral leaps, but I'll return to them when I discuss symbolic behavior. But now, the story.

Cats aren't supposed to be able to taste sweet, though Meesh used to open the Entemann's donuts package and eat the chocolate from around the cake. Well, it was dark chocolate, though whether dark or milk I've always been told that dogs aren't supposed to eat it at all because it makes them sick. But H.D. loved it and took it off the coffee table or even a counter top if a chocolate bar was left close enough to the edge. For us humans, the solution was simple. Push the chocolate to the back of the counter or, upstairs, where we ate, push the chocolate to the back of the dining table where, when not entertaining, we pushed the table against a wall. Now H.D. couldn't reach it. Nonetheless, that didn't solve the problem. When we got up in the morning or got home from work, we found a candy bar wrapper on the floor, battered and empty.

Talk about behaviorism, did we change our behavior? No. We just marveled at the disappearing chocolate bars and wondered how it happened. Then one day, I guess I came home unexpectedly, I caught the culprits in the act. There was Mucha Plata on the dining table pushing the chocolate bar to the edge of the table where H.D. sat waiting below. Mucha Plata spotted me, stopped, walked away from the chocolate bar and jumped off the table. I guess everybody was really disappointed I'd shown up.

Let's just look at this. This was before the Counter Culture when the cats weren't permitted on the counters and tables. Of course, all that meant was that the cats stayed off the counters when we were around, e.g., Meesh had to wait until we left to ascend a counter in order to get to the donuts. That kind of behavior doesn't require a lot of intellect, though it does require the bare minimum of perceiving the difference between when we were there and when we weren't. Because we don't have cupboards, but open shelves above our counters, you might expect our food supplies to have been ravaged by the cats, but aside from Meesh and the donuts, the cats didn't go after crackers or cookies or chips or cereal or, for that matter, not even bagged cat food or snacks.

Mucha Plata didn't eat chocolate. H.D. did. And Mucha Plata didn't knock down chocolate for Piccolo or any of the other cats, nor did she bring it to her kittens. She got it for H.D. And as far as I'd seen up till then, the two of them shared nothing else in common, but for the fact that they were both domineering females.

More so, Mucha Plata wasn't the type of cat who went up on counters and just knocked stuff off randomly, as some cats do, especially when they're kittens. She was always very precise about what she knocked down, another story for the symbolism chapter. So she didn't accidentally knock the chocolate on the floor, observe H.D. eating it, and then do it again, though that in itself would be a rather selective cognitive step. Why would she feed H.D. at all? Cats don't share food, per se, though mothers do feed kittens.

The simplest explanation is that Mucha Plata had been weaning her kittens. A number of animal psychologists have suggested that our pets treat us as some combination of their children and parents and that's why cats bring us mice; even the male cats sometimes brought rodents for kittens. Meesh even babysat. Music Batty, who was not an attentive mother, often left her kittens soon after she fed them. Meesh went in the closet and slept with them (if I were really pushing the cat culture thing hard here, I'd suggest that Meesh's behavior was another example of filling community gaps). So Mucha Plata's behavior wasn't a complete anomaly in terms of feeding behavior; even before she had kittens she brought in mice and rats for us.

But she didn't bring H.D. a mouse, though there were times when the dogs ate dead rodents if they got to them before anybody else did. She could have noticed that as easily as she noticed the chocolate. She didn't get H.D. table scraps from unwashed dishes. I'm sure the cats cleaned any unkempt plates when we weren't around and sometimes those were left on the table for a while, but Mucha Plata didn't knock any of that food down. No, she got H.D. something very specific and something H.D. really liked.

In one of my uncontrolled experiments, I opened some dark chocolate and left a little in the wrapper on the dining table, then I left the room and hid around the corner. In no time at all Mucha Plata was up on the table and H.D. was at its edge, looking up. Mucha Plata knocked the chocolate from the back of the table to the front, then off the table, right to H.D. H.D. picked it out of the wrapper and ate it. Mucha Plata hung her head over the edge of the table and watched.

Maybe it had something to do with domination or hierarchy. Both were domineering females. By feeding H.D., Mucha Plata might have been asserting her domination. Or was she acknowledging H.D.'s? For H.D., having Mucha Plata feed her might have been hierarchical, though maybe she was just getting fed no differently than if I gave her a table scrap. Whatever was going on, no matter how unself-conscious, it wasn't simple.

Mucha Plata, who didn't eat chocolate, had to notice that H.D. did. How it evolved, I don't know. I'm trying to get to how Mucha Plata perceived the chocolate, which she didn't eat, as something that H.D. would eat. Possibly the chocolate was perceived, somehow, as a food stuff easy to swipe and move. But that's a big cognitive leap, acting toward something as if it were food, even though she didn't eat it. Mucha Plata did not randomly knock things down, nor did she eat chocolate. How could she recognize something she didn't eat as food for another animal, another species?

Animals do beg for food while watching you eat, and cats more than dogs might turn it down if you offer it to them. Arguably, an animal can learn that our eating behavior leads to them being fed and have a rote response to that stimulus, separate from the sight and smell of the food, then reject the food when it's offered. That occurs most often at the places I eat, like in the kitchen or at the dining table, though they are quite capable of recognizing eating behavior in other contexts, at my easy chair or even when I'm walking and eating. It might be cued by smell or other recognizable contingencies, like the refrigerator being opened or my taking something to the cutting board.

In other words, Mucha Plata could recognize the chocolate as food by the fact that H.D. ate it, even if she did not. However minimal, that requires abstract thought. Maybe she just knocked it down once and H.D. noticed it, smelled it, and got up and ate it. Even if it were that accidental, at some point Mucha Plata had to make a connection more general than the iconic and act on it. Reasons, i.e. politics, aside, if seen as a semiotic sequence it's easy to explain. One icon connects to the next. Dog eats this. Knock it down to dog. Dog eats it. But that the chocolate is food in the abstract, or food for a dog, might not necessarily be an explicit semiotic link in that sequence. But it must be an implicit one or the act couldn't be carried out.

Reasoning aside, there yet had to be reasons why the behavior occurred, and however inapproachable those reasons might be—motherhood, feeding, domination, or alliance politics—something in Mucha Plata's behavior had to be an act of understanding or she could not complete the behavioral sequence. The act of feeding a dog chocolate had to contain a kind of general understanding of food, an understanding more complex than a single icon, but a general understanding that something she herself did not eat was yet something someone else ate, and so a general or symbolic understanding of what food was. And H.D. had to anticipate getting chocolate or she wouldn't go stand at the edge of the table to wait for it. As the gangster says in the Bugs Bunny cartoon, "I don't knows how ya done it, but I knows you'se done it!"

I don't mean to complicate what for many people is simply common sense, but unfortunately the commons sense of animal behavior has been rejected by science, religion, and linguistics for quite some time. A close analysis of common animal behavior reveals a dialectic of cognitive behavior and physical behavior in which some physical behavior is preceded by cognitive behavior. Like Frans De Waal, who argues that human morality has evolved from sophisticated cooperation demonstrated in groups of primates like chimpanzees, bonobos, and gorillas, who live in social communities, I'm suggesting that the fundamentals of semiotic consciousness exist in animals, in this case our domestic animals, and that it explains a number of behaviors, including, here, behavior among domestic animals living and acting with each other in groups. Those behaviors are political in the most fundamental sense, to gain advantages and acquire protection. That is the root of human political behavior. And though cats and dogs and horses aren't making pots and telling stories, species pass information from generation to generation biologically and semiotically. Sometimes these groups of domestic animals operate together in group patterns, however fundamental or however fleeting, and here are the evolutionary fundaments of tradition and culture (Please see *The Question of Animal Culture*, Kevin N. Laland and Bennet G. Galef, eds. for a more technical spectrum of defining the animal culture debate).

THE AVOCADO
LEAF OF PEACE:
SYMBOLIC BEHAVIOR

SINCE THE SIXTIES, when the Gardners first taught Washoe sign language for the deaf, the battle over chimpanzee cognition has raged. The line in the sand now appears to be syntax, and the non-conceptualists hold rigidly to the argument that if the higher primates (and gray parrots, whales, dolphins, etc.) can't create new word combinations adapted to new contexts, then their apparent symbolic responses and requests are likely rote, i.e. as automatic naming or cue responses, as mechanical as Pavlov's salivating dogs. It requires no self-consciousness or self awareness, likely not even conscious memory, therefore there's no reason to presume that they think.

This argument conflates several different terms and issues, among them syntax, symbolic thinking, self-consciousness, awareness, consciousness, and cognition, as if they were all one thing and syntax was the answer to all of them. In fact, as I've argued, awareness is not necessarily syntactical behavior, nor does the use of syntax necessarily imply awareness. One can use syntax without being aware of it, or without being self-conscious, though the capacity to use syntax increases an organism's potential to be both self-conscious and aware. All these terms need to be distinguished from each other and more tightly defined, something I've tried to do here.

Though most animals think semiotically, few use symbols, though I've seen it on occasion from extremely bright ones like Mucha Plata. One poignant example was when she weaned her kittens. When a mother cat removes herself to hunt for mice it accomplishes two things, first it removes/releives her for extended periods, second she brings the mouse back for them; before there was cat food, that was pretty essential to survival, learning what prey was. Birds hunt for their young, as well, and non-conceptualists would have us imagine that they are "hard wired" for it, and that they do so without any thought that their hunting for food is followed by or anticipates returning with it for their young. They just do it, somehow, without eating it themselves, without anticipating returning to the nest with the food, without picturing the nest they return to and its location. (Griffin addresses this rather assiduously in *Animal Minds*, and though he argues that it insinuates cognition, he doesn't offer a theory of cognition). I've argued here that the explanation of behavior as hard wired is irrelevant to whether or not cognitive behavior is involved and that, as well, *hard wired* is a very imprecise explanation.

Of course, kittens associate their mother with feeding. As Mucha Plata began weaning her kittens, when they came to suckle she got up and went to the food bowl on the upper porch. Kittens will eat hard food and suckle both, and though her kittens made no explicit association between suckling and food bowls, it seemed that Mucha Plata did. She removed her breasts and went to the food bowls, her kittens following, and there she refused them her milk. This got more explicit when she brought in the first dead mouse. The kittens spotted her and ran to her. She took the dead mouse and put it in a food bowl. She did this several times until she finally brought in a live mouse. That went in a food bowl, too, and I remember that little mouse, standing up in the food bowl, surrounded by Mucha Plata and five kittens.

That, along with feeding H.D. chocolate bars, led me to believe that Mucha Plata had some concept of food, a generalization or an abstraction distinct from any particular food in front of her that she ate. Moreover it was an abstraction more complex than an icon or a sequence of icons; it was a symbolic gesture, in the sense of Peirce, an understanding of food, and in that sense, contained the index, putting the food in front of the kittens, and the icon, the mouse itself (mouse in the food bowl is a sign from Mucha Plata, the mouse in the food bowl a sign for the concept/object, food, to the interpretents, the kittens).

I haven't seen other mother cats do this, though they all weaned their kittens in approximately the same way, by not permitting them to suckle and by bringing them mice. They didn't lead the suckling kittens to the food bowls, nor put mice in the bowls, but Mucha Plata's behavior led me to believe that there was semiotics involved in weaning, particularly mouse hunting for the litter: intention to get the mouse, anticipation and waiting in the hunting, and, of course, returning with the prey for the kittens; it all required iconic sequences.

I don't know what increments there are in the intelligence of domestic animals, but I know that some are smarter than others, and the smartest seem to make this ever-so-slight leap from icon to symbol.

Some cats are lap sitters and those who are will typically place themselves between you and other things you might place near or on your lap, newspapers, books, laptops. Yoko does this, and now Jughead. Mucha Plata did, too. Romeo sits on Gail's newspaper when she puts down the crossword. Now he sits on the paper as soon as I bring it in the house. As for Mucha Plata, she developed another unusual behavior; she began knocking the land phone and the Rolodex off the phone cabinet. It took me a while to realize that I held the telephone up to my face and I stroked the Rolodex to find phone numbers. Veronica tends to ignore my lap unless I put my laptop on it.

Aside from getting the chocolate for H.D., Mucha Plata only knocked one other thing down and that was the first thing. Gail had inherited a beautiful, large Deco statue, a foot tall, from her great grandmother. The statue was of a woman in a blue gown walking two Borzois. When Mucha Plata got big enough to jump on the dresser, she knocked the huge statue off.

Gail immediately interpreted that as a symbolic attack on the dogs. I was much more skeptical until all the other stuff happened. Not only do cats not knock down things that are bigger than they are—generally it's small things in that make-it-move-make-it-move game they do; oops, it fell off—Mucha Plata didn't play that random knock things down game.

Two other incidents. She liked me; she followed me; she watched me. It didn't take long for her to connect my putting on my running shoes and tying the laces on them to my leaving the house with Piccolo and H.D. (for runs, which she didn't observe, she only saw the sequence of my dressing and leaving with them). She ate my shoestrings. Tore them to shreds. After the third time I figured it out and hid my sneakers.

On another occasion Gail and I saved a fresh water turtle, a red slider that we found on the beach in Malibu. People release them in streams and they wash out into the ocean and sometimes wash back in. I took the turtle home, named her Suerte (Luck), and got her a twenty gallon aquarium. When I came home with that turtle and put her in a bucket Mucha Plata tried to get at her, so I bought a screen for the top of the aquarium. Mucha Plata sat on top that screen and watched Suerte for hours. Predation, a natural response. But the next day began a lizard killing campaign and for a couple of weeks I found a dead fence lizard in my shoe every day until Mucha Plata just got tired of the whole thing and began ignoring the turtle.

In the case of Mucha Plata there were just too many complex behavioral incidents to attribute them to coincidence, though back then I hadn't thought out an explanation; the behaviors just seemed too intentional, and though it wasn't behavior that required great amounts of abstract thought, it did require abstraction; it required making connections; it required having some kind of cognitive behavior that preceded the physical behavior and it required behavior that sought to settle an emotional state by removing an instigative stimulus, either by direct action, like the phone, or implied, like the lizards, or like the mice and the chocolate, a general understanding of feeding or food.

These stories aren't offered to prove anything; they're unabashedly anecdotal, but they tell the story of what got me thinking about animal cognition. But if you are a pet owner, then you likely have a lot of this kind of behavior surrounding you daily and icon semiotics explains much of it.

I've never had a dog that imitated any human sounds, though I've tried to teach them to do it. I've had a lot more animals who recognized words, another issue. In my life, two cats used words. Mr. Puff, very late in his life, was accused of saying "hi" when we came home or guests entered. Gail's mother pointed that out. "That cat says 'hi'," she said. Well, he seemed to. But cats make a lot of sounds. The one word he did use was "no." And as he aged and found that more and more things bothered him, like being picked up, well, he just said, "No." That was way before the counter culture, when my cats heard that word from me a lot more often.

My other big, orange cat, Littel, spoke two words, it seemed. "Out." Easy and natural enough for a cat who naturally makes "ow" sounds, and likely easy enough to a human to mistake "ow" for "out", though he made many sounds and "ow" or "out" always came in front of a door. Other cat owners will attest to their cats doing this (we should take a survey!). More markedly, Littel sat in the bathtub, under the spigot, and looked up at it and said "water-water-water-water," until you turned on a stream for him to lick. Twice I had house guests come running out of my bathroom yelling "A cat is in the tub saying 'water-water!'"

"Well," I said, "did you give him some?"

Okay, just more stories, but our animals are around us a lot and they're tremendously focused on what we do as it pertains to their needs. Let's move to some more paradigmatic behavior exhibited by dogs.

You've walked into the kitchen and your dog has followed you because, well, if you're reading or watching TV in your living room and you get up, where else do you go if not the bathroom, than the kitchen? If you're a cat owner you know that one of your cats is as likely to follow you to the bathroom, as well, where they've got you stationary and sitting and alone, a good place to corner you for some affection. If you have a lot of cats, then the lowest in hierarchy will likely be the one to notice this because she gets pushed out of other food and affection contexts, so in my case it's Yoko who follows me; I don't close the door tightly, leaving it ajar so she can open it, and sometimes I sit, though I needn't, so I can take a few extra moments to read a book and pet a cat.

Let's say you don't feed your dog from the refrigerator, but on the counter nearby you keep dog snacks. Your dog gives a little "urf" and looks up at the dog snacks. Your dog might not even be able to see the dog snacks, but moves her head toward where they are kept. If you have dogs, then you know that some dogs don't do this, but many do. Piccolo didn't, but H.D. did. Nadine didn't for quite some time, but now she does. As an aside, all domestic animals seem to prefer what you're eating over what they get; they even prefer what another animal is eating over what they're eating, even if it's the same thing.

Back to the dog snacks on the counter. Remember the squirrel? Does your dog know that there are dog snacks on the counter? Of course. Knowledge does not require self-consciousness, nor does it need to be correct all of the time. I could go to the counter knowing that the dog snacks are kept there and be wrong; they could have been moved or we could be out of them. Your dog, as well, knows that's where they're kept. Your dog's nose is not pointing at nothing at all, but at that place, though she can't see the snacks themselves. Maybe she smells them. But your dog isn't just looking at that spot, but indicating to you where the snacks are and that she wants some; she doesn't just wander downstairs and stare forlornly at the counter; if she were alone and could get to the snacks, she'd likely do so.

Any number of people, including several of my acquaintances, have argued that animals don't understand indices because if you point at something they just look at your finger. Well, for one, it's your hand that usually holds the food. If you have cats, then you know that often your cat won't bother to wake you up to get petted, he'll just put his head under your hand. Secondly, animals don't have fingers. Pointing fingers don't translate at all. Animals point with their heads or noses. If your dog was simply barking at the counter you might consider that pretty rote. But she doesn't. She gets your attention by grumbling or touching you, then looks in the direction of the snacks. If you're far enough away, she might come to you, get your attention, then go to the counter. Likely she'll look at you, then at the snack spot, then look at you again, then at the snacks. When your cat meows at you and beckons you to follow, she's pointing with her body, likely to the food bowls.

H.D. exhibited this behavior in several other circumstances. On cold nights she stood in front of the wood stove, barked, got my attention, then looked at the stove, looked at me, then looked at the stove. She wasn't asking me to take her to the movies. She wanted me to make a fire, make heat. If I got up to do so, the cats circled and lay down around the stove in anticipation. I don't think a dog would bark at a thermostat; that's too abstract. I generally made the fires, not Gail or my daughter, so H.D. barked at me. More so, the process of fire building was prolonged enough and done with and in front of the thing that produced the heat. She had to have a clear understanding that I instigated the eventual result that she desired: heat. She connected the source of the heat, the stove, with the heat, easy enough, but she also connected my behavior in front of the stove to the heat that followed. She then indicated to me that she wanted it done. She looked at me and then looked at the stove. Piccolo didn't do this.

Our animals typically connect us to things that they want done; the best example, of course, is feeding, another, opening a door (or window) to get in or out. After a few days of hard rain, my cats commonly go to the door and cry to get out, but when I open the door they spy the downpour and think the better of it (though Veronica likes the rain). But it doesn't stop there. They look at the open door, then turn and cry at me. I do everything else. Why can't I stop the rain?

H.D. didn't like to travel or visit other people's homes, in fact H.D. didn't really like other dogs or other people. If you took her to someone else's house, after we were done eating she'd walk up to Gail, put her paw on Gail's thigh, and look toward the door, or if we were not near the door, then she'd simply point away, in the direction we'd need to go to leave. This was done emphatically. If she had to, if the door were in sight, she'd go to the door and come back and do it again. If you have dogs living with you, then you've seen this kind of indexical behavior repeatedly.

At the ranch, Jackie O consistently displayed the dog snack behavior, going so far as to butt me with her head and then look at the tack box where I kept the carrots. Near other people's corrals, if we rode by, she knew where they kept their carrots or feed. She nudged them with her nose, or later, as she learned that people loved it if she kissed them, she'd kiss them on the lips and then look at their feed bin. I'd taught her "give me a kiss" to get apples or carrots. A non-conceptualist would have to argue that she mindlessly looked at the food bin without any attempt to get someone's attention, kissing aside. She just looked at the place where food emerged previously, with no anticipation that food was inside the bin or that I was the person who could get it. Though Jackie O, if you didn't go to the bin and get her carrots, would walk over and take the lid off herself. It's hard to explain how she could do that without the slightest notion that a specific thing she desired was in the bin. The cognitive behavior, iconic cognition, was inseparable from the physical.

Cats are much more likely to come and get you, call, and then have you follow them to the food unless, like the Cheese, they drop the "come and get you" portion of the behavior.

Here's a good H.D. symbol story. As much as H.D. disliked leaving the house (except for runs), she disliked being left there alone. She didn't regard the cats as company, nor later, Piccolo. She wanted people there, preferably Gail. One holiday season when she was still quite young and we'd all left for a good part of the evening and night, we came home to a disaster, a living room ankle deep in trash: statuary and musical instruments chewed, stuffed animals eviscerated, not a thing left standing. I guess she was really mad, though her rage had to have continued for quite some time.

Did I scold her? You bet I did. Many argue that dogs don't have a conception of time, so scolding them outside the immediacy of domestic violations accomplishes nothing. But animals make connections to contexts by means of icons. I was trying to impress upon H.D. that this was an undesirable context. When housebreaking a dog, even after some time has lapsed, the dog recognizes the smell of her poop, the living room is not a place for her poop and she can be reprimanded verbally near it, then taken outside, and yes, better if caught in the act, good or bad, reprimand for bad, reward for good, and more so for puppies than older dogs, of course.

I dropped H.D. in that mess and yelled like crazy. She cowered, because I was yelling. Did she make a connection? Well, the next time we left she just took a dozen stuffed animals from my daughter's room and tore them up. I put her amidst the carnage and yelled again. The next time she only destroyed one. I put it in her face. The next time, when we came home, we found one undamaged stuffed animal outside, inside the gate at the top of our steps (remember, H.D. could get out of the yard anytime she wanted). That's where the dialogue ended.

If we stayed out too long, there'd be a stuffed animal waiting for us outside at the top of the steps. If we came home within what I assume she considered to be a tolerable amount of time to wait, she emerged from the house wriggling and carrying an avocado leaf. Why an avocado leaf? I don't know. But to quote an old cowgirl friend of mine, "It were symbolic."

There are plenty of people who say that however much a dog seems to display guilt, they likely are just responding to your yelling and if you yell at one the others around him will cower, too. That's likely quite true often enough. But H.D. had a preemptive cower. After greeting us with an avocado leaf she might go in the house and cower in her feeding corner if something was amiss. If she went to that corner, then we knew somebody did something, even if it was a cat knocking something off a counter or table or Piccolo eating cat poop and leaving remnants on the floor.

Domestic dogs are yet pack animals and they slowly identify with their family as they would their pack. If you watch film or video of wolves, of a hunting group returning to their pack, then you'll see the same kind of bending and wiggling and smelling from your dog when you come home from work. They're members of your pack. In my house, I'm the big dog, the power, the discipline, what there is of it. Yet however much I take the dogs for runs or even feed them, I'm not their favorite, not their solace or comfort, not the person they want to sleep next to. That pack member is Gail. A dominant dog, like H.D., regarded my daughter, Marlena, as someone she could dominate in the hierarchy and attempted to dominate her. I had to step in and scold her for that.

As that identification with the family grows, so does the identification with their territory, your property, your house, even your things. Dogs develop astute discriminations as to what is what and whose things are whose. H.D., who didn't play with dog toys, yet gathered all of Piccolo's toys under the dining table and lay down on them. Nadine assiduously protects her bones and dog toys, down to the last shreds, from the cats, and with kittens around that can keep her pretty busy.

True to Ridgeback nature, Nadine is extremely playful. She loves real bones, fake bones, leather bones, and any kind of dog toy but especially squeaking ones, including toys that look like an animal, in fact stuffed animals that she shakes the life out of, tearing them apart and spreading the stuffing around until she liberates the squeaker. If you watch nature films, then you've seen mother animals eviscerate prey for their young. When Gail comes home with shopping bags, Nadine's nose rapidly inspects the bags, looking for her treat or toy. But if some prospective boyfriend of Marlena's gives my daughter a stuffed animal, Nadine leaves it alone, even if it's left out in the living room.

I don't think that Nadine makes any connection between a stuffed squirrel and a real one, however much the kill behavior, that hard shaking to break their neck, is similar. Nadine might just as well shake a stuffed bone. But my animals are acutely aware of where I place my affection in regard to other household members, visitors, be they human or animal or, in Mucha Plata's case, my Rolodex or telephone. This applies to stuffed animals for dogs in regard to both possession and affection given to them. Nadine recognizes the difference between her stuffed animal toys and Marlena's. And H.D. did, too. In terms of her preemptive guilt, it might simply have been that she wasn't sophisticated enough to disassociate from a household miscue; but she had to recognize a miscue, something outside the normalcy of how things operated, how things belonged in the house, the house she identified with, and she acted guilty in anticipation of our finding it.

The argument that it's senseless to scold an animal for, say, defecating on your rug, because they have no sense of identifying with a past act, is based on our human sense of causality through time and over-reliance on the sense of sight. As natural as time might seem to us, subjectively it's a pretty abstract concept and requires cognitive skills that animals don't possess. Of course, they learn that one specific thing follows another, but they don't have general notions of cause and effect or the passage of time in the way that Mucha Plata *did* demonstrate a general notion of food. That doesn't mean they can't identify with a past act based on iconic memories, for dogs in particular, olfactory icons. A dog recognizes his own poop and knows the difference between his poop and other poop. In other words, contrary to dog training dogma, you don't have to catch your dog in the act; if the offense is recent, they'll connect that it's their poop and it doesn't belong there; it belongs outside where you take them after scolding them in front of their poop.

If you've spent any time in zoos, then you know that the animals of higher intelligence will throw their poop at you: monkeys and chimps, elephants, too. Back in the cage days, lions would turn and spray at me. Jackie O used to poop at Gail. Shit is the universal icon of mammals and it means about the same thing to all of us.

H.D. was as housebroken as a dog could be. She knew where her poop belonged and, house habits aside, didn't even defecate or urinate in our yard, but took it to the lot next door or saved it up to mark the trail on our walks. In those days our animals didn't sleep with us so they waited for us in the living room outside our bedroom door. If we somehow failed to meet one of H.D.'s. expectations, say her run in the woods that day, in the morning there'd be a huge dog poop outside our door. When she pooped in front of our bedroom door she was, well, really pooped-off about something. It was an opinion, a demonstration of displeasure. On those mornings, instead of waiting outside the door for a morning greeting, as she and Piccolo most often did, she'd be downstairs sitting in her guilt spot. So guess who pooped there and who didn't.

Piccolo simply responded to being scolded. I don't think he ever made the connection between the repercussion of something he'd done and the fact that he'd done it, though he did develop a sense that some behavior was risky because when he stole food or tried to sneak into the cat room to feast in the cat litter he arched his back and tip-toed like a dog in a cartoon. Cats, notoriously conscienceless, yet learn that there are kinds of things not to do in front of your face.

Anybody who spends time with animals knows that they communicate with urine and feces and it's generally explained as sexual and territorial, though it's somewhat more complex than that and, like H.D.'s poop in front of our door, it contains elements of symbol use. If I was running H.D. and Piccolo on a trail and I stopped to urinate, H.D. always turned around and urinated on top of my urine. I figured any dog trainer would tell me that I shouldn't let her do that because the implications are obvious, but I just didn't want to fight about it. Back in Salt Lake City, where I met Gail and lived alone with Mr. Puff, if I didn't come home at night he urinated on my pillow. Jackie O, who didn't like Gail, didn't just pin her ears and bare her teeth at her, she didn't just poop at her, she turned and urinated at her, popping her vulva when she was done.

These are examples of kinds of behavior that I've witnessed constantly and anybody who spends time with animals has seen it. The interesting thing about domestic animals is how frequently it's exhibited across species, more particularly from the animal toward a human, that is, though cats and dogs seldom communicate much to each other unless one is actively inconveniencing the other, dogs and humans, and cats and humans, do. And not just about food, but about affection, and affection bleeds into the sensual, the territorial, even the sexual.

I've found, particularly among ungulates, that I can incite demonstrations from dominant males or affectionate behavior from females by imitating movement, body placement, and tactile signals, though it doesn't take much to get some dominant males riled up. Herd animals are tremendously sensitive to these kinds of gestures, either up close or at a distance, and this is why you can control a horse's movements in a bull pen simply by stepping left or right, backward or forward. The general rule with any species is: watch what they do and then do it. You won't get to pet your neighbor's skittish cat by walking up to her. Sit still on the floor quietly and she'll walk up to you.

Much of inter-species communication has to do with context and purpose. There's generally no reason or context for a cat to communicate with a cow. But it can happen. When I lived in the northeast with my bell ringing cats I used to get my milk by walking up a dirt road to a dairy farm. Outside the milking stalls was a big tank where the milk was deposited during milking and you could draw yourself a half gallon of fresh milk, still warm, for fifty cents. In the summer the cows were pastured, but they spent the winter in a huge barn where they were kept and fed in stalls. In that barn were a dozen or more barn cats, obviously there to keep the rodent population at bay.

There wasn't any heat in that barn, so where do you think was the warmest place for a scrawny barn cat on a cold winter night? On the back of a cow. But cats don't find a nice place to sleep and just curl up. No, they have to pace and curl and go into their suckling ritual where they knead their bed with their front paws. If you have any lap sitters of your own, you know that can hurt. The cows hated it.

When the cows got back from milking, several cats immediately jumped to the top wrung of the pen. The cows bellowed at them and tried to knock them down with their noses. Sometimes they succeeded, but if you've ever tried to stop a cat from doing something he wanted to do, then you know the outcome. Eventually the cows had a cat or two on their backs, cats purring and cows bawling in protest until the suckling stopped, though occasionally a cow got so frustrated that she lay down and rolled. The cats yowled, took off, then came back when she got on her feet.

I wasn't thinking ethologically then, but I noticed that some cats seemed to prefer the same cow and if I were to go back and study it I'd want to know the development of those pairings. Were some cows softer or warmer than others? Broader or easier to mount? Was there hierarchical competition among the cats for certain cows? Were some cows more sensitive to the clawing? Did some cats claw harder or softer than others? How much of the choice was up to the cat and how much up to the cow? Was there any anticipation among the cats for the arrival of the cows on the first frigid or snowy day? Was there a cow-cat culture like a cowboy culture or a cat-cow culture like the Counter Culture? Was there a system of repeated behaviors passed down through generations? How did the first cat find out? How did the second? Does this happen in all dairy barns in the winter? Does it have to be cold? How cold? I'd like to put some cats who'd never seen a cow in barns with cows, at least one warm barn and one cold barn, and watch.

Anyway, the cats wanted to get on the cows' backs and the cows didn't want the cats on their backs; that's how normal people would say it; to try to break that down into simple behavioral contingencies would take a lot of complex yakking. So how is that a more simple explanation? It was a conversation of gestures. The cats moved to solve one cognitive emotional disposition, to get warm, and solved it by getting on the back of a cow; the cow moving from another disposition to prevent that from happening. They were both behaving toward the same event that had yet to occur, the cat trying to create it and the cow trying to prevent it. They were both responding to and anticipating an event that operated cognitively as an icon they behaved toward, otherwise they wouldn't behave at all, or would just as likely be doing something completely different. Animal behavior is purposeful and doesn't proceed from a *reductio ad absurdum*. They do what they can do in the context they have to do it in.

You might not think there was much communication going on there, but if you listen to most human conversation you'll find it has a lot more in common with the cat-cow model than you think. As a fiction writer and a student of dialogue, I've learned that people talk at each other, they don't listen. Seldom is anything communicated that changes anyone's behavior. People talk *from* themselves, with agendas about themselves, and the other person tends to do the same, often barely holding to a topic. It's faster and syntactically more complex, but watch people's bodies during conversation; the cats and cows are communicating much more directly. More to my point, there's no reason for cats and cows to communicate unless they're thrown together in a context where their needs meet or come into conflict. When that happens, communication, a conversation of gestures, develops, and rituals, i.e. mutually repeated behavioral sequences are established and even adapted and changed. With humans and domestic animals, this happens a lot.

Our domestic animals have many sequences of behavior that are human specific and are not replicated among each other. Nadine might wriggle like a wolf greeting a returning wolf when I come home, but she doesn't share food with or beg from other dogs. Yet now, when she and Yoko Dodo sit near each other next to my chair at the dining table, if I offer food to Yoko, Nadine lets her take it. She might, soon after, whine at me for her portion. Cats don't pet each other while they eat. If I sit down in my mission chair, Jughead will run to me and jump into my arms, rolling over to have his belly rubbed. Maybe he did something like that in the litter with his mom, but he didn't jump in her lap and roll over. Jughead will grab my hand with his paws and put it on his head to be rubbed.

Briefly, recently, I had a rat. I kept rats as a boy and trained them to run through a maze for a school science project. They learned their way through the maze in a day and could race through it in seconds. But rats are extremely curious and despite knowing (there's that *know* word again) the way to the food, they sometimes wandered into other parts of the maze, sniffing and pawing. When Marlena was a child and wanted pets of her own, besides the cats and dogs (and the requisite gold fish) we bought two rather unremarkable rats who were unaffectionate. Still, I grew attached to them and mourned their deaths, but rats do not have much longevity, only about two years, so I vowed not to keep rats again.

In the same vein, we bought Marlena two newts, Uno and Dos, who lived to be seventeen. They were rather lethargic creatures, except at feeding, but I was surprised to learn that newts have habits and apparently preferences as well. Sometimes they even do surprising things. Not too long after Dos died, Uno, after seventeen years, made a break for it and escaped the covered aquarium. I never found him. The two of them seemed to recognize me, in fact they would only eat if I fed them; they would eat for no one else; and they ate from my fingertips.

When my precious daughter reached college age and was ready to go off to school, we gave her a small checking account and the first thing she did was buy a wig and a python. For my part, I like reptiles, but feeding live mammals to them is where I absurdly draw the line. I can't watch it. As I've said, just as absurdly, though I cohabitate with five cats who actively keep the rodent population down, if they bring a mouse in alive I try to save it, though rats I try to ignore. You grow older and learn to accept your endless contradictions. But you can imagine my dismay when after spending a semester in India our daughter decided to move in with us again, python in tow. The python's name was Eve and she ate live mice. And as the Eve grew the mice got bigger until it was time to eat a baby rat, which

Marlena brought home in a brown sack.

Unfortunately, Eve didn't eat the baby rat and after two days of watching the little rat scurry around the snake terrarium or sit on the snake's back, Gail couldn't stand it anymore and pulled the rat. Off to the Petco for a rat cage. He was a male rat, white with a pale brown head and shoulders. Gail named him Ratsky Wronsky-Rosenthal.

Well who knows, even after twenty years, what your partner is going to do, but Gail, who claimed to have an aversion to rats, began taking Ratsky out of his cage and carrying him in her breast pocket, claiming that he was an unusually handsome and intelligent rat and wouldn't I like to hold him. No, I said. Oh here, hold him. No. Come on, hold the rat. No. Plop, on my lap. Ratsky scurried around my lap, climbed up my chest and sat on my shoulder. I tried to give him back to Gail. He didn't want to go back. He likes you, she said. And so it came to pass that every evening after dinner Gail went into our room where she kept Ratsky near the bathroom so he could see people coming and going and as you passed by his cage you might give him a Cheerio or a gold fish cheese cracker, Gail went and got him and then gave him to me and I let him sit on my shoulder until he peed and then I put him back.

Except that the peeing only happened twice. Not only did Ratsky stop peeing on me, but when we forewent the ritual of Gail getting him, and I went to get him every night, he'd jump down from the cage door where he was waiting for me, take a long pee, then jump back up to the door for me to take him out. And when I put him back he immediately urinated. Ratsky housebroke himself. And he did it in a blink.

Intelligent and handsome, Gail said. And really affectionate, too. He liked me to pet him and scratch his cheeks, though his most interesting habit was his drinking. One night as I sat in my chair with a glass of bourbon and soda sitting on the chair arm, Ratsky ran down from my shoulder and tried a little. Then a little more. And a little more. In no time Ratsky was blotto and crawled up my arm to pass out on my shoulder, legs splayed. Turns out he liked potato vodka, red wine, and beer too. Eventually, as Ratsky sat on my shoulder, I just lifted my glass and let him drink. People came from far and wide to see me and Ratsky get drunk together (there's probably a You Tube of it) though he never got so drunk that he didn't hold his pee.

Ratsky seemed to really look forward to our evenings together. He got excited when I arrived and scurried for minutes on my lap when I sat down with him before finally settling down. If I missed a night because I was away, when I picked him up he bit me. Then I put him back, waited, and brought him out again. No biting then. I learned that no matter how late I got home, Ratsky was waiting there at the cage door and I always took the extra half-hour before bed to hold him. After a while, he let Gail and Marlena hold him, too, and then he became a family rat. If I was holding him and one of them came into the room and sat down, he grew excited and crossed from my chair to the next, to the end table and onto the couch to sit in their laps. Then he'd return to me. He was lucky because I didn't have any lap sitting cats then, though the great rodent killers, Cheese and Romeo, were bringing in Ratsky's cousins, dead or released for the chase, on a daily basis. Everybody, even territorial Nadine, left Ratsky alone, another example of animals responding to context, but for Italo who, as a kitten, jumped on my lap with Ratsky aboard and Ratsky attacked him. Italo ran away. But it was only a month later, when Ratsky was eighteen months old, that he died from a heart tumor.

Most of those are just so many cute rat stories, but I was not inclined to own, let alone love, a rat. If you're around household animals, then you know that they can vary widely, within species, in disposition as well as intelligence. Ratsky was a remarkably affectionate, sweet, intelligent animal. Among all those anecdotes, I'm going to pick out one that's paradigmatic. If you've had pet rats, then you know they can be housebroken. I talked to dozens of people who have done it. In Ratsky's case he had to make the connection between his behavior, urinating, and being put back in the cage. Then, in order to move from an unwanted disposition, being in the cage, to the desired disposition, being on my lap, he adjusted his behavior, both anticipating having to urinate in the future by urinating before he left the cage and then holding his pee while staying with me.

My horse trainer, Paddy Korb Warner, was a brilliant horsewoman and like anyone who spent a lot of time around animals, she wondered about animal thinking, though like most of us most of the time, she didn't wonder about it very systematically. One of her beliefs was that animals didn't understand any words. My position was, well, it depends what you mean by that.

She meant that if you left the training context, a horse who might walk, trot, lope or gallop on command in the bull ring or on a lunge line, wouldn't do so if you stood outside the ring and yelled those words. I said, of course not, the context was completely different, but within the context my horse knew exactly what I was saying and behaved accordingly. In fact, she might *choose* not to behave accordingly despite knowing what I was requesting.

Paddy said, well, issues of choice aside (and let's put them aside for now) there were other non-verbal, body-positioning signals in the bullring context that my horse was likely reading. That was a good answer. Horses are really good at that.

Paddy was right about her first point. If I stood outside the bullring and yelled, "Lope!" Jackie O didn't do anything but walk over the door and butt it with her head to try to get out. But inside the gate, even if I stood perfectly still, she often responded to my commands. She might ignore them, as well, but I could be standing in the middle of the ring with a whip and she might ignore me, too, depending on, well, I'd conjecture, her mood, which seemed sometimes to be related to the weather; horses are generally more active on cool days compared to hot ones, though Jackie O wasn't necessarily more obedient on cool days, even if more active.

That wasn't a very controlled experiment, but it did indicate to me that Jackie O responded with the correct behavior to words alone. She also did so to "Take a bow," "Give me a kiss," "Spanish Dance," "Come," dozens of foot and hand signals while on the ground or on her back, and even "Do a trick," to which she usually responded by taking a bow, though if that didn't get a carrot she'd give me kiss.

Admittedly, responding to sounds and signals does not imply animal cognition. Nadine responds to dozens of words, the usual dog words, of course, like *come, okay, no, walk, toy, bone, snack, snack toy, dog, she*, etc., but also *Momma, Dad, Sister, dinner?* I could go on and on, but let's stop with *hot tub*. Most of these words occur in phrases like, "Want to go for a walk?" or "Want some dinner?" But the words that perk her ears are *walk* and *dinner*, so the phrases might be irrelevant, though there are those, like Temple Grandin, who suggest that dogs respond or cue to phrases, not individual words, and it's better to speak to them like adults, not babies. Just the other day, Nadine was bothering Gail in the living room, throwing a toy at her to try to get her to play, and Gail said to her, "Go tell your Dad to take you for a walk." Nadine ran to me in the bedroom and began nudging my hands and nosing my running shoes.

The dynamic by which a dog picks out the essential word in the phrase might be worth studying. With both *walk* and *dinner*, in these cases the essential word is the last one, though I don't think they were learned that way. In my case, I started using the phrase after I noticed that my dogs were responding to the word.

Those who contend that dogs respond to intonation and expression more than the words themselves are likely correct, but dogs do respond to specific words. If anyone says "hot tub," around my house, without even intending to get in, Nadine jumps up and runs to the hot tub, then if we proceed to the tub, she runs up the stairs to Gail's office and onto the roof of our house where she stands guard, watching over the hot tub user and barking into the canyon. If I simply get up and go into the bedroom she follows and watches me closely. I can cue her as to what we're going to do by either saying "hot tub" or "walk." As well, if I get naked, she'll assume I'm going in the hot tub. If I reach for my sweats or socks, she goes into walk frenzy and tries to nibble my socks. I'm sure the physical cues are more meaningful to her than the verbal ones. If I say "walk" but get ready to get in the tub, she'll change her behavior and get ready for a hot tub. Like any good behaviorist, for Nadine, what I do is more important than what I say.

If Marlena or Gail is absent and I say "Sister" or "Momma" Nadine jumps up to look for them, though if she doesn't hear them she sits back down. She was particularly attached to Marlena's ex, Gareth, who lived with us for over four months and who we'd called Boyfriend, and when we did she'd jump up to look for him, too. Now that he is no longer a presence, she still looks for him if we use the word, in fact, when Marlena received a phone call from him and went in her room to take the call, Nadine heard his voice on the phone and went into a frenzy, crying at Marlena's door. Boyfriend does not mean the new boyfriend, who Nadine didn't accept for quite a while—two months later she still growled and barked at him—but the old one, specifically. Boyfriend was Gareth. She doesn't understand *boyfriend* as a concept generally applied, say, the way Mucha Plata seemed to wordlessly apply the concept of food. So, though icons can operate as signs without the use of words, attaching a word, a sound, to an object or an event doesn't imply generalization.

Nonetheless, the great symbol user H.D. could string together a few words. Early on, if I was waiting with Piccolo and H.D. for Gail to come home and they heard a sound outside the gate, they'd launch themselves down the stairs. If I knew she was going to be gone for days, not hours, I said, "No Momma," when it happened. It didn't stop Piccolo, but it stopped H.D. who looked at me. I said, "Momma no come," all words she knew separately. She sat back down. After that, if they heard a sound at the gate, Piccolo ran to it and H.D. looked at me instead. I said, "No Momma," and that was it. If Gail was, in fact, coming home, I got up and said, "Momma," and H.D. ran down the stairs.

You could argue that she cued on "no", but she wasn't the kind of dog who always listened when you said "no" or "come". She was the kind of dog who'd look at you when you said, "come," and then, well, decide. Most dogs seem to have some kind of distance gauge. The farther away they get from you the less chance they'll come back when you call them. Even Piccolo might not come if he got far enough away. If you have dogs, you know this. They'll pick up their heads, take a look at you, and not come (I'll talk more about decision making next chapter). In H.D.'s case, with "No Momma," she'd have to disregard the "Momma" and only regard the "no" or link "Momma" and "no". Likely she read my body language, as well, but Piccolo did not. Piccolo could sit, sit up, stay, and rollover on command, but he couldn't separate himself from a stimulus. H.D. refused to learn any tricks. If you held a treat and tried to push her butt down to sit, she'd walk away.

Animals don't speak in languages or understand language. But as dozens of experiments with chimps and gorillas have shown, they can manipulate symbols and signs, including arbitrary ones, to communicate desires and intentions. These capacities don't come out of nowhere, but from the building blocks of a semiotics that those animals *already* possess. But those building blocks in primates didn't come from nowhere either. Mammals and birds possess the ability to use icons and indices, and sometimes even symbols, and to remember them and apply them in suitable contexts. In fact, iconic cognition explains animal memory and makes it possible to talk about animal emotions.

THE ROAD NOT TAKEN: DECISION MAKING

ASIDE FROM BEING THE TITLE of one of Robert Frost's most misunderstood poems, coming to a fork in the road does necessitate a decision. Recently I had my right hip resurfaced and had to curtail my walks in the mountains for a while. But after about three weeks, when I found that I could drive, I grabbed my cane and took Nadine for a walk. Gail came with us the first time. We walked about a quarter mile to a lookout point where I always stopped and bowed to the natural world. Now, of course, Nadine had become accustomed to the ritual and she ran ahead and waited for me to show up there, though on this day, this first walk after almost a month, I was already a little sore so we turned back. At first Nadine started down the trail, but when we turned and called her, she turned around, ran past us and took off for the truck.

Of course, you could ask what was remarkable about that; you call your dog and she comes, but any dog owner knows that isn't always the case. Even after a two-mile run, sometimes Nadine wasn't ready to go home and when we reached the truck she wandered. It sometimes took five or ten minutes to coax her back. One thing that might have cued her in the current context was that when Gail walked with me we never traversed the whole trail; we always turned back at some point, so Nadine might have been susceptible to turning back early because Gail was with us; however mechanically one might wish to interpret that, it still required some level of discernment. Her behavior with Gail and me was different than her behavior with just me; when Gail was along Nadine was more cooperative, even though we didn't walk as far and, if there was any disciplinarian in our pack, it was me. Possibly we were more of a *pack* when there were three of us and that made her more conducive to following with the group; that's utter speculation.

I'm going to digress here and point out that there are some remarkable symbiotic events that occur when you live in a house of animals. Nadine is a big wild dog and when she gets excited she can be hard to control, throwing her huge forelegs at you, even snapping (that's right, we're bad dog trainers). One of my worries about returning home an invalid was that she'd hurt me. But during my convalescence she never bothered me at all. It wasn't until I was up and about that she returned to rough housing with me.

Of course, she might have simply read my activity level as a cue to her play behavior, but she still had to read it. More to the point, now that I'm recovered, if I'm sitting quietly and Nadine wants to play, my inactivity does not cue quiet behavior on her part; she'll bring toys or bones or whack me with her paw to instigate me to play with her. She apparently read the difference between my quiet behavior and my convalescing behavior.

When Jackie O died and I lay weeping on our bed, Nadine came into the bedroom, put her forepaws on the bed, and left her pig's ear at my face. The day Mucha Plata was killed, Gail, who found her, brought her to the ranch where I was riding. I took Mucha's corpse home wrapped in a towel and placed it on a picnic table. I couldn't face burying her yet. I'd wait till morning. But that night, her son, the Cheese, came into the living room and for the first time in his life lay down on my lap.

These are completely anecdotal examples, though there are dozens more. Those of you who live in a family of domestic animals have experienced this kind of inexplicable synchronicity of emotion, behavior that suddenly and momentarily transcends the everyday habits of interaction, metaphorically speaking, something of the heart that verges on the mysterious, that little bit of what's left now where humanity and nature interact. I'm not talking about mystical oneness. I'm talking about unselfconscious sympathy resulting from the daily rhythms of caring and watching each other. We function, in a sense, like a family, like a coordinated living entity. Many of the problems in talking about animal emotions comes from confusing the difference between sympathy and empathy. I'll return to that.

99% of the stories I've heard about animals are baloney. Dogs don't call 911 unless they've been selectively and repeatedly trained to do it and have really big phone buttons to work with. They might also poop on your pillow if you stay away from home too long, and that without any training at all, except to the contrary.

Because animals don't think like we do, humans tend to take one of two positions regarding animal cognitive behavior: that, in fact, they do think and feel like we do, that they're stupid people with a few talents exclusive to their species, or that they don't think and feel at all. Imposing dualisms to explain things is deep human cognitive behavior and we probably need to spend more time analyzing human thought using behavioral models, based on the way I'm talking about the processes involved in cognitive and physical behavior in animals, behavior that, in fact, can't be separated into two distinct categories.

For humans, separating phenomena into two kinds is the first and most fundamental way we categorize: Aristotle's first law of logic. Something cannot be both A and not-A in the same way in the same place at the same time. A or not-A, is or is not. There are two kinds of people, don't you know, ones who love animals and ones who do not; there are things that can move and things that cannot, thinking minds and unthinking bodies, on and on. You might say we're hard-wired to think in dualisms. The thinking versus non-thinking dualism still tears at the heart of cognitive ethology because it accepts the terms of non-conceptualists: if animals aren't thinking like us, well, then they're not thinking. There's no model, no theory, for thinking that isn't like ours.

Before dualistic concepts got hold of us humans, our first tier of explanation, our first cognitive impulse, was mytho-poetic, not scientific. We used metaphor (technically metonym), i.e. stories. If the stories are about the really big stuff it's called religion. There's something about the life of Jesus that speaks to what it means to be human, something essential, something true, about forgiving and receiving forgiveness, whether Jesus ever existed or not. It's a big leap from that kind of story to the stories about pets that people send to the Comics Page, but if you jump, that's where you land. Most of what people talk about and believe operates on that level, from reincarnation to alien abduction. I don't believe in dogs calling 911, but I believe the metaphor in that anecdote and how the need for that metaphor expresses an essential fact about our relationship with animals, a relationship that lies within all the other illusions and stories we live inside; in this, our deep and personal interdependence with the other that we bring into our homes, our lives. We are not alone.

Two days after that first walk with Gail and Nadine I went out alone with my dog and walked a little farther. Two days after that I walked as far as a foot bridge that spanned a stream, now dry, though there was a waterhole under a palm tree down there where Nadine loved to race down the cliff and jump around in the neck deep muck. Generally I didn't wait for her but continued up the hill. Soon she'd have run back up the cliff side (about a 50 degree angle; it's stunning what dogs can do with their four-legged drive) and caught me on the path, again racing ahead. But today, not wanting to get too sore, I turned around at the foot of the bridge and didn't cross. Nadine crossed the bridge. I would have let her go down to the waterhole, but after she stood there a while, waiting at the top of the ledge, I called to her. She didn't go down to the water; she turned, ran to me, and then we headed back.

When Nadine and I walked alone, we'd never before turned back at the bridge or anywhere else, but did so in both previous contexts, in the second while she stood above her palm tree bog. Again, she's not necessarily a dog who comes when you call her.

After a day's rest I figured I'd try to stretch the walk to a half-mile out and a half-mile back. When we reached the bridge I crossed it and Nadine charged down to the waterhole. She hadn't been there for some time and so lingered down there, jumping and splashing. I went ahead up the trail as I'd done hundreds of times before, though several minutes later I realized that Nadine hadn't followed me. I called. Whistled. No Nadine.

It's usually pretty safe out there, but dogs, even big dogs, disappear in Topanga Canyon all the time. There are rattlesnakes up to six feet in length (H.D. was bitten once, through her ear, which saved her from absorbing a lot of the venom), coyote packs, mountain lions. Gail's cat, Elizabeth Taylor, was taken by a mountain lion from right outside our front door. Nadine and I had run into a huge rattler on a different trail just before my surgery. So when Nadine disappeared, I worried a little bit. Once, from a thicket at the bottom of the ravine, she'd retrieved two deer skulls, so I knew pumas had been in the territory. I turned around and began to walk back. She wasn't at the waterhole, but two women who were crossing the bridge said that they saw a red-brown dog running toward the Santa Maria trailhead from where we started out. I was relieved and headed for my truck. About two hundred yards from the trailhead I spotted Nadine already heading back up the path toward me. We greeted each other. I walked toward our parking place and Nadine sprinted ahead to wait for me there.

So Nadine came out of the waterhole and up the cliff, didn't see me, and at some point headed back to the truck. What I found interesting was that though in almost all of our walks prior to my surgery we'd followed the pattern of continuing onward up the trail from the waterhole, possibly five hundred times or more, but when she emerged from it this time and didn't see me, she headed back, not forward; in my absence she did what we'd done the last time, not what we'd done five hundred times previous. More so, among the few times in those hundreds that we did turn around, I was with Gail who seldom completed the full circuit, so if Nadine possessed a behavioral pattern it was that she turned back when with Gail and me, gone forward when just with me.

In the last three times we'd gone out and turned back, the first was with Gail, the second with just me before we got to the bridge, the third with just me again, from the foot of the bridge. I could speculate that Nadine didn't remember the first five hundred times we took the walk, she just automatically turned around like the last time. But there are problems with that explanation. The other times I turned back, she proceeded forward and I had to call her back to me. Each of those times she assumed that we were going forward, not turning back. She hesitated, and then I called her back to me. Why, in my absence, did she turn back? More evidence that she did not simply run out of the waterhole and thoughtlessly head back is that when I found her near the trailhead, she was already coming down the trail again. She'd arrived at my truck and finding me not there, headed down the trail in the original direction. Was she was just a dog running around heedlessly or was she was looking for me? (HD, by the way, in the same circumstance, would simply have waited at the truck; she was one of those dogs who moved until finding a possession of yours and then waited there with it; if we got separated in the woods, and we sometimes did on trail rides with Jackie O, I could put my shirt on the ground and proceed forward, a half-hour later on my way back I'd find her lying on it).

As I was walking back to the truck to find Nadine I asked myself what I would have done in her place. Well, in fact, the same thing. I'd have hesitated, looked around, and figured that my partner had headed back like the last time, not the five hundred other times. But why would I have figured that? Partly because it's what we did the last time, but also because the truck was a certainty, the place where we always returned. One possible difference is that I would have gone forward a little ways, calling for her, and if she didn't come, then I'd have turned back.

Indeed, when I noticed that Nadine wasn't following me, I called for her and then turned back. If I ever thought, "Oh, she likely ran back to the truck," I did so after I called for her, then turned back, thinking to find her at the waterhole. When the women told me they saw her I was relieved and hoped for and pictured her running back to the truck and trailhead. Maybe I did more worrying than she did. But my behavior wasn't the result of syntactical analysis or logic. It was a jumble of noticing her missing, calling for her, picturing her back at the waterhole, then heading back before ever figuring anything verbally, in fact, if I began some kind of syntactical thinking it came after my behavior pattern commenced.

I don't know how long Nadine hesitated after she came out of the waterhole or if she bothered to look for me up the trail before turning for home. I do know that regularly she charged up the ravine and immediately sprinted up the trail. She did this when she could spot me, but she did this when I was out of sight, too, and ran to catch up to me depending on which direction we were headed at the time, out or back.

I don't know if Nadine emerged from the waterhole and hesitated or if she charged up the trail and didn't find me, or if she immediately headed back, but at some point she had to choose one direction or the other, and if hundreds of times she'd correctly assumed that I'd gone ahead and continued to run to catch up with me, this time she assumed incorrectly that I went back like the last time, the same assumption I would have made, and I would have made it just as wordlessly and instinctively, choosing the certainty, the truck where we always ended up, over the uncertainty of continuing up the path ahead.

Analysis aside, at some point Nadine was faced with two directions and chose one. Whatever the cognitive steps involved for me, I would have made the same choice she did. I know for certain that there were cognitive-emotional steps involved in my choice because I experienced them. In fact, however jumbled, immediate, emotional, and wordless my reasoning was, it contained an evaluation of one direction over another and a choice. Why describe my behavior, my choice, as cognitive and not hers?

We could disregard my cognitive processes, as well as speculating about hers, and regard them as behaviorally irrelevant, i.e. choice is determined by biology, the history of my conditioning, and by context. The feeling of making a choice based on cognitive processes is an illusion; just because I reasoned, doesn't mean my reasoning caused my action. That's an ontological position, determinism and behaviorism. It's a possible explanation. But any ontological position, even a reductionist one, draws a metaphysical line in the sand; as ontology it's a position unproven and not provable. Further, though reductionism might be the simplest starting position, in regard to sentient behavior its explanations don't always result in the simplest solutions; for example explaining animals with complex food storage and retrieval behaviors, often explained as some combination of conditioning and instinct, though instinct is at least as mysterious and impenetrable as cognition when it comes to explaining behavior.

Yet as far as my argument is concerned, it doesn't matter whether or not reductionist determinisms are true. Whether or not, ultimately, my choice was conditioned by other factors, that I experienced a series of cognitive-emotional processes can't be denied; even behaviorists have them, and most philosophers would admit that now. The issue for them is more about locating intellect in the bio-chemistry of the brain and whether or not that solves the mind-body problem. Does electro-chemistry cause cognition? Do electro-chemical processes and thoughts co-arise? Where are thoughts anyways? Where are they? I don't experience electro-chemistry, I experience thought. (Back to dualisms; behavior and instinct is another dualism, by the way).

The steps I took in choosing to go back to my truck were wordless, intuitive, and semiotic and the logic of what I did might have confirmed my choice more than guided it. Yet however much I might wish to disregard my cognitive processes, I can't deny I had them. As I've stated in a number of places already, I'm not interested in arguing that those processes caused my behavior, nor am I arguing for parallelism, that cognitive and physical events occur simultaneously in separate spheres, i.e. the brain and the mind—all of that is speculative ontology—but that my cognitive behavior and my physical behavior are part of a dialectic, or better, a *pluralecitc*, of several intimately related behaviors, desires, emotions, memories, worries, images, some of which occur during, some before, and some after my observable physical behavior.

A colleague of mine who recently learned that I was writing a book about animal cognition said to me, "That's fascinating, I always wanted to know what my cat was thinking." I said to him, "Look at your cat. That's what she's thinking." Or as a student of mine said, reading aloud a completely opaque sentence by Derrida, "Why doesn't he just say what he means?" Well, that is what he means!

Some philosophers have suggested that animals, and machines, too, because they can't report on their reflections by means of language, are, at best, *alien minds*, because we can't know them. The behavior of animals and machines must be examined by experts using strict definitions, controlled experiments, and highly qualified lexicons. They contend that most speculation about machine and animal intelligence is conducted by naïve observers using *folk psychology*, and such folk know nothing about computers, robotics, biological robotics, physiology, psychology, philosophy, zoology, ethology, comparative or animal psychology (see *Guilty Robots, Happy Dogs*, David McFarland). These fields of study consistently prove that what appears to the naïve observer as intentional or goal oriented behavior, for example mound building in termites, is actually quite mechanical and accidental and then, at best, eventually habitual. The hunter who "thinks like a deer" has simply learned its habits and anthropomorphized the deer's reasoning. Most of us are like ignorant, non-technological bushmen. Because we don't understand the phenomena in front of us, we impose intentionality like our own on machines, animals, and even nature in general. We anthropomorphize.

In the end, the argument goes, even the experts can't know whether animals and machines are subjective or rational or whether they can hold representations (icons) in their heads, though we can explain their behavior without assuming that they do. To believe in animal cognition is simply anthropomorphism and this is what most human speculation about machines and animals and nature in general amounts to, imposing what we do, in our minds, onto the world at large. This is the rhetoric of monist materialism and of religion, as well. Yet, as Marc Bekoff contends, it refuses, quite self-consciously, to look at intelligence as part of a biological continuum.

So though I might understand my cat, Cheese, better than I understand Derrida, I assume Derrida means something when he says *trace* and Cheese means nothing when he says *meow* at the bottom of my stairs. I'm cheating here. That's rhetoric, not philosophy. Derrida might be able to re-explain what he meant to mean, the Cheese can't. Both Derrida and the Cheese might know how to get me to come downstairs and feed them, but the Cheese only has procedural knowledge, *knowledge how*, while Derrida has reflective knowledge, *knowledge that* he's doing what he's doing. So far, I've tried to expose how the assumptions of these kinds of dualisms make the obvious inapproachable. Highly qualified lexicons, invaluable as they might be, often do that, too. We might further ask why *knowledge how* is not conceptual knowledge.

Humans, because of language, have developed sophisticated "inner worlds" where we plan, contemplate, remember, practice deceit, even lie to ourselves. Humans can do this because of our capacity to think in symbols operating in adaptable rule-laden systems, i.e. language. Sophisticated emotions, for the most part, are perpetuated, i.e. continued in time, by a dialectic of syntax and imagery that consecutively maintain our attention to our wishes, fears, feelings, that allow us to keep those emotions in front of our faces, so to speak. The jealous lover *holds on* to his jealousy by reliving the act of betrayal over and over, the way I did when Gail had dinner with the Nobel Laureate.

Without the dialectic of language and imagery, most animal planning, remembering, and choosing occurs temporally more closely to their solutions. This means that their emotional responses are generally not as prolonged, as well, though it doesn't mean that an emotional response cannot recur if a representation sparks it in their memory. Nadine, frightened on a running trail one Halloween by a half-dozen teen-agers dressed as goblins, became frightened again every time we came to that spot, in fact, anticipated it and began to run through it to my truck.

When it comes to humans, people often loosely use the term *body language* to say that posture and facial expression can expose what a person is thinking, but this once again divides the dessert into frosting and cake and nothing but.

When someone lies to me, they might mean exactly what they say. I comprehend that they are lying by a combination of understanding human gestures, the history of the individual's gestures and the history of their behavior, as well as the context, and what's at stake for them. That allows me to gauge whether it's gossip, storytelling masquerading as fact, exaggeration, self-justification, or a protest of innocence (that often implies guilt). Based on these observations I can judge, at least vaguely, what I need to come away with in that conversation.

Verbal behavior is behavior. Much of the precise meaning of what people say is irrelevant. It's why I tell my students that even though I'm a writer and a teacher, I don't believe in communication. I tell them, as well, that they don't write with their minds but with their hands, i.e., they can't decide to write well (or play the piano well, or dive off a diving board well), it's a matter of practice and repetition.

Meanwhile, back at the bog, Nadine made her choice and decided to run back to the truck. Does choice imply cognition? Not necessarily. A hardened philosopher of the mind would point out that machines are programmed to evaluate situations and make choices all the time. Do we want to say that our video recorder is conscious? Well, maybe we should, depending on what we mean.

So I began to observe Nadine's behavior around the waterhole more closely. I noticed several behavioral patterns. Farther down the trail from the bog there's a stream that goes dry in the summer. In the fall it runs after a rain, but if it doesn't rain again soon after, then it goes dry again. I thought that I noticed that Nadine apparently preferred the stream to the bog because after a rainstorm if she discovered water in the stream, the next time out she skipped the bog and ran to the stream. On the way back she played in the stream and skipped the bog again, this time without any hesitation. She did that until the stream went dry again and, finding the stream dry, went back the next day to jumping in the bog, or so I thought.

Then I thought I noticed that she had an additional behavioral pattern toward the bog when the stream was dry. On cooler days she hesitated at the top of the ridge, sometimes even going down a few steps, then stopped, stood, and turned and ran ahead. She did this while running in front of me, so it was possible for me to observe it. On the way back, when she was heated up after running for a few miles, she often ran down to the bog without hesitation, but not if it was colder still, say in the 50's. If there was water in the stream and she'd been in the bog once and the stream twice, she likely skipped the bog on the way back, simply running past the bog without stopping.

I suppose I could put a couple thermometers in a robot and take it for a walk and it might go into the bog or not depending on the variables of the outside temperature and, if I rigged it to heat up internally as it moved, its internal one. I suppose I could program it, as well, to remember if the stream was running and not go in the bog if it was. Given what we've got crawling around on Mars now, I don't think we have robots that sophisticated yet, but I imagine some day we will.

In the meantime I'm waiting to see if Nadine makes the connection between rainstorms and the stream flowing. I don't think she does, though yesterday, after a big storm on the day previous, she skipped the bog and jumped in the stream. But it was pretty cold out for Southern California, 50 degrees Fahrenheit, and she might have skipped the bog because it was too cold, though if so, why go in the cold stream?

What I want to do now is to introduce another model, a human one. I don't jump in the bog because I don't want to flop around in a stinky, muddy bog, though bogs aside, when I was younger I pretty much jumped in any water deeper than my waist and wide enough to spread out in, anything from a waterhole to the ocean. Even when I lived in the northeast I was pretty good for a quick dip in a lake or a quarry, or better, a waterfall, well into November. When I moved to Los Angeles I immediately learned to surf and, as soon as the ocean got cold, I bought a wetsuit. But as I got older I began to measure my comfort levels, the temperature outside, the temperature of the water, the bother of getting dry or, worse, being cold, wet, and covered with sand, as well how I'd dry off if I didn't have a towel. I'd hesitate in front of the water. That hesitation occurred before I thought about it.

When that happened, after my hesitation, my response came in a sentence. "Should I go in?" Then I felt the outside temperature, touched the water, imagined how quickly I'd get used to it or if I ever would; then I contemplated the process of getting out. Most of that occurred very quickly in a series of images. Of course, being a cognitive organism, I might have known I was going to encounter water and begun some of these evaluations earlier.

Though I imagine that I'm thinking about a lot more consequences than Nadine thinks about, it's that moment of hesitation I'm focusing on, that moment just before Nadine chose to run back to the truck or chose not to jump in the bog. Though I imagine I could program a robot to hesitate at the bog, that hesitation would have nothing to do with the decision making process of the machine. Its decision was already made by the calculation of the temperature. As well, I doubt that I could program the robot to enjoy jumping around in the water, though I suppose I could program it to behave as if it did, to jump around in the bog and make gleeful sounds, to come running to me when I called it, shaking itself dry and sprinting up the trail. As of yet, we have no machines capable of this, however well they might play chess or Jeopardy.

One might argue that Nadine is as programmed by nature, by natural selection, as the robot is by its designer. However true or false that might be, these are very different concepts of design and I don't need to postulate an anthropomorphic deity into natural selection to find them incomparable. More so, Nadine doesn't just go in the water or not go in the water. She goes in because she enjoys it. That's the only reason for her to go in or for me to go in. And that moment of hesitation is a moment of sentience, a moment of hesitation similar to mine. An enjoyment calculation is made, a very near future scenario imagined. In the other case, the case of Nadine's turning back for the truck in my absence, an objective is imagined, the truck.

I decided to keep a log of Nadine's behavior when she encountered the bog. *(You might wish to skip or skim this portion, i.e. the log itself, and proceed to the summary on page 134).*

Nadine's Dog Bog Log

December 15—It's Tuesday and it rained very hard into Sunday morning. The ground is wet in spots, muddy in others. It's cool, 62 degrees. Nadine sprints past the bog, jumps in the stream. On the way back she jumps in the stream again, hesitates at the bog but doesn't go in, sprinting over the bridge.

December 16—It's still wet. The sand on the path is already drying where the sun hits it. The mud is beginning to harden. 64 degrees. Nadine hesitates at the bog, looks at me, then sprints ahead. But at the stream we run into two couples who have children and dogs. Nadine runs past them and the stream. On the way back she jumps in the stream, hesitates at the bog but doesn't run down to it.

December 20—I've been holiday shopping and missed a few days. The path is now dry, the mud hardened. It hasn't rained for a week. It's warmer, 68 degrees. Nadine hesitates at the bog, then runs down and jumps into it. The stream is dry at the crossing and she runs by it, ignoring waterholes to her right and left. She does so again on the way back, but when she gets to the bog she hesitates, looks at me, and then runs over the bridge.

December 22—It's cold and dry, windy; 54 degrees. Nadine runs past the bog without hesitating. Though the stream crossing is dry, there's some water in holes on either side and Nadine spots them, then jumps in the hole to our left. She jumps in the same hole on the way back, then runs past the bog.

December 26—Gail's mom went into the hospital on the afternoon of the 22nd, so it's been a few days. It's dry and 58 degrees. Nadine hesitates at the bog, but doesn't go in. Though there's water in the waterholes, she runs past the stream on the way out and the way back. At the bog she hesitates, looks at me, then runs down and jumps in briefly before darting back up the cliff.

December 28—Dry, cool, some breeze. 60 degrees. Nadine races past the bog and the stream, but on the way back she jumps in a waterhole downstream. Then she races to the bog and runs down to it and jumps in.

December 29—Dry. 64 degrees. Nadine skips the bog and jumps the dry stream, but on the way back finds a waterhole downstream and jumps in, then races ahead and goes right down to the bog without hesitating.

December 31—Dry, 60 degrees, but very calm and sunny. Nadine hesitates at the bog, looks at me, then runs down and goes in. The stream is running (I don't know why; it hasn't rained); she plays in the stream on the way out and the way back, then races past the bog.

January 2—74 degrees, sunny and warm. Nadine races down into the bog. The stream is dry and she jumps over it on the way out and back without looking for a waterhole. She hesitates at the bog on the way back, then goes in.

January 3—74 degrees. Oddly, though it's sunny, Nadine hesitates at the bog and skips it. The stream is running and she plays in it both out and back; races past the bog on the way back.

January 5—72 degrees. Sunny. Nadine races into the bog, jumps the dry stream both times, then skips the bog without looking at it.

January 7—Sunny, 74 degrees. Nadine stops at the top of the bog, looks at me, then goes in. Though there are waterholes on either side of the crossing, she runs by them, but jumps in one on the way back to take a drink, then skips the bog.

January 8—Dry and warm, 72 degrees. Nadine hits the bog, uses the waterholes out and back, skips the bog at a run.

January 11—72 degrees, a bit windy. Nadine hesitates at the bog, then goes in. The stream is dry with waterholes right and left. She skips it on the way out but stops for a drink on the way back, then runs past the bog.

January 15—70 degrees, calm. Because it's warm and we haven't been out for a few days I predict that Nadine will go into the bog. She hesitates at the top of the path, looks at me, then runs down and jumps in. At the dry stream there's a waterhole downstream and she runs to it, but stops at it and doesn't go in. On the way back she runs to the waterhole and jumps in. I figure that means she won't go down to the bog and I'm right; she runs right past it.

January 16—70 degrees. Almost the same conditions. Nadine runs right down to the bog. At the stream she goes to the waterhole, stops, and takes a drink of water. On the way back she jumps in and predictably skips the bog.

January 17—(The first anniversary of Jackie O's death). It's cold, 54 degrees, and drizzling. Nadine runs past the bog, jumps the streambed on the way out and the way back; she ignores the bog, as well.

January 18—It's been raining constantly since our walk on Sunday afternoon. Rain is expected for the week. There hasn't been enough rain this winter to judge whether or not Nadine assumes the stream will be full after a hard rain and so skips the bog on the way out. Of course, how cold it is on that first walk could be a factor. My assumption is that the connection is too abstract and too much time passes between the end of the rain and the walk, though if Nadine understands 'water' or 'wet' in the way Mucha Plata understood 'food', then I imagine that signals like the muddy path and humid air might make some combination of connections possible.

The pattern of behavior here, so far, generally follows my more casual observations. Nadine seems to prefer the stream to the bog. On cooler days she often skips the bog on the way out whether the stream is running or not, though not necessarily. If she goes in the stream, she generally skips the bog on the way back, sometimes hesitating and sometimes not. Anomalies occur on December 28, 29, and 31 sequence when the temperature was 60, 64, and 60. The first two days she behaves predictably, passing the bog and stream on the way out because it's cool, using them both on the way back. But on the 31st, despite it being cool, she followed her warm day pattern, going in the bog and the stream and passing the bog on the way back. She seems more likely to go in the bog on the way back if the stream is dry, less likely if there's water, even a waterhole, though on January 3, despite the warmth (74 degrees) and the dry streambed the previous day, she skipped the bog and looked for waterholes in the stream.

As well, she sometimes races past the bog, sometimes stops and looks at it, then goes in or does not and, as well, sometimes races ahead to the bog and jumps in without hesitating. The racing behavior is possibly more telling than her hesitation, implying that she has made a decision about the bog while not in front of it. This holds for the stream, too, where she sometimes looks for the waterhole and sometimes does not. The waterholes are not something she can see until she reaches the streambed, but she must have some disposition to skip them or go to them and, if she goes, she chooses to skip them, take a drink, or jump in. Further, she is much more likely to race ahead of me to the next water area if she hasn't used the last one, implying anticipation.

What's more interesting to me than the pattern of Nadine's behavior is its variations and how often, under very similar conditions, on different days, her behavior varies. Once again, I'm not interested in finding environmental or physiological causes for why her dispositions might change from one context to the next. Whether or not her behavior can be explained is irrelevant. Nor am I interested in arguing for separate cognitive processes that guide Nadine's behavior. I'm trying to demonstrate that whether we are considering humans or animals, behavior and cognition are linked, a movement from one disposition to the next, to satisfy dispositions, seek enjoyment, find pleasure, avoid pain. These are cognitive acts, however one might choose to quibble about how much cognitive awareness or abstract thinking precedes them, and much of this behavior is best explained by the pluralectic of dispositions and semiotic responses.

Jackie O's behavior when I arrived at the ranch was pretty ritualized, especially in her later years, but her readiness to come to me when I arrived was often weather related, too. On any normal, southern California day, sunny and warm, she saw my truck, walked forward, urinated, and then came to me.

If I was busy at the tack box and didn't come right to her, she nickered (a low, throaty rumble), I'd say to get my attention. Though less loosely, what else would be the point of making the noise?

I haven't seen thousands of horses in thousands of circumstances, but I've observed nickering in a number of contexts. Recently I briefly leased a mare that I contemplated buying (a blue-eyed, Overo Paint quarter horse that I named Barbarella). She was housed in one of a series of open-air contiguous stalls. After my second time with her, i.e. the third time I showed up, she nickered to me when I got out of my truck. The other horses, who I didn't spend time with, did not nicker.

When Jackie O hurt her leg and had to be stabled for a month, she nickered as soon as she saw me. As I've related earlier, Tasha began to nicker to me, too. There's a sound similar to a nicker that horses emit before fighting or sex, but it's a deeper, more throaty, aggressive sound. Further, it's not a sound of satisfaction like a cat's purr, although purrs are a little more ambiguous than just expressing being sated. A horse doesn't nicker when she eats or when you pet her; if you scratch her withers she might stretch her neck out and purse her lips or even prance. At first I thought only mares did this, but I've found that geldings do it too.

The nicker is not a call like a scream, which occurs when a horse is separated from someone she's attached to, like Tasha screamed for Jackie O. The nicker is a gentle, anticipatory call, a kind of "come hither," although Jackie O, being a very emphatic personality, had pretty demanding nicker. Nickering does not occur in a vacuum. It happens in a context, and a result is expected; one disposition, nickering and pressing against the fence, calls for an expected disposition of my presence, my carrots and apples, the smells, the sounds, and the tactile rituals of our reuniting.

If it was spring, and grass grew outside the pasture, Jackie O might pass up the bowl of carrots and trot off to a spot on the hill where the grass grew thickest, a spot she had to remember because it often couldn't be seen from the dressing area outside the gate. All else aside, this behavior is at the very least demonstrative of my horse *wanting* to get out of the pasture and go eat some carrots or grass. Wanting is a disposition. Something has to be wanted. It's cognitive behavior like my getting hungry and going to the refrigerator.

If I came when it was wet and cold Jackie O hesitated, sometimes for quite a while, standing under the shelter with the other horses, body to body, keeping warm. I began to understand it when one day I waited a long time and she eventually came to me, standing in the wind and rain, shivering. I felt badly for having caused her discomfort and I didn't come in the rain anymore. If it rained for days in a row, I waited for a break in the rain to go see her, feed her and clean her. Even then, it was cold and wet, if not raining, and so more comfortable for her to stay put. It's interesting to note that in this situation she might have been facing away from the gate, that is, she saw my truck come up the road, possibly heard me get out. But she stood under the awning at the other end of the pasture, some thirty yards away, with her butt to me, surrounded by other horses. She couldn't see me at all. I doubt very much that she could smell me across thirty yards of mud, wind, and manure. Then she had to back out from the little herd, turn, see me, and come to me. But standing there for several minutes, the *decision* to come to me had to be made without any physical stimulus from me.

The other circumstance where she hesitated was when it was really hot, in the vicinity of 100 degrees. I'd wait at the fence, holding a carrot, and she'd stare across the pasture, looking at me. In the end, she'd come, sometimes after quite a long time, five or ten minutes. Let's reduce this to a bare minimum like the horse is warm and comfortable and doesn't want to move. Yet she is staring across the pasture at me. What is she looking at? Nothing? If she doesn't anticipate a future preferable disposition, why would she leave a place where she's comfortable and walk thirty yards to come to me? In fact, it's more complex, because on any normal day she just came. If she's simply too hot to move, why then would she ever move? What changes in those minutes that she stares across the pasture? More compelling, when she comes to me I will not just give her carrots or let her graze. I will, as I always did when I arrived alone, saddle her and mount her and ride, as I did 300 times a year for fifteen years. The price of my companionship and carrots was work, sometimes hard work

I can't read one of my horse's behaviors without reading her other behaviors. If her behavior changed from mobility to immobility simply because it was too hot (or too wet and cold), then she would come to me when the weather was pleasant and not come when it was inclement, or she'd come immediately no matter what the weather. In any regard, however mechanically one might wish to envision it, a choice must be made to stay put or come, one behavior must occur or the other. In her hesitation—and being a huge vegetarian her hesitation can last a lot longer than that of a predator like a dog—we see the semiotics of decision making. A transition occurs. One disposition is left for another anticipated one, and more so in the circumstance of cold, wet weather when her back was turned to me. It's impossible to reduce this below the level of memory and anticipation.

Nadine's Dog Bog Log

January 23—The day broke clear, cold and sunny after six days of hard rain (we lost 80% of our bottle brush tree, our electricity was out for six hours and when it came back on the computer in our new split system for heating and air conditioning couldn't reconfigure and we lost heat downstairs for a week). After breakfast, Nadine begins her morning ritual: she snarls for a pig's ear that she takes upstairs and runs out the back door, down the outdoor steps and back into the kitchen, then up the steps and out the back door again, then coming in she races up to the living room, puts the pig ear down and gets her snack toy and brings it to Gail who fills it with Milk Bones, though sometimes Gail prompts her by saying "Where's your snack toy?" and Nadine tries to find it and sometimes Nadine will bring the snack toy and then run away repeatedly, trying to get Gail to chase her; when Nadine gets the filled up snack toy she extracts the milk bones from the toy and eats them (she squeezes one end of the toy with her teeth and shakes them out the other end; she had to figure that out), then she goes to her toy box and pushes toys around, eventually emerging with a soft toy fragment that she takes to Gail; Gail tugs on the toy and chases Nadine around the house; that over, Nadine jumps up on the hassock in front of my chair and puts her front paws on the arm of my chair; I hug her around the neck and chest; she'll also do this if I say, "I want to hug my dog," or "Want a hug?"; now she's ready to eat her pig's ear and then lie down next to Gail on the couch (Romeo already perched opposite). This is generally what she does, specifically, every day has variations. What's unusual this day is that she gets up from the couch and requests a walk, standing in front of me and offering a short woof, than bounding toward the stairs; she does this several times.

It's interesting to note that Nadine did not request a walk while it was raining. I know she would come for a walk with me in the rain, because we've done it before, but I don't go when it's raining hard. She goes outside in the rain to urinate and defecate. I can only conclude that on this day she noticed that it stopped raining and asked for a walk.

I take her. It's cold, 51 degrees, but sunny and calm. The path is muddy. By my calculations she should skip the bog. It's too cold. Furthermore, if she knows the stream fills up after it rains, she should run to it. In fact, she does neither. When we reach the ledge above the bog, she hesitates and looks down at the bog, then looks at me, then the bog, then me, and then sprints down to the bog. She doesn't run to the stream. When she gets to it, she paces up and down the shore with her nose down, then jumps over it. She doesn't go in at all. But on the way back she races about forty yards ahead of me and jumps in the stream, running back and forth, playing hard until I reach the shore, then she sprints up the hill. She skips the bog on the way back without hesitation.

January 24, 25, 26—These days she behaves almost the same each day; the temperature is in the mid-fifties everyday, sunny on the first day, hazy the second, drizzling the third. Nadine runs past the bog and sprints ahead to the stream to play, then on the way back sprints ahead to the stream, plays in it, skips the bog without hesitation. On the third day, in the drizzle, she skips the bog and trots to the stream, stands in it and takes a drink, but on the way back runs ahead and plays in it, then skips the bog.

On the last three days Nadine behaved as I would have predicted. January 23 indicates that she does not conclude the stream is running after a rain, even though she seems to recognize the difference between a rainy day and a dry one. The other days indicate that she remembered that the stream had been full and anticipated it being so, even so much as to skip the bog and run to the stream long before she could see it. The semiotics of memory and anticipation are obvious, the tactility of the water, the smell, the taste, memories of jumping around (memories similar, I imagine, to when she dreams, and for those that doubt that animals dream, icon semiotics explains it). The joy is palpable.

January 23 is wonderfully complex. For one, the temperature was far below her behavioral pattern for going in, but we hadn't been out in a while, she was excited, and went in despite the cold, though she hesitated to do it. She seemed surprised by the stream, inspecting it, maybe jumping it because she was already wet (and cold) from the bog, but on the way back she raced ahead to it with joyous enthusiasm, getting there way ahead of me and playing even as I arrived.

Later in the week, on the 28th , a warm, dry day (74 degrees) Nadine skipped the bog and ran to the stream, then doused in the stream on the way back and skipped the bog. She did the same the next three days in a row. Then, after two days of hard rain we went out on the third day, February 6. It was so cold I could see Nadine's breath (54 degrees); as well, we ran into a family with two dogs just ahead of the bridge, then a woman with a child on the bridge. Previously Nadine always skipped the bog if there was somebody there, but that day she ran down into the bog without hesitation, then ran to the stream on the way out and the way back, then skipped the bog on the way home.

She repeated this same behavior on February 16 after I'd been out of town for four days, when the temperature was 80 degrees, much warmer.

Many of my theories about Nadine's behavior toward the bog and the stream weren't confirmed. She doesn't seem to skip the bog after it has rained. She doesn't deduce that the stream will be full because it has rained. Nor does she go in the bog or skip the bog simply because of the temperature. In several cases she went in the bog despite it being cold outside and with people and dogs nearby when I predicted that she wouldn't go in when somebody else was present or when it was cold. She sometimes skipped the bog when it was quite warm out. The only consistency I observed was that when we went on the trail on a daily basis, she apparently remembered from the day before that the stream was full and so then skipped the bog on the way out, then after going in the stream on the way back she almost always skipped the bog. She apparently does prefer the stream to the bog and if we go out on a daily basis remembers that the stream is full and skips the bog. Though her occasional hesitation at the bog can't be explained, it seems to indicate a decision process. Other times she seems to have clearly decided to go in or not go in well before we get there. Her general pattern is to go in the bog on the way out, hit the stream on the way out and the way in, then skip the bog on the way back. She only goes in the bog on the way home if the stream is dry. Most of the time, she's made her decision well before she arrives at the bog or stream, because she runs ahead and jumps in without hesitation.

(GETTING COFFEE)

This morning, as I sat in my armchair reading the sports, Yoko Dodo on my lap and Jughead waiting his turn, I ran out of coffee. The coffee pot was across the room on the dining table. I put Yoko on the hassock and asked Gail, who sat across from me on the couch, if she needed more coffee, too. She said, "Yes." In less than two seconds I pictured myself getting up and getting the coffee pot, walking to Gail's cup and filling it, then walking to my cup and filling it, then returning the pot to the table and then walking back to my chair. Next I pictured taking my cup to the table and filling it, then filling Gail's cup and returning the pot, then walking back to my chair with my filled cup. I immediately decided the second alternative was more efficient and that's what I did. I did this all in pictures and made the decision without a moment of verbal cognition.

More interesting, the iconic cognitive process I employed when I chose the more efficient method is one I've employed time and time again, day after day. Whatever its causal relationship was to my behavior the very first time I made the decision, now it is less a cause of my behavior than a process that accompanies my behavior. You'd think that by now, after thousands of times, I wouldn't bother to think about it at all. Why would I ever bother to think about the less efficient method of filling the cups? But I do. The cognition and the behavior aren't separable behaviors. Thinking the process through in those icons and choosing the more efficient method is what I do every time. Likely I have already chosen the more efficient approach and begun enacting it before I've completed thinking it through in pictures. This is because the apparent division between the cognitive aspect of my behavior and its physical aspect doesn't really exist. It's an abstraction imposed by verbal analysis occurring after the behavior. The decision is not made in language, nor is the iconic cognition a cause of my physical behavior. *They are the same behavior* and the result of repetition and pluralistic circumstances.

Much of the *figuring* I do in a new circumstance, like fixing a door knob, is very similar; the pictures and the manipulations of my hands accompany each other. Now I am looking at a stapler on my desk. I contemplate picking it up. I do that in pictures. I see my hand touching it, clasping it, lifting it. I choose not to pick it up but instead I've written about thinking about picking it up. As I type, now that I'm thinking about typing, I can picture my hands typing at the keyboard even as I watch them typing.

If you've ever spent much time trail riding than you know that your horse always seems to know the way home and, it might seem, the fastest way, too.

Jackie O was a fiery young animal, but even in her old age she could blow up on the trail over anything—voices yelling in the distance, a helicopter overhead, a butterfly flying too close to her face—bucking and crow hopping and trying to race home. In the early days I'd try to confuse her by spinning her around and taking her in a direction away from her pasture or barns, but she'd usually try to spin back in the direction of home or try to refuse to walk in the other direction. I'd also work her, making her run backwards or sideways or spin in tight circles or find somebody's corral where I ran her furiously until she calmed down. Some of these disputes could last an hour. If she bucked me off and ran home I'd walk back and find her, get back on and take her back out. Eventually I won these fights because to lose one would be a disaster. If Jackie O were a basketball team, she'd consider going 1-27 the same as being undefeated. Call me a lousy horseback rider.

Horses are a fascinating combination of cooperation and obstinacy, fierceness and flightiness. Most riders will tell you that the first thirty seconds on their back are crucial. In the days when I kept Jackie O at a huge training facility, my trainer, Paddy, would have us show off in the ring for new riders and she'd tell them, "See that horse. If you don't get control of her in the first few moments, in fifteen minutes she'll be riding you." That was Jackie O, my first horse, the hell between my legs that I loved.

As she aged her disobedience more often came in the form of sloth. Even a young horse might try to take over a ride by sloth and if you let her do it you're liable to get a big surprise at an unwary moment and end up on your toosh. This was how my rent-a-horse Barbarella behaved. If I didn't let her act up at first, she'd later try to walk a little slower than I asked, then a little slower, then trouble. I swear that Jackie O could slow down so incrementally that if I wasn't paying attention (something that happened sometimes as we both got older and went out poking around on sunny warm days in the hills) we'd be standing still before I noticed. This would imply that a horse uses tactics during a ride. Almost anybody who works with horses would agree with that. Some of the tactics are only seconds ahead, others minutes.

Out on the trail, whenever we came to a fork Jackie O always tried to choose the one that took us home or took us home more quickly with the least effort. I tested her hundreds of times and if I gave her the rein she always chose the short way back. Coming back from a trail ride there was one fork off the main loop that led up a steep hill. Not taking it, we would loop back toward her pasture.

If we ran up that hill, then at the top we could go in three directions: a long run to the top of the mountain, a road around the ranch, or a path back to the corrals, though a choice loomed ahead there, too, either down to her pasture or up around another hill above. Given any of those choices, she always picked the easiest if I left it up to her.

If we'd already been out on the trail and we were heading back, Jackie O employed a number of tactics. One was to break into a gallop when we got in sight of the hill (but long before we could see the trail), that is, try to run by it. Another was to walk calmly toward the fork and make a break just as we approached. This was behavior that anticipated the trail up the hill. Why didn't I break that habit by always heading up the hill? Well, sometimes I was tired and wanted to go home, too. My policy was to try to make her walk past it if I didn't want to go up it. She displayed this same behavior in front of the gates to the riding (workout) rings. My new horse, Nikki, does now, too.

If we were coming from the other direction, then usually it was early in the ride. Now the choices we more complicated. To pass the fork meant we were heading out onto the trail. To go up the hill meant either a run up to the top of the mountain, a hard run to a windy, open place she didn't like. Or instead of that we might take a leisurely coast around the ranch and, if so, we'd go past my friends Nick and Adele's stalls where there were carrots. If they weren't there, Jackie O could take the lid off their garbage can and get them herself. But that direction could also lead to a workout in one of the big rings, though sometimes it meant we'd turn right back for home and have a really brief, twenty minute walk. I tried to never do the same thing twice in a row because once Jackie O knew what we were going to do, then she had an opinion about it and, like Mr. Horse on *Ren and Stimpy*, it was usually "No sir, I don't like it." That writer must have owned a horse.

Faced with any of these choices that involved more exertion, she'd pick up speed and try to run past them—the bottom of the mountain, the gates to the riding rings—preferably in the direction of home, but at that fork, where all of those choices lay ahead of her, she'd stand like Zeno's ass. It made me laugh. What she really wanted to do was just turn around and head right back home and if I waited there long enough she might try to do that. Too choose the preferable over the uncomfortable is yet to choose one over the other and to do so one must anticipate, contemplate, shall I venture imagine (picture), both.

The fork meant different things to Jackie O depending on the direction we were going and whether we were at the beginning or the end of the ride. She couldn't run past the ring unless she was avoiding what she anticipated would happen inside it or gallop away from the mountain base unless she didn't want to run up it, however rote or determined you might think it. Nor could she trot toward Nick and Adele's corrals unless she anticipated carrots, or head for home without having something she was heading for. Horses anticipate and remember. That patch of dandelions under the oak tree, just off the trail, well, the next time I was there she'd look for them, and she'd look for them next spring, a year from then, too.

MORE FOLLOWING, MORE ANTICIPATING, MORE SYMBOLS

NADINE AND ROMEO SLEEP WITH US NOW. The others choose not to. Generally, when Gail and I sleep, we spoon. When we awaken, Nadine gets up from her spot at Gail's feet and licks her face, then mine. After the licking ritual, Gail gets up and Nadine jumps down from the bed. She frolics in the room, often trying to pounce on Romeo who ignores her. Gail says, "Oh Nadine, jump up and get a hug from your dad." And, in fact, she then does. She responds to *dad* by looking at me or coming to me, even if Gail says it; she also responds to *hug* by coming to me or jumping up and putting her front legs around my thigh. This behavior is prompted as well by Gail and me hugging each other. Of course, you're not supposed to let your dog hump you, it's bad manners and considered to be part of sexual domination behavior. Some female dogs do hump, though it's considered a male sexual behavior, and some, like HD, lifted their leg like a male did when they pee, just as submissive males, like Piccolo, squatted to pee. I watched Nadine hug me or Gail for quite some time before I decided it wasn't domination. It might be crossover sexual behavior; again, animals have limited behavioral repertoires, but her humping is generally a response to our hugging and/or the word *hug*, leading me to interpret it as following behavior; we hug, she hugs.

Often, in the morning, she's pretty playful. She'll feint at the bed and bound away, put her paws on the bed and then bound away again, but eventually she jumps up and throws her back into my chest, spooning, it would seem, just like Gail. I hug her, rub her stomach and the inside of her thigh. She pushes the back of her head under my neck. She might lick me. Her tongue drops out and she bares her teeth in, well, it looks like a grin. Her eyes are goofy, she makes a pleasurable groan.

Today Gail had a luncheon appointment. Before showering, Gail selected some clothes and put them on the bed. Nadine, who always spends her time with Gail if the two of us are home, came to my office and lay down, as she does when Gail is not home. She anticipated Gail's leaving by recognizing her pre-departure behavior and behaved as if Gail had already left. She reads our leaving behavior and anticipates our leaving in numerable contexts: before we leave for trips (suitcases); when we go out to eat or shop (we lock up and open the balcony door); in these cases she goes to the corner of the couch and mopes; when I prepare to go riding, take a hot tub, or take her for a walk (she follows me to the bedroom and watches what I'm going to wear), riding clothes, she walks away; running clothes she goes berserk and nibbles at my hands and feet; naked, she races outside to spot on the roof overlooking the tub.

In the morning, after Nadine's eaten her pig's ear, Gail will stand up and say, "Where's your snack toy, Nadine? Where's that snack toy?" And when it's found, by Gail or Nadine, "There it is!" The snack toy is the purple rubber thing I've mentioned earlier that can be opened enough to put Milk Bones inside, then closed. Nadine retrieves the Milk Bones by biting one end of the toy so other end opens and the bones drop out. In the early days Nadine would stand very still and wait for Gail to get it, but now she might look for it and bring it after finishing her pig ear. She'll bring it to me if Gail isn't there. As well, she might just stand near it and stare intently into the air. I knew that Nadine obviously recognized the sounds *snack toy*. We all know that dogs match up sounds to things. But recently a significant change has occurred.

Often, when I was about to take Nadine for a walk, she headed out the door and ran behind a huge elephant ear plant. She sat there perfectly still and was, in fact, immovable. No amount of pleading, tugging, or pushing would move her. If I said "Walk," or Let's go for a walk," or "Come on, Nadine, let's go," or even "Hot tub!" all exclamations which usually excited her, in this situation she didn't budge. Not until I walked down the stairs, opened the gate, walked out, and then closed the gate behind me would Nadine bound from behind the plant and run to the gate. Gail noticed this behavior as well. I said that I thought it was some kind of crossover behavior. Nadine was a hunting dog and when she got all excited, as before a hunt, her impulse, I thought, was to go into a hunting mode, i.e. hide and sit absolutely still (though, of course, she wasn't really very well hidden). I presumed it was hiding behavior because she sat behind the big leaf while I was present, and bound out from behind it when I left, no longer there to hide from. This displayed a cognitive/emotional transition based on my being there and then not being there.

Nadine has a number of what I call *behavioral holes*, behavior that she falls into, like wild play, licking, or suckling, and in each case she is so intent and intense that you can't penetrate her, you can't communicate anything to her at all. I speculated that the hiding behavior was like that. She fell into a hunting behavioral hole of some kind.

Yet something very unusual happened recently. When Nadine ran behind her giant elephant ear plant, instead of tugging and pleading with her (Why did I always do that? The same behavior? It never worked.) or just walking down the stairs and out the gate, I raised my arms, ridiculously, and shouted, "Where's Nadine? Where's Nadine hiding?" Nadine jumped from her hiding place and ran to me, practically jumping into my arms. She did it the next time, too.

I experimented a little. When she was behind the plant, none of the other coaxing worked. If I just asked, "Where's Nadine?" she remained hidden. But three times in a row when I said, "Where's Nadine?" she burst forth. Then, the next two times she didn't budge. So I added, "There she is!" She burst out again. Now when she hides behind the elephant leaf she might jump out when I say, "Where's Nadine?" or wait until I say, "There she is!"

The only verbal connection here is "Where's that snack toy?" And though it would be interesting enough if Nadine made the connection that *Where's* followed by an object meant go search for the named object like bone or toy, and in fact, if I say, "Where's your bone?" or "Where's your toy?" she might find one on the floor and bring it to me, or go to her toy box and bring one, though sometimes she might find it and not bring it and sometimes she might not search at all, but instead stand, motionless. But to respond to "Where's Nadine? There she is?" it seemed she must connect the idea of *where* constituting a search with the idea that I'm searching *for her*, and connect *there* with the act of *finding*. That's a very different response, or I might say, a different understanding of *where* than simply hearing the word as a cue to go look for the object that follows it in the phrase. I don't know why she sometimes only needs to be looked for, i.e. "Where's Nadine?" and others waits to be found, "There she is!"

In the case of finding her, it's possible that she responds only to *where*, that is, she gets excited when asked "Where's your snack toy?" because the word where simply gets her excited. But in fact, indoors, she can respond specifically to what I ask her to search for, the snack toy, a toy or a bone. Behind the elephant plant she gets excited when I say "Where?" or with the finding word, *there*.

When we say an animal *knows her name*, we simply mean that the name, the cue, draws their attention because we use it around them all the time, just like *dog* or *she*. Because Nadine responds to her name doesn't mean she knows what a name is, though she associates the sounds of the cats' names with the individual cats, as well; if I say Romeo she'll likely look at him. If Gail says "Dad," Nadine looks at me. Yet responding to "Where's Nadine?" implies a much more intimate connection to the appellation. Nadine means her, not some other person or animal, in the same way that her toys are hers, so is her name. It's not self-conscious possession, but a cognitive/emotional sense of *mine*.

To respond to "Where's Nadine?" Nadine must comprehend that *I am* searching for her like she has been asked to search for things. In fact, when I ask her to search for her snack toy, I'm likely to go into search gestures myself, so that there's following behavior going on between us, both of us falling into search behavior. So though I exhibit search behavior when I ask "Where's Nadine?" I'm not asking her to search, but expressing searching and specifically *that I am searching for her*, for a particular possession of hers, her name, i.e. her. It's a primitive syntactical comprehension requiring an understanding of the sounds as symbols, even if the word *where* produces icons of her searching for things, in this case she had to apply it in a very different context, one in which the thing being searched for is her. Then it would seem she responds to being found, as well, though one might argue that she simply responds excitedly to my gestures of finding, "There she is!"

In other contexts, say when Nadine is lying in front of me in my office, if I say "Where's Nadine?" she might look up, then put her head back down. And then, "There she is!" No response, even if I behave excitedly. So it would seem it isn't the phrases themselves or the words *where* and *there* that get her bounding around, but the context of her hiding and my using the phrase.

I'll discuss empathy a little later in this essay, but I have enough experience with animals to acknowledge that they don't empathize, i.e. put themselves in our shoes, though they do recognize our emotion behaviors and it's only a small step from that recognition to another kind of following, emotional following, or sympathy.

CAT POETS

Recently Gail and I have been watching 1950's sci-fi movies and writing down some of the dialogue. We then type up the lines and cut them into strips. We place the strips in a bowl and, on the dining table, each take a handful of lines out and put them on the table. From these piles we select lines and try to construct sci-fi poems. Some are pretty good. We've been placing them in magazines. The Fifties were quite existential times, and in reality, at the dawn of the nuclear age, the fate of the earth was constantly at stake, and it always is in those movies as well; alien invasion schemes are well-documented metonyms for Soviet invasion. If you watch "Iron Curtain" sci-fi films from the period they're usually about space travel, and not to Mars, but Venus.

Very early on, Romeo jumped up on the table and tried to put himself between us and the poems. We shoed him away. He sat. Watched us. Then he began to paw the strips in the bowl. Soon he had his own little pile of sci-fi lines in front of him. When we got done, he crawled into the bowl, curled up and went to sleep. In another week, Yoko Dodo began to do this as well. Both those cats might beg at meal time, sometimes even from the table top, so it seemed a possibility that when they first saw us at the table they assumed we were eating or, more simply, just went into begging behavior. Not finding food, Romeo dominated the bowl the way he dominated computers and newspapers and books, by sitting on them, though Yoko doesn't exhibit that kind of domination behavior in any other context. Another week later, Veronica, who doesn't beg or dominate things, jumped up on the table and did the same thing, pawed at the strips, then slept in the bowl. Now we might find any one of those three sleeping in the sci-fi poetry bowl with a pile of sci-fi lines lying outside. We investigate the pile when we find it and construct a poem. Now our sci-fi poem book has an appendix of cat poems. Okay, they don't write poems, but they do reach into the bowl and knock strips of paper out of it just like we do, and each of them approach the act from different behavioral matrixes, different cognitive/emotional attitudes that result in their following behavior, pawing at the strips in the bowl like we do. Sleeping in the bowl full of paper strips might appear to be typical domination behavior for Romeo, who did it first, but not for the females, who don't sleep on things to claim them, though they might sleep in places that are important, Yoko on my hassock, Veronica, at night, comes in the house and sleeps on my chair.

I would assume that this kind of following behavior is produced in the intimate circumstances of pride or pack or family, or whatever the complex group a bunch of people and domestic animals becomes, so it would not lend itself to laboratory experiment, but I'd be interested if other animal owners could corroborate similar following behavior in their domestic animals.

THE KING
OF CATS

MY YOUNGER BROTHER, Pete, used to call our house Rancho Catsamongus (cats-among-us). Meanwhile, back there, Jughead and Veronica were growing up. Here are some interesting cat community stories.

Jughead had become a little bit of a miracle because at about twelve weeks old he came down with a high fever and retreated under a dresser in Marlena's bedroom, a room where she "stored" things, for lack of a better word; she didn't sleep there, she slept on a futon downstairs in the Tiki Room. When cats retreat like that they're really sick. He refused to eat or drink.

I took Jughead to the vet the next day; she hydrated him and put him on antibiotics. His temperature was 107 degrees (normal cat temperature is about 100). He didn't get better. If I dragged him out and put him on my lap, he purred, but eventually jumped off and staggered back under the bureau. I took him to the vet four days in a row, but he refused to eat or drink and his temperature went down only one degree to 106. On Sunday the vet would be closed, though I could take him to the Valley to an emergency clinic, but I was starting to wonder, why bother? He was going to die. In fact the vet speculated that he had F.I.P., a fatal intestinal virus that is now very common in rescued cats. Monday was my birthday.

I started to force feed him water using a dropper and I put baby food on his paws that he licked off very slowly. His body was very hot. In desperation I called the old woman, Lisa, from whom I'd adopted him.

"The vet thinks it's F.I.P.," I said.

"That's baloney," she said. "Where do you live? I'm coming."

Lisa drove across the breadth of northern Los Angeles in her old Datsun station wagon, twice getting lost. I navigated her through the canyon by cell phone and met her outside my yard on the road. When she arrived she grabbed

Jughead and put him on her lap. She pulled out a number of herbs, crushed them, and mixed them with the baby food. Then with her finger she repeatedly pushed the food down his throat.

She gave him Baytril, a drug many vets regard as too dangerous, then pulled out a bag filled with water and connected it to a hypodermic needle. She showed me how to inject him with fluids subcutaneously. "I'm leaving all this here," she said. "Do this every four hours, and the Baytril twice a day." She refused any payment. I told her to keep the $200 that she was supposed to refund us when we had Jughead and Veronica spayed and neutered. She offered me only the slightest smile.

So that evening we dragged Jughead out again and did all the things that Lisa showed me. That night, before bed, we did it again and gave him Baytril. In the morning, I heard Jughead crying at the bedroom door and when I opened it he stepped out. He could barely walk, but the fever was broken. He was so weak that he staggered for a few days after his recovery, but he lived and he's one of the most affectionate cats I've known in forty years, second to Italo.

"A cat witch," said Gail. "Bruja de los gatos."

So I got a miracle for my birthday instead of a death. Aggressively affectionate, when I came home Jughead ran to me and hugged my calf.

Veronica is a slower miracle. When I got her she refused to be touched. If anyone took a step toward her she ran away. Even at the food bowls, if I touched her she jumped down. But slowly she began to let me pet her while she ate. The problem with that became that she seemed to equate eating with affection. She tended to hide under the futon in the Tiki Room and only come out when she saw me in the kitchen, then she rolled on the floor in front of me, though when I stopped to pet her she ran to the food bowls in the cat room. At first I went along with it, but soon she was getting fat. The only time she let me touch her was while she ate.

I reinforced it at first and followed her into the cat room for a week, but then I started not to follow her to the food bowls unless she let me touch her in the kitchen, which she eventually did. She'd roll on the floor in front of me. I petted her and then she jumped up and ran to the food where I petted her some more.

Then I began to stop following her half the time, then two-thirds of the time. Slowly she began to let me pet her in other places in the house. At the top of the stairs, on the living room floor, then on the hassock in front of my chair, (though at first she lay on the hassock and ran away when I approached), then on one of the dining chairs, in fact, Gail's. But now she let's me pet her anywhere and has begun to let Gail and Marlena pet her, too. In the morning she follows me to my office where she waits outside and rolls over when I come out. Just last night she jumped up next to me on the bed and now she follows me sometimes and mews, then we have great affection orgies. It took eight months. After ten months, one evening she came to my chair and jumped in my lap. She's still quite timid. She's still chubby. And if Jughead sees me petting her he runs over and throws himself in between us. Some people might call that jealousy.

Veronica is yet quite sensitive. Recently I grabbed her and had Gail clip some of the fur clumps that had accumulated under Veronica's chin. After that she avoided me for two months. Slowly she began to come upstairs again, and in a week was following me around. Today she came into my office and discovered my water fountain on the end table. She sniffed the water in the bowl. When I got up and turned the fountain on, she fled, but five minutes later returned, came through the door and immediately leapt to the fountain. She had to remember it was there to return to look at it again, exhibiting memory and curiosity. Temple Grandin talks about curiosity and fear as companion emotions in ungulates and I've noticed it in my horses. Both Jackie O and Nikki were very bright, so very curious, and very flighty, as well.

As the kittens grew older and larger the Counter Culture shifted. Jughead, whose constant play once seemed frivolous, became more possessive and political. The big cats, Cheese and Romeo stepped up to the challenge. This was most evident in the morning ritual.

We sleep with our bedroom door open but remarkably no one chose to spend the night with us very often. Nadine slept on the floor beside Gail or waited in the living room for Marlena to come home. As well, she patrolled the decks and the roof. Sometimes, then, Romeo slept with Gail, and if not he came in at dawn. If you have a hand outside the covers he'll bite it, then he settle down on top of me and watch Gail. Of course now they both sleep on the bed. When Gail began to stir, Nadine flew into her ritual, bounding back and forth from the bed, then when Gail got up, jumping off and on the bed until she let me catch her and give her a prolonged hug. In the meantime, Jughead entered and often I was hugging Nadine with one arm and playing with Jughead with the other. Then Veronica entered and raced back and forth around my feet.

You might think it's just about food but it's not. If Gail goes downstairs to the kitchen and I go to the bathroom, Nadine, Jughead and Veronica will wait upstairs with me, Jughead at me feet, Nadine outside the bathroom door. Romeo and Veronica wait in the living room. When I emerge there's a lot of chaos. Nadine races back and forth, lunging at cats who jump on chairs and tables or run under bureaus, then they all rumble downstairs where Cheese might be waiting on the counter near the food bowls. I check Eve, Marlena's python, go down the stairs and turn on my frog, Cisco's, light.

Veronica and Jughead follow me into the cat room. Sometimes Romeo joins them and sometimes he jumps on the counter next to the Cheese. I put food in the cat room bowls. Veronica purrs wildly. Sometimes the Cheese comes into the cat room, but generally waits in the kitchen. This self-imposed segregation often breaks down on Saturday when I open a can of tuna. After I've filled the counter bowls, Yoko Dodo, who has waited for the chaos to settle, comes down the stairs. Though she can make the jump, I lift her up to the cat shelf and fill a bowl for her. Meanwhile, Gail has fed Nadine, though on Saturday, tuna day, she follows me around because she wants to lick out the tuna can.

After they ate, usually Romeo, Cheese, and Veronica went outside. Jughead loved milk and waited on the window sill next to the dining table. If we weren't eating cereal and there was no milk, then he left, too, eventually, but in any case he's quite a nuisance and I took to bringing a small bowl of milk for him and placing it on the other end of the table so he'd leave us alone. Yoko started waiting upstairs too, on the floor to the right of my chair, and I let her lick milk or butter from my finger.

I get up and read the sports page in my chair and Yoko follows to sit on my lap. Jughead waits on the window sill behind the couch. When I get up to get more coffee, Yoko moves to the hassock and when I sit back down Jughead gets on my lap. Meanwhile, Nadine has gone through her rituals, her pig's ear, her snack toy, some stuffed toy, and her hug, though sometimes Yoko swats at her if she gets too close. Now Nadine goes to her toy box and brings Gail a toy, woofing at her, shaking the toy, placing it in Gail's lap, pushing the newspaper with her nose until Gail succumbs and chases her around the room.

Nadine stays with Gail, lying next to her on the couch or following her up to her office, but if she leaves then Nadine comes down to my office and sits outside my door or inside it. Right now, Romeo is in my office, sitting behind my screen on the writing desk, having a bath. After the bath he might sleep in a desk drawer and, in fact, he just finished up and crawled into the big drawer on my right. He might do this once a month. Gail is heading for work and comes to my door to say good-bye. Romeo leaps out and goes to the door. Jughead follows her to the gate and then comes inside the office. Nadine is sitting outside my door, Romeo is having a bath on top my printer, and Jughead is rolling around knocking things off my desk. Seldom do I have two cats in the office at the same time and nothing good can come of it. Jughead has just jumped in the drawer and Romeo is glaring at him. He got out. Now Romeo is watching him roll around and knock things off my desk. Recently, Veronica has begun coming into the office if no one else is around.

Jughead doesn't really like the office, though there are lots of places to hide and lots of things to knock over in here. The problem is that I give all my attention to the computer. He jumps on my lap, he jumps on the keyboard, he cries to get out, but when I open the door he won't leave. He doesn't want to leave, he wants *us* to leave. His last visit he did a very Maine Coon thing. After twice trying to get me to leave with him, he jumped on my desk and knocked everything off. I had to take everything and put it on the floor to continue working. Then he left and he hasn't been back, till now.

The rainy season has come and it's brought some changes. Like Nadine, the cats know the difference between raining and not raining. Even during big storms the cats urinate and defecate outdoors, but for old Yoko who will now settle for the litter rather than deal with the rain. Romeo will wait for a break in the rain and go out and get it done and come back in. Both Cheese and Veronica really prefer to be outside and will often get caught in a downpour. Then I won't see them again until the rain stops. They must have places they where they hang out because they usually come in pretty dry, though if the Cheese is wet he'll go to Gail and cry at her until she wraps him in a towel and holds him. Ordinary folk like us think he's requesting that. Music Batty, who lived outdoors, found a way to sneak into my neighbor's house. He said that during rainstorms he woke up at night with her sleeping on his chest. The Maine Coons, Cheese, Veronica, and Jughead, don't really mind the rain and are willing to go out in a drizzle or light rainfall.

I think the soaked earth in the neighboring lot has forced the ground moles to the surface because I've found a different dead mole on the floor of the cat room for last five days straight. They're about four to five inches long, pretty big. I assume it's the work of the Cheese because that's his hunting territory. If I don't get it cleaned up right away somebody, I think it's Veronica, will try to eat it. The placement is interesting. Cheese is the son of Mucha Plata who weaned her kittens by placing mice in their food bowl. Currently Cheese doesn't eat in the cat room very often, but on the kitchen counter (actually, he will eat in the cat room, though not with the others, only if he can get me to himself and that, of course, is not hard and fast). Though Veronica is slowly being weaned from equating affection with eating, she yet spends a lot of time in that part of the house. The Cheese tends to place his prey in the area where the person, for lack of a better word, it's intended for spends time. A bird in the bathroom is for Marlena or Gail. Is it nurturing? Domination? Community behavior? Well, those are fine lines to draw, human lines.

Regardless, this theorizing about the Cheese was refuted last night when Veronica paraded through the living room with a huge rat. The rodent was so big that she had to raise her head to carry it, prancing like a leopard with a gazelle. More so, she could have brought the animal directly to the cat room, where it ended up, much more directly by coming in the downstairs kitchen door, but detoured up to the pet door in the bedroom and came into the living room, stopped in front of the television to burrdle at Gail and me, and then headed down the stairs.

"A display," Gail said.

Well, for us folk psychologists it's hard to argue otherwise. In the morning I found her in the cat room munching on that rat. I'd underestimated her and misread the Cheese who is a birder, not a mouser. So it's chubby Veronica catching the moles. That kitty likes to eat. And she's not fat and lazy. She's just fat. Though I've watched her with mice and she seems the most lackadaisical of hunters. Most cats chase rodents as frantically as they chase a ball of aluminum. Veronica barely chases her quarry, but sits and casually directs the running animal with her paws. The mouse is running around and Veronica seems barely to move. It looks physically impossible, though it's the way she plays with Jughead, too. Jughead jumps on and off of her, bounces off walls, off and on chairs, sliding, rolling, somersaulting, while Veronica casually swats and rolls, barely invested.

But the cold, rainy season has brought everybody inside a bit more and power issues have arisen. Cheese reentered the Counter Culture with bluster. He pushed Romeo off the counter. He pushed Jughead and Veronica off the cat room feeding bench. He whacked them when he encountered them in the living room. He chased them off chairs. He went into Marlena's room where Yoko slept and chased her out of there. He even sat in my lap. He was being a big bully.

And then one morning after breakfast he came upstairs, surveyed the living room and slipped into Marlena's bedroom through the crack in the door. Only this time Romeo followed. He pulled the bedroom door more open and walked in. Romeo *never* goes in there. In a matter of moments the place was filled with yowling and the zzzt of claws. It went on for fifteen seconds. That's a long time for a cat fight, in fact the longest I've ever heard between two familiars inside my house. Things quieted. Romeo walked out tail up. Walked through the room and down the stairs. I went to the bedroom to check on the Cheese who sat straight up and wide-eyed behind a stuffed toy.

After that the bullying ended. The Cheese, who didn't abandon his winter reentry into the household, slept with Marlena on the futon in the Tiki room at night and in the morning waited on the kitchen counter while I fed the others in the cat room. Sometimes Romeo joins him and they don't fight.

Like any seasoned combatants, cats usually don't pick fights unless the odds are clearly in their favor or there's a lot at stake. If you've ever owned a small dog, then you know that dogs seem to lack that survival mechanism. Romeo is a big cat, almost fifteen pounds with huge forearms, but the Cheese weighs twenty pounds, lives outdoors for days at a time and has been through some great scuffles, sometimes returning with large wounds on his forehead. When cats get wounds on their heads it tends to indicate that however things turned out, they didn't back down. Losers have wounds on their thighs and butts. And though Nadine and Romeo face off over Gail's lap all the time, they seldom fight. If Nadine gets really aggressive, Romeo usually just turns away, although he immediately comes back. On occasion he'll hiss and strike, she dodges, then it's over.

I guess I hadn't been watching closely enough. Romeo changed where he slept. He began sleeping on the end of the dining table. That places him directly across from where Gail works or relaxes on the couch, or he sleeps on my dining chair. These are two powerful positions. And at dawn he comes in and sleeps on me, facing Gail (Nadine stopped sleeping with us at night; she patrolled the decks and the roof; she slept with Gail during a daytime nap, then, as Romeo's presence became more persistent, she returned to the bed next to Gail). Cheese slept on Gail's dining chair and when he didn't, Veronica did. As well, Romeo began to spend more time with me, especially when Gail wasn't around. In other words, there were subtle changes in his behavior as he reasserted himself at the top of the cat hierarchy. And though Jughead might have appeared to be the most irrelevant cat I've ever known, he seemed to get bigger everyday and one morning, while Romeo chose to have breakfast in the cat room, Jughead jumped up on the kitchen counter and ate breakfast next to the Cheese.

There is little that's empirical about this chapter; it's just story telling. But it's a story about a community of sentient beings, of anticipation, plans, desires, and yes, emotions. Sadly, as all life is sad, one morning Jughead left the house and didn't come home. He seldom roved, I assumed he went next door to the realtors' office and threw himself on some customer's feet. "Look at this giant, fat, neutered cat. Must be homeless." It happened a lot. Sometimes we put up a sign and got the cat back. When Veronica disappeared I put notes in my neighbors mailboxes. She appeared the next day. Not so a year later with Cheese, who notoriously left for days at a time. One day he didn't come home.

THE
EMOTIONS

LOVE

Some time has passed. I've turned down several opportunities to replace both Jughead and Cheese. Yoko is old and needs my attention. I've developed a close relationship with Veronica. Romeo now follows Gail everywhere, as does Nadine.

I finally got new horse after eighteen months, a six year old buckskin, Morgan mare I've named Nikkita. She's a very sweet animal; she's learns quickly and she's affectionate, unlike Jackie O, but yet very stubborn and high strung. Marlena moved to Australia to pursue a career as a performance artist. I was stunned how viscerally this broke my heart. Then I was diagnosed with prostate cancer. I've been through surgery and radiation, but that didn't get it all. I have miniscule levels of antigens and I'm on very close watch for recurrence. I hesitate to accumulate more pets that I might not outlive.

Some relatively recent popular books on animals flirt with the idea of animal consciousness (I shall use *animal* here to designate non-human sentient beings). Journalist Tim Friend's *Animal Talk* is basically a survey of recent discoveries and observations of animal communication in the wild, most of it explicit, intra-species communication, but a little implicit inter-species, like a scavenger bird who learns to follow a predator. The book is devoid of theory or speculation on how animals do what they do and it offers simple, reductionist Darwinism as the ubiquitous explanation of animal behavior. It's kind of one of those "Oh those amazing animals" books. A very similar work was published by National Geographic in 2017. Neither of these texts dealt with domestic animals very much.

Temple Grandin, the autistic, innovative vetinarian and author (with Catherine Johnson) of *Animals in Translation*, though Darwinist and reductionist as well—she is a scientist—uses her own autism as a means of explaining emotions and learning in a number of domestic animals, most extensively slaughter or prey animals like cows and pigs, but sometimes dogs, horses, and others. Borrowing from her own autism she speculates that animals think in pictures, more accurately, images, not language, and in combination with understanding their hard-wired instincts we can use this understanding to read their primal emotions:

1. rage
2. prey chase drive
3. fear
4. curiosuity/anticipation

She adds four more primary social emotions:

1. sexual attraction and lust
2. separation distress (mother and baby)
3. social attachment
4. play and roughhousing.

It only takes a second to see how basic these are and how reliant on *prima facie* behavioral observation. For example, is "play and roughhousing" an emotion or a behavior? If I were observing humans, might I not ask what the participants were *feeling* during play? (though if I were a behaviorist, I might not). Of course, *I* would say that they *feel play*, rather than saying they feel playful. Words like "sexual attraction" or "play", in terms of emotion, vaguely describe a little about what anyone might feel. For example, curiosity and anticipation might result, or maybe better, arise with, similar behavior, but should I classify them as the same, vague emotion? Grandin does so because she observes both fear and curiosity in the behavior of ungulates and sees the combination as evolutionarily advantageous. Yet, even in behavioral terms, anticipation is different from both fear and curiosity, and arises differently in different kinds of animals, particularly prey and predators.

Grandin's work, particularly in its resulting humanitarian changes in slaughter houses is invaluable, but without theories of consciousness, emotions, or language, her understanding of animals, as well as her own "thinking in pictures," which she uses to explain almost everything, is restrictive.

Animals do often and even primarily think in icon images, but how? (I prefer *image* to *picture* because those images could be tactile, auditory, or olfactory, as well as visual, as Grandin would admit). What is the difference between human and animal thinking, given that human thinking often occurs in language? Aside from the mystery of instinctual behavior, like the migration abilities of birds, why and how do they do some things so much better than we do and why are they incapable of doing other, simple things, particularly abstract ones, like simple addition? What is the role of emotions and consciousness? Why are we failing to do what would seem so simple, understand the animals who have been living with us, some of them inside our homes, for thousands of years?

Let's return to Jackie O. I wondered what she remembered about my car and how quickly she learned it. Did she quickly learn my car or did she look for me inside the cars that drove by? The simple explanation at the ranch was, "She loves you." The other pastured horses didn't have someone who "loved them" or, more significantly behaviorally, didn't have someone who came almost every day to feed them, groom them, ride them (not that she enjoyed being ridden, in fact, though she enjoyed a bath, she didn't really even enjoy being groomed and we finally reached a compromise, after years of annoying each other about it, by my letting her graze or eat carrots while I brushed her). Whether or not Jackie O loved me is difficult to unpack.

Once, a boulder hit my Jeep and I had to rent a car for a few days until I bought a new one. I wasn't paying very close attention, but it seemed that Jackie O recognized the car almost immediately, at least by the second time. I arrived. She looked up and moved her head up and down as if saying *yes* (though I never assumed that was what she was saying, head nodding is just something horses do); she turned and urinated, then walked to the gate, nickering at me after I parked. If I dallied in my carrot gathering, she pawed the ground or kicked the fence. Not thinking very self-consciously about it, I began to slow down when I approached her pasture, trying to catch her eye when she looked up, because I wondered whether she quickly learned what vehicle I came in or, rather, looked for me inside it.

The intensity of my relationship with my horse aside, I reasoned like this: My horse likes me and she likes carrots and apples (is *like* too anthropomorphic a term?). She seldom hung out with other horses, i.e. my arrival was important, more than, say, for a herd-bound horse, i.e. one who likes to hang around with other horses and panics when separated from them. Horses have good memories and are very habitual (in fact, we all are); if a horse does something once in one place, she is very apt to do it again and again, notoriously, as horse people say, they learn bad habits immediately and it takes forever to break them. Simply, bad habits are more immediately gratifying than good habits and horses are stubborn; some would say stupid. But it's not that simple. Horses have a narrow focus within a small spectrum of desires and behaviors. They repeat behaviors determinedly within contexts: the desire to eat (grass on the ground, carrots in your pocket), to flee, or spontaneously run and buck (called vacuum behavior in cats), to do nothing, to have sex, etc.

So a car appears, I get out of it and I always bring carrots. Carrots taste great. Jackie O remembers the car. Again, simple positive reinforcement, yes? No. Jackie O is making a number of abstract associations and choices in that process. And part of the problem here is that we don't understand how we think, so it's really hard to understand how they do. As well, humans condescend to everything, even each other; you can't condescend and understand at the same time; when you see "stupid behavior" you see the stupid and not the behavior.

So I tried an experiment. I had my daughter drive me to the ranch in her new car, a car Jackie O had never seen and, incidentally or not, I sat on the passenger side, not the driver's side. We slowed down. I looked out the passenger-side window and then we drove by. Standing by herself on the opposite side of the pasture, about 50 yards away, Jackie O looked up (the other horses did not). She nodded her head up and down and, as we turned to park, she walked to the gate. An interesting addendum to this is that she did not urinate. Whenever I arrived at the ranch with someone else, I didn't ride her. She urinated, I speculate, in anticipation of having two hundred pounds on her back in a few minutes. No matter how habitual, she displayed one habit for one context, or anticipated context, and one habit for another.

This was not, of course, a controlled laboratory experiment, nor did I repeat it hundreds of times with grounds and variations, though I believe that controlled experiments often create more problems and complicate more issues than do observations in context. But after my experiment I thought that the following assumptions were creditable:

1. Jackie O watched cars
2. She looked for me in them
3. She recognized me
4. She chose to come to the gate (leaving aside the question of whether that *choice* was *determined*, or how); this is based on the fact that on a number of occasions, if it were extremely hot, or cold and wet, or another horse happened to be swatting flies from her face, or she was lying down, then she might not come to the gate, at least not right away.

5. On the occasions when I brought guests, I didn't ride her. I assume she didn't urinate because she assumed, correctly, that I didn't plan to ride her in that context.

6. Jackie O thinks about me when I'm not there. This isn't an observation. It's a battle line for animal consciousness.

As I've said, a lot of what I've been talking about here has already been suggested by Temple Grandin (*Animals in Translation*). Born with autism she originally only thought in pictures and proposes that this is how animals think, too, adding that those pictures are likely occur in touch, sound, smell, and taste as well. Humans are often unaware that we think in pictures because of the post-lingual evolution of *verbal shadowing* whereupon we reason in language and ignore the pictures that accompany it.

Grandin's speculations are based on her observations of animals, given this assumption, and scientific evidence which seems to confirm it. The difference between her analysis and mine is that I've extended the idea of "thinking in pictures" to the conversation of gestures and semiotics in order to explain how thinking in sense-images allows animals to interact, anticipate, hunt, hide, remember, predict, figure things out, and decide. Instead of scientific studies, I have, in several particular cases, used phenomenology to examine particular paradigmatic behaviors of domestic animals.

I have my disagreements, but Grandin's work, like mine, is heuristic, that is, interested in provoking a conversation about animal cognition by means of observations and conservative speculations based on them.

As I've pointed out, Grandin identifies four basic animal emotions: rage, prey chase drive, fear, and curiosity/interest/anticipation. She lists four primary social emotions, as well: sexual attraction and lust, separation distress (mother and baby), social attachment, play and roughhousing. Lacking here are behaviors related to claiming territory, joy, depression/disappointment, non-sexual emotional attachment, anticipation/hope, jealousy, possessiveness, loyalty, sympathy, some of which can be seen as derived from or versions of Grandin's basic classifications, some not.

Are these emotions that we folk psychologists observe among our animal affiliations anthropomorphic impositions? Are we making them up? Can they be reduced to Grandin's core behaviors? Do they exist? Have they evolved from anything? Are they distinctive, real emotions comparable to ours?

The two emotions I hear most commonly attributed to pets are *love* and *jealousy.* These emotions are often seen as accompanying each other in the human sphere of behavior, but neither is a necessary nor sufficient condition to the other. Interpersonally, we can love without jealousy and become very jealous about someone long before love ever sets in. But then, what kind of love, or loves, are we talking about? Love of God, of humanity, of my child, my lover, my parents, my friends, my dog, my horse, my cat, nature, my car, my land, my house?

In general, emotions seem simple when, at first, we just name them, but become more complicated when we turn the lens of inspection on them. In the *Symposium*, Plato's famous dialogue on love, Socrates winnows the reader away from where love seems apparent, the lust of infatuation (in the Athenian case, of a man for a beautiful boy), toward a more ethereal desire for beauty itself, something, for Plato, that transcends the physical, even human, object. Generally the *Symposium* is read as one of Plato's unresolved Socratic dialogues, but if you've read all of Plato then you know where the *Symposium* is leading: to the love of Justice, Plato's highest virtue, realized in the State, i.e. Plato's *Republic*, the state transcending the individual, and even this only an embodiment of true Justice realized on the level of the Forms, because for Plato, reality, ala Parmenides, is permanent and unchanging; we won't find "true love" down here in the shadow world of impermanence and change, even in the *Republic*.

This might seem quite ephemeral, but our impulse for permanence goes as deep as Brahma, God, Allah, and our own immortal souls, if not over the Rainbow Bridge, as well, where all of our pets are waiting for us like our friends and relatives are waiting for us after death, on the other side of the tunnel of bright light. Yet even down here, among us sentient beings, in our mortal lives, whatever the *feeling* of love, in the end we measure love by years of performance, and as time passes that performance is gauged as much by loyalty and generosity as by passion. How does my dog love me? Let me count the ways.

What I've left out here is the concept of romantic love, that is, mutual love. When my daughter, at fifteen, turned to me and said of her first boyfriend, "But Father, I love James. We love each other," I said, "Of course you do," understanding that they wished to be with each other all of the time, were sad when they were apart, that they thought about each other a lot and, being modern humans, called each other on the phone constantly, chattering, and gave each other presents, and when together, touched each other constantly, and when alone, made love. Phones aside, I imagine mating birds exhibit similar behavior and go beyond it, often mutually building nests and caring for young, if not mating for life, all of which I thought Marlena and James quite incapable of doing and it turned out I was right. In fact, soon they broke up; Marlena dumped James. In her own words, she "outgrew him." He threatened suicide. She wept inconsolably for two days, taking his calls, apologizing, but holding fast, eventually not picking up the phone. He didn't kill himself. She fell in love with the next young man and broke up with him somberly with considerably less histrionics. Am I making light of it all? Is *Romeo and Juliet,* a prototype romance common to most cultures, a tragic infatuation story? Do we give more weight to *Anthony and Cleopatra* because they are adults? In fact, we don't, because Romeo and Juliet love innocently and sacrifice their futures, giving up their lives for love or, more, refusing to live without it, while Anthony and Cleopatra die with love at their backs, to immortalize its loss and the loss of empire. Maybe it's as simple as our attraction to baby mammals: kittens, puppies, foals, bear cubs, pandas! Yet though I find baby animals cute, I don't love them ("Oh, I love puppies!" the young woman says, but in fact, she doesn't *love* them, not really) and, in fact, I don't like babies or even children, though I am deeply attached to my own daughter. None of this, philosophically or psychologically, is new ground.

Prejudice, I have found, generally exhibits a combination of the over-evaluation of oneself or one's status and under-evaluation of the object/person I am biased against. As a young man in my first philosophy graduate school, I once attended a lecture by a famous utilitarian philosopher who advocated, among other things, the eradication of all pets (all domestic animals who did not contribute directly to the production of food for human consumption) because they were competing species eating up valuable food and utilities.

This position immediately becomes more complex than it might seem, the emotional sustenance of pet owners aside, if, in fact, we should put it aside. For example, we might consider a species like cows who, despite their production of dairy products and meat, create tremendous environmental impact on the erosion of our water and air, or oxen and horses used for plowing in the third world; the utilitarian equation, greatest good for the greatest number would be modified by context, without even considering religious issues. Of course, the famous utilitarian was an atheist but, as we've found in our most recent world conflicts, it's difficult to throw religion out of the human behavior basket, however scientifically useless it might appear, or whatever the drawbacks of righteous violence, again, like our pets, there are emotional payoffs in religious belief like ontological security, guidance in moral decision making, etc. Spenser thought to have defenestrated religion in the 19th century. Not.

Anyway, after the lecture I raised my hand and said to the utilitarian, "But humans love animals," i.e. the emotional sustenance argument. "That could be seen as something that's the greatest good for the greatest number."

He saw that as less important than the physical survival of the human species in terms of food and shelter. My argument was that you couldn't separate that from the emotional issues, domestic animals were part of the gestalt of urban and agricultural existence since its inception, in terms of our emotional wellbeing and their utility. Well, he said, for the survival of our species, it had to go. We don't need dogs or birds to hunt or cats to kill mice anymore. Science would control rodents (What about eating domestic guinea pigs in Peru?). Urban planning. The new *Republic* would not have them.

More directly to the point, as I left the lecture I ran into my mentor, a libertarian, who said to me, "I see that you disagreed with him."

"He's a species-ist," I said.

"I think that sums it up," said my mentor.

Of course, this is yet another argument. A number of animal rights activists that I've met do not unequivocally regard human life as more valuable than non-human life. Why do we? Because even if we dispose of our immortal souls, humans tend to regard themselves as superior to the other animals because of our intellects, our cultures, our emotions, our morality. We have them, they don't. Their individual lives are thus not as intrinsically valuable, though for a utilitarian it might be reducible to a more Darwinian line, in the survival of the species battle, it's us versus them, which disregards the possibility that without *them* there might be no *us*, i.e. this is an interdependent eco-system. Further, let's consider that death sustains life as much as life does.

Circling back, for my part, I find the act of devaluing something generally requires two impulses, (1) the devaluing individual's overestimation of his/her value and (2) the underestimation of the thing devalued. You don't need to look far, even in the human sphere; racism and sexism are fine examples. Though whatever the connection there is between superiority and oppression is quite beyond me. I'd think the opposite would be the case, that we should care for inferior beings, but we only need look to Victorian values to see how protecting women and other races quickly turned into oppressing them for their own good; religions are pretty good at it, too: the caste system in India, slavery's justification in the Bible, the slaughter of unbelievers in the Koran, polygamous marriage among the Mormons.

In this vortex of morality and logic, we can only end up, as David DeGrazia does in *Animal Rights*, as vegetarians. We shouldn't kill and eat creatures who possess thoughts and feelings, however much they kill and eat each other. As any Buddhist or Hindu would point out, whatever they do to each other is irrelevant because we're morally and intellectually superior to them; we should know better. Once again that means our decision to refrain from the slaughter of animals for food is based on our superiority, not their equality. As well, all this requires other fine lines being drawn, the division between animal and vegetative sentience for one (that's why devout Jains don't eat anything at all!). How about contextual parameters? Oh Arjuna, facing your brothers and cousins on the battlefield, dharma says slay them, but do you spare their elephants and horses? In my classroom now I teach veterans returning from Afghanistan and Iraq. Most of them made some very difficult choices about whether the person in front of them was an enemy combatant or an innocent civilian or something in between. For my part, I try to contain my meat eating to fresh caught fish and free range fowl, but when my best friends, who are Argentinian, serve an asado, I say a prayer and partake. They spent four years on death row under the dictatorship and saw 30,000 of their comrades slain. I've lived around enough farmers who raised their animals with affection, named them, and ate them.

Let's leave these moral conundrums and return to love. Most of the time when we use the word *love* we do so pretty loosely. I don't love my truck any more than Nadine loves her toys, do I? In fact, in some ways I might, because my ability to recognize and articulate my relationship with my truck, through language, creates an accumulation of feeling, as when I think about how it makes me seem more masculine or I remember the time it got me through a police road block of our flooded road because I had high road clearance and 4WD.

Actually, I don't love my truck. So I'm looking around my office now and trying to find some inanimate object that I *feel love* for. What I see is a number of things for which I have some emotional attachment. As I make my perusal I find that it isn't the thing itself that seems to draw me toward it but, generally, if it is not some picture of Gail or Marlena or my horse, then it is something they gave me that provokes memories of them, and these memories produce a feeling of longing to be near them. Likewise, there is a photo of my mother on the wall, a photo of her wedding day, and to my left the only object I have as a vestige of her life, a spelling book entitled *20,000 Words* that she used on her desk when she went back to work after raising six kids. I used it much more before there were computers with spell check, but I still keep it beside me; a gift from her from when I aspired to write, long before I published anything, and she died before I did. I am yet a bad speller. And now I'm flooded with memories of my mother.

Back to the days of Jackie O when people at my ranch would say to me, "That horse loves you." And I'd respond, "I love her." As I've said, Jackie O watched cars in anticipation of my arrival, came to me when I arrived, preferred me to other horses and other people. She liked to spend time with me, preferably just standing around eating grass and you could argue that it went no deeper than that, with my arrival came apples, carrots, and grazing, though what came as well was my cleaning her, tacking her, and getting on her back to train, perform, or worst of all, go for a ride in the woods, none of which she liked to do, in fact she didn't enjoy being touched and early on would even try to bite me when I groomed her. Under saddle she always tried to run past the entrance to the ring and once inside she tried to leave. On the trail she always tried to turn for home, if not run home. You could argue that she came to me thoughtlessly when I arrived, at best thinking only of apples and carrots and that every time I groomed her and saddled her up it was a total surprise to her, but for the fact that when I rode her the apples and most of the carrots came *after* the ride. If she didn't come to me and call to me because she *liked* me, than at least she seemed to be able to delay her gratification for carrots and apples beyond being groomed and ridden.

My trainer, Paddi Korb, once argued that much of Jackie O's negative behavior was something she enjoyed, i.e. they were acts of engaging me, just as her acts of superb performance, like dancing on command or changing leads on the fly, were insincere; her point being that some horses enjoyed performance and some unique others, like Jackie O, could perform brilliantly while holding back an essential part of themselves. She called that performance behavior *counterfeit* behavior (surmising that Jackie O was sincere when she misbehaved). Of course, this kind of horse trainer talk falls under the rubric of folk psychology, but it's an attempt to explain a constellation of related and apparently complex behaviors. It could explain why Jackie O came to me when I arrived, getting rid of the postulate that she came to me despite anticipating a number of things she didn't like to do. That, in fact, despite demonstrating a lot of irritable behavior, it was all gratifying to her in some way. Or was she willing to get through the irritating stuff in order to be gratified at the end of the ride? Another possibility would seem to be that she just saw me and came without ever anticipating anything. Or another, that she liked me, liked the attention, and the more she misbehaved the longer I stayed to work things out.

I'm looking for that ineffable thing, that feeling I have when I see Gail, separate from my desire for her, though we have made love thousands of times, separate from the habit of attachment; that feeling, that cognitive-emotional event that accompanies my going to her, *that feeling*, that longing for my daughter 9,000 miles away in Australia, something more than the screaming of the mares in the high pasture on the day the ranchers forcibly wean their foals (Grandin's "separation distress"), though that is feeling, too, but more, that in Jackie O's coming to me lies a core feeling similar to my love for her, a feeling on my part that produced commitments that she was incapable of making: my cleaning her hooves and her body despite her dislike of it, paying her board and vet bills, that moral commitment that humans make because of love, perpetuated by, yes, language-bearing consciousness from which morality and duty arise. On that mark, Jesus was right (and St. Paul), love is the first emotion, but that feeling, taken to hyperbole by the language of romance, in cheap movies or great literature, that's what the people at my ranch recognized when they said, "That horse loves you." It doesn't require verbal articulation to be recognizable.

If real love, true love, in friendship or romantic companionship, is demonstrated in commitment over time, love that does more than survive, but supports and persists through births, deaths, child rearing, illness, disaster, economic turmoil, conflicts over money and family, life goals, business interests, and much more, than it is indeed human love, love made capable by our ability to consider and weigh our commitments and it is, in fact, as intrinsically human as language, because it's language that allows human beings to perpetuate emotion toward the other in the other's absence, to transform the abstract into the fact, and this is, of course, in theory, what the marriage vow is, though we know that the marriage vow is not love, but an hyperbole of purported commitment that, as often as not, fails.

Yet in the beginning and the end, however much love is constituted by the concept of *love*, it doesn't begin or end with language, but with behavior. The words, "I love you," as we all know, can mean very little. I might use them loosely to seduce someone or even to perpetuate a sexual relationship to which I'm not committed but which I want to continue for the time being, both, in some ways, lies, maybe to the other but maybe to myself, as well, or maybe, in that moment, I feel I could make that commitment, as well as any broad spectrum within those dispositions, but the words themselves really mean very little upon inspection, though very few people bother to inspect them. As a species we are really much less reflective than we propose ourselves to be; many humans don't reflect at all about anything; but that even the most unreflective of us regards himself as a thinking-feeling being, and that animals are not, is part of the overvaluing that creates the prejudice against animal emotion. (Unfortunately, it can permit us to mistreat them, as well). This is not to deny that there are some very unreflective human beings who overvalue animals in some very anthropomorphic ways.

For my part, I have learned that the act of being in love is very different from the act of falling in love and I never ended up being in love with anyone I immediately fell in love with. Early on I learned to be skeptical about my infatuations, however much they were accompanied by fantasies about the future and rationalizations about my psychological and intellectual compatibility with the other person. If it's happening right away, be careful, it's probably grounded in Grandin's "sex drive/lust." Of course, for humans it becomes immediately more complicated—read Freud or Flaubert—but now we are in the empire of language: literature, dreams, social psychology, symbols, the worlds of the human animal. Let's circle back again.

Let's play the game you see so often in romantic comedies. Go to a restaurant and watch the couples around you. But instead of making up stories about them (something that usually demonstrates the dire imagination of the screenwriter), just watch them. You don't have to enter their lives or make anything up or hear a word; just watch. You recognize a first date, one that is succeeding, one that is failing, one that is working for one person and not the other; you can see a relationship that is working and one that is not; just observe the postures, the movements of the head, the hands, watch the lips, observe who is talking, who is listening, whose eyes are wandering, who's spending all of their time watching their phone. I seldom teach a fiction class where a student doesn't bring up their "restaurant moment" when they look across the room and spot an older couple (though older for them could mean anyone over forty) sitting together, eating silently. "How sad," says my student. "They have nothing to talk about." In fact, they're probably very much in love and don't need to talk about it. Watch the dance of their eyes and hands. Shared silence is an art of experienced love.

But this isn't an exercise in *body language*. The concept of body language is as problematic as the act of translating animal behavior, translating a non-language into language. Of course, being language users, it's how we must do it, but we must be very careful. It's difficult enough translating one syntactical system, say English and Spanish, into one another.

When it comes to cognitive-emotional behavior, the first moment of comprehension is immediate and intuitive. But it's also obvious. An angry dog is angry. The joy your dog emotes when you come home is joy. To deny animal emotion is to say there is no difference between an angry dog and a joyful one. The bond my horse feels with me and not someone else, however deeply it is found in the biology of the herd, is a bond, a feeling. Our affection, my petting and her nuzzling, is affection for each other. Human love has complicated and enriched it with a few million years of symbolic culture.

My relationship with my new horse is a very different relationship than the one I had with Jackie O. Nikki is as affectionate by nature as Jackie O. was furious. Like any horse, she is obstinate and flighty both, like most mares her moods or emotions, so to speak, are complicated by her sexual cycle. If you've dealt with any animals then you know that the responsibilities of bearing, birthing, caring for, and separating from their young produces a different cognitive-emotional organism, a female organism, with a broader, more complex set of concerns than the male whose behavior follows pretty univocally from sex, territory, and food.

I've known Nikki now for only a little more than a year; eventually I knew her for eight, another story. I knew Jackie O for fifteen years. Whatever Jackie's nature, by the time I knew her she was deeply suspicious of all things human, though she bit, kicked, and struck out at horses as well as people. Even in heat she was selective as to what stallion she'd approach. Over time—it took over ten years of almost daily contact—that fear and anger transformed into her fierce loyalty to me and, if I was on her back, a tolerance of others. There is nothing fierce about Nikki and I speculate that however close we become over the years, it won't be a bond forged in sweat and fire as with Jackie O. At one point, Jackie O. *felt* toward me that core of the cognitive-emotional element we identify as love, something that Nikki does not feel when she sees me, not yet.

JEALOUSY

This morning after doing the crossword, Gail, on the couch, opened her laptop on the coffee table to go to work. Romeo lay down next to it, facing her. Nadine jumped on the couch. She lunged at Romeo, who barely stirred. Nadine lay down and pressed against Gail's thigh, facing Romeo, her snout in the gap between the coffee table and the couch, their faces six inches apart. Nadine lunged again. Romeo didn't flinch. She looked at me, made a small yelp, almost a whine, then lunged toward Romeo again. He licked his leg. Then they stared at each other.

I realized, in that moment, that at this point neither one would hurt the other. Nadine would have to touch Romeo to rouse a hiss or instigate a paw placed on her forehead, but that's at best what she'd get. Escalation is rare. In the last year Romeo has begun sleeping with us at night. He roams back and forth from my side of the bed to Gail's, and Nadine, who had stopped sleeping next to Gail, has now returned, yet patrolling the yard, but when she re-enters the house she jumps on the bed. I assume her return is in response to Romeo's recent incursion.

Cheese, before disappearing, had a period of about a half-year when he left the house again. It started just after Marlena, his person, so to speak, left for Australia. That's Cheese's common response to any disruption in our routine or, I suppose, his: guests, their pets, a new animal. But the Cheese returned to the house recently for a new round of conflict with Romeo who hounded him relentlessly for days. He began to bully Yoko Dodo, too. It got so bad I resorted to the squirt bottle to stop him. But after one squirt, Romeo recognized the bottle before I barely picked it up, almost, it seemed, anticipating that I would. He ran away from Cheese, Cheese ran away from him, then Romeo followed. But my having entered the fray seemed to re-align the politics. Romeo began to leave the Cheese alone. He calmed down.

In all of this, among the cats, of whom there were only four now, the issue arose as to who eats where, when. The Cheese preferred not to eat with the others unless there was tuna involved. He generally entered the house after feeding. Romeo might eat with the females and might ask to be fed on the counter culture. The Cheese most often went where Romeo was not, but sometimes joined him now at the counter culture. Sometimes Romeo hissed at him, sometimes he ignored him, and sometimes he left. In all of this, however combative or domineering Romeo might be with Nadine, Cheese, or Yoko (our house sitter calls him Ulysses S. Asshole), he has always been kind of sweet on Veronica. If Veronica wants to join him at the counter culture, that's fine. She walks up to him, sniffs him, licks him, rolls on her back in front of him; the same behavior she displays with me, though in my case she'll use it as a prelude to luring me to the cat room to pet her while she eats.

Like the Cheese, Veronica will request my presence at the food bowls whether they're full or not. If I stop petting her while she eats, she'll stop eating and turn around and look at me and squeak, until I start petting her again. Often, I heard the Cheese meowing in the cat room. I went in, and there he sat, his back to five full food bowls. Meow-meow. I petted him. He sniffed a bowl and began eating.

As I've said, as well as species differences in a number of behavioral nexus, there are anthropological reasons for our different relationship with house cats which includes much more recent domestication and the kinds of needs we require from them. Watching Veronica has made me increasingly aware how closely her behavioral displays with me run with litter behavior and sex demonstrations.

When Music Batty was young and courting she once had a prolonged mating with a big gray tom. When they saw each other, he yowled, that kind of frightening baby cry; she raised her cheeks and chattered at him. They sat in the sun together for hours, then rolled on their backs head to head in a kind of dance before she righted herself and they began the mounting ritual; she raised her butt and tail, he groomed her ears, then mounted, bit her neck and eventually entered; copulation culminated with his withdrawal, she screamed, then turned and bit him.

When I leave my office, Veronica is waiting. She arches her back and squeak-mews, though she might chatter. When I pet her, she raises her tail and back end, walks forward, then rolls in front of me. We'll do this several times on our way indoors to the cat room, though if I stop to pet her, she'll raise her butt in the air, then spin to bite my hand, just like a copulating female. If I'm in my reading chair, she'll enter and leave the room several times before circling me, then chattering (the sex call) and rolling on her back in front of me. Often, she'll stop, as if to see if I'm looking, and stare at me between her raised hind legs before rolling some more. This all might earn me a visit on my lap, where she'll bite my hand if I pet her, or it might be a prelude to her jumping up and heading for the food bowls.

Veronica didn't do this for Gail at first, though she performed a version of it for Romeo. Now she does it for Gail, too, if I'm not around. Before he was neutered, Romeo was daring, violent, and extremely sexual. There was no sitting or rolling in his mating ritual. It was grab the female, do it, grab her and do it again. If his behavior toward Gail is not explicitly sexual, his attention toward her is constant and unequivocal. He will challenge for her lap with Nadine, Cheese, or Yoko. Gail simply has to fight him off, then he'll sit close by and watch. Though Veronica would never challenge Romeo for space, she'll follow him anywhere without regard, even to the counter culture. In the living room, she often rolls in front of him and chortles, raising her cheeks. This is her behavior toward the two dominant males, one a human and the other a neutered cat, though Romeo will on occasion raise his cheeks at her and quiver them over his incisors. If one leaves the room, the other is likely to follow. "Jealous, Gail?" I ask. She hates when I say things like that.

To digress briefly, cats knead before lying down and do so before or during eating sometimes, just as they do as nursing kittens. In fact, when Nadine is deep into Gail's lap, she does a version of this, too, licking and pressing, then gently nibbling; her eyes shut half-way, she emits a pleasurable groan, falling into a nursing zone.

It's long been said that our pets, particularly cats and dogs, behave toward us as if we were both their parents and their children, but this is, again, a mistranslation. Certainly, litter behavior and sex behavior are deep behavioral zones. We have them, too, and the better you get at recognizing them, the more control you can gain over your behavior, even if recognizing behavioral zones is just another kind of training, another kind of zone. Some zones are more enjoyable and productive than others; again, the ontology is irrelevant.

Nonetheless, understanding these zones in your domestic animals, horses included, can help you get along with them in more free and open cooperation; it's why I'm not a fan of systematic training, i.e. imposing a kind of *philosophy of discipline* on your animal. In the equine world, this kind of *understanding the horse* engendered the first seeds of *horse listening* (at first misnamed *horse whispering*).

Again, one of the premises of this book is that however deeply the behavior of our domestic animals is rooted in their biology, and then conditioning, much domestic animal behavior toward us, interspecies behavior, is not demonstrated when they interact with each other intra-species. My female cats might catch mice for their litters, for themselves, and for me. Males don't catch rodents for litters, but eat them themselves or leave them for me. Do toms catch rats for females that they're courting? Possibly. I haven't seen it. Though Veronica has eaten rodents that Cheese or Romeo have brought in, I haven't seen them present the catch to her.

Veronica's hunting specialty leaned to moles and voles in the rainy season, though nobody ever ate them. As spring settles in she starts catching rats and mice again. These she usually *exhibits*, in that she enters the house through the pet door in the back bedroom and parades them through the living room where Gail and I are sitting. In another recent change, Nadine has asserted herself and attempted to dominate the cats, particularly Romeo. Veronica's response to this, though you'd hardly think she needed to respond, has been to parade her prey in front of Nadine, too, in what would appear to be an obvious gesture to her perceived order of the domination hierarchy.

When my brother, Peter, lived with us for a year and a half, Marlena was a small child and on several occasions I had to scold H.D. for growling at her in what I perceived was a scuffle for family positioning. Pete slept downstairs on the futon back then. When he left for New York, H.D. began sleeping on the futon. When Pete returned for a visit, H.D. first growled at him, much to his surprise, then she tore up the futon sheets and pillow. H.D. could be viscerally territorial. She destroyed two hot tub lids, much in the same way as Mucha Plata attacked the telephone.

In a quantum leap in sign behavior, Nadine began using her bones, toys, and pig ears to mark territory. The most interesting semiotic transition was the pig ears. When Nadine got her pig ear in the morning after breakfast, she'd run out the kitchen door and circle the house with it several times before eating it while we prepared breakfast. After that, later on, she began saving the pig ear, placing it in front of her and waiting until we went upstairs to eat. She took the pig ear upstairs and ate it there, near the table. After eating the pig ear she requested her snack toy; I don't use the word *beg* here because begging behavior is somewhat different than requesting behavior. Animals beg for things, usually food, that's right in front of them; they request, the snack toy, a walk, to be petted while they eat, things that are not present, and those are iconic abstractions.

In time, Nadine stopped eating the pig ear, laying it between her feet and growling whenever a cat entered the room, this though no cat has ever shown any interest in pigs' ears. Slowly she began to put distance between herself and the pig ear, leaving it in the center of the room while she lay at Gail's feet, though yet she growled at any cat that approached it, jumping up and pouncing precipitously toward it as a cat entered the room. I should qualify the word *approach* here, because the cats didn't approach the pig ear. The cats weren't interested in the pig ear. The pig ear was a means through which Nadine became aggressive toward the cats, much the way she would if she were lying next to Gail and a cat, usually Romeo, but any of the others, as well, tried to get on Gail's lap. This was a small transition, protecting something at a distance. Soon, Nadine was sitting next to Gail on the couch and protecting the pig ear from there.

Accompanying this, Nadine started positioning herself in transition points throughout the house, at the top or bottom of the stairs, in the doorways to the living room where Gail and I sat. It wasn't coincidental. Sometimes she even placed herself in the cat room doorway at breakfast time, ignoring her own food in trying to prevent the cats from getting to theirs. This was the first indication that there was more involved than simply protecting something of her own, like the pig ear or her food. In fact, she wasn't protecting her food, but preventing the cats from getting to their food, and willing to postpone her own breakfast to do it!

For their part, the cats made associations about Nadine's eating. Everyone was fed breakfast, but only Nadine was fed dinner. Nonetheless, Veronica noticed when I fed Nadine dinner and began requesting me in the cat room when I fed Nadine. Now, during Nadine's dinner, any or all of the cats might rush to the kitchen and ask to be fed in the cat room. I give them dry food and pet them while they eat. However mechanical, Veronica had to associate Nadine's feeding with her own; she had to recognize *feeding*, by sight, sound, or smell, and then the others had to notice or follow or both.

Whatever the cat room *meant* to Nadine was indiscernible. She knew that the cats ate in the cat room; though she never ate there, she had to smell the food and recognize eating. On Saturday, tuna day for the cats, I let Nadine lick out the tuna can, but I only gave it to her outside the cat room. Even if blocking access to the cat room was simply motivated by domination, it had to be motivated by a drive greater than eating her own food, food that sat in front of here ten feet away; she was, instead, preventing them from getting to their food, and it was done in the doorway, implying an understanding of the access to the room, i.e. she didn't stand in front of the cat bench, in front of the food itself, food she couldn't reach and never ate; she was preventing them from getting in the room by blocking access to it. Precisely what she was doing, I don't know, but it required a synthetic string of icons to do it. Anyway, I chased her away; in other cases, other situations where she began blocking them, the cats simply entered a room some other way or jumped up onto something.

Then another set of transitions occurred. Eventually, Nadine stopped eating pigs' ears altogether and began leaving them around the house, in the doorway between the living room and the bedroom, the doorway to Marlena's room (Cheese's favorite room), the front door and back door, both of which we left open when we were home, the pet door, even the doorway to the cat room. When I stopped giving her pigs' ears, because there were unchewed pigs' ears everywhere, she started leaving her snack toy in the strategic spots, then went to her toy box and began leaving old bones and stuffed toys in the doorways or at the top or bottom of the stairs. If I moved them, she put them back.

The cats either failed to perceive or ignored these gestures, walking right past these objects if Nadine wasn't present to "protect" them, though as I've noted, Veronica's behavior changed toward Nadine; besides demonstrating prey in front of her, in Nadine's absence she began rolling on her back in front of the toy or pig ear and even grabbing stuffed toys and placing them on her stomach and rolling around with them. Nadine responded to this. While continuing to harass the other cats when they approached her toys, she let Veronica sniff them and pass by. In any case, there were too many marked places to guard them all and the cats, taking advantage of not understanding Nadine's "signing" just ignored the toys if Nadine wasn't there to "protect" them.

Again, it's too easy to try to unpack that sequence by using folk psychology, i.e. that Nadine somehow acknowledged Veronica's deference. Gail speculated that it might be because the other cats tried to sit on her lap while Veronica only sat on mine. Then again, though the last to arrive in the ménage, Veronica has most clearly claimed me; she's *my* cat, and in the politics of alliance, Nadine might be deferring to me. Cats, especially female cats, as I've argued, can be politically sophisticated. More simply, if I were to scold Nadine for harassing a cat, and I sometimes do, though without any consistency, I would be most likely to scold her for chasing after my kitty, Veronica. Given all the varieties of interaction and chaos around our house, even if Nadine's response is simply behavioral, it at least requires discernment, and then there's Veronica's response, sniffing things to which she previously showed no interest.

But what I wanted to talk about, though it's taken me a long time to get there, is the transition in Nadine's behavior from *protecting* an object like the pig ear to using it to protect something else, as well as the demonstration of a number of other cognitive-emotional transitions. Dogs often behave possessively around food, they'll protect what they have or even take it from others, other dogs, certainly a cat, even a child. This is done with aggression, growling, even snapping if it comes to that. They sneak and steal food, too. As well, they develop similar protective behavior concerning objects, demonstrating possessive behavior toward objects they perceive as their own, though there are variations. H.D. did not play with toys, yet she'd gather all of Piccolo's toys under the dining room table and lie down with them, Piccolo whining in the center of the room.

Nadine has a toy box where we put her toys when we clean up. Aside from showing depressed behavior if she perceives that both Gail and I are preparing to leave the house, that is, moping and retreating to her spot in the corner of the couch—she doesn't get up to follow us to the door to say good-bye—she might gather the toys she has laying around the house in the center of the living room, including a pig ear, and lie down with them, her chin on the ground, her eyes, well, doleful. As well, she'll protect these objects from other dogs who visit. She'll even fight for them. More so, Nadine demonstrates that she distinguishes the difference between her objects and Marlena's, Gail's, or mine, even if those objects resemble hers, say one of my rubber dinosaurs as opposed to her rubber chicken.

This act of taking possession of and, further, distinguishing between objects as hers and not hers, is cognitive-emotional and requires a semiotic process. She must distinguish *kinds* of objects and respond to them as hers or not hers, even if these objects are similar, possibly interpreting our behavior in regard to them. Her toys are given to her, mine are not, though if it were a bone, i.e. food, she might cross the line and snatch it if it were left alone. But her behavior in such a case is very different from her behavior in taking a snack from my hand or taking a toy from another dog. She will, in fact, move with a degree of stealth, glancing around to make sure she's not being watched. Once snatched, she'll skulk off and hide with it. Different behavior is displayed in this case because very different cognitive-emotional processes are at work in regard to her disposition toward the object. Again, this is behavior that any dog owner observes commonly, every day.

In the case of Nadine's use of her objects to mark or protect, a transition from making iconic distinctions to enacting symbolic behavior occurs. From identifying an object as hers, and protecting it with her body, she moved to protecting the object at a distance. Somehow, at that point, she made the transition that the object itself, the pig ear, was warding off the cats, not her own aggressive behavior around the pig ear. That's the inexplicable leap. Her behavior toward the pig ear, which she originally guarded, was now transferred to the ear itself, as if it would ward off cats on its own. That power was somehow transferred to the pig ear itself, and then to any other object she perceived as hers. In that cognitive-emotional leap she moved from perceiving the object as *mine* to perceiving the object as *me*, possibly a basic, mammalian totemic leap of imbuing objects with our meaning so they might operate in our stead.

In the process Nadine had to recognize places of entry, doorways, pet doors, stairways, for placing the pig ear or toy there. And in the way that Mucha Plata generalized individual instances of food into the concept of food in general, Nadine had to generalize from the pig ear to all of the objects she identified as hers and use them the same way. This is a leap from iconic recognition to symbolic behavior, in this case, even communication, even if her interpreters, the cats, appeared oblivious, at least at first. Soon at least one other sentient creature in the house, besides Gail and me, perceived something was going on because Veronica began behaving toward the pig ear and toys the way she did around me, flipping and demonstrating her stomach near them. Then, not too long later, dead rodents began appearing next to the toys in the doorways. It's hard to speculate on the level of the semiotic miscommunication, but I surmised the perpetrator to be Romeo who often goes out on the poop deck and leaves his feces next to Nadine's. Twenty-five years ago, my cat Mr. Puff, who by attrition briefly became our only cat, did that in our yard every time we adopted a dog. Back to Nadine, after four years of running the trails, she's became more domineering and began to respond aggressively if another dog was aggressive toward her. Much like H.D., she's now begun urinating on top of other dogs' urination and defecating on top of their feces.

I am yet trying to talk about territorial behavior translating into jealousy, an emotion that requires a little more than mechanical/instinctive territorial possession behavior, whatever that it is. Jealousy seems to have its roots there. For domestic animals there are core behaviors that change in the domestic context, behavior *toward* us and because of their interaction with us. Sitting on my lap or sitting on the back of a cow or sitting on blanket or warm pad or sitting in the sun all might be part of a natural behavioral nexus of seeking comfort, seeking heat, but my cats often come to my lap for affection as well, not just heat. At times it would appear that sitting on my lap is a political alliance.

You could speculate that it comes from a core combination of heat seeking and grooming, though, in fact, most cats won't stay on your lap for long at all because you move around too much. Mine, when the petting is done, move off my lap and sit on the hassock, next to my feet. That's a power spot, in terms of territory, though not as important as my chair when I'm not in it. At the dining table, Gail's open chair is Romeo's. Cheese might try to occupy it, but more often he sat in the chair Marlena once occupied.

A spot in the sunlight is not perceived as territory and one cat, regardless of hierarchy, will lie down next to another to sleep in the sun. In terms of the cats, most of the power spots in the house are defined by Romeo and those are defined by his relationship to humans: the counter culture, the edge of the dining table across from Gail, the coffee table across from Gail, his "spot" on the bed now, even Gail herself, though these are not permanent, but fluid. If Cheese found a spot that Romeo generally ignored, say, near the wood stove, Romeo might decide it's important enough to chase him away and occupy it. Cheese would find another spot, say my dining chair or Gail's, then Romeo might challenge that. Of course, not even Romeo can be several places at once, but he never made the transition, like Nadine, to marking his spots with objects, in fact I've never seen a cat do that. Gail is more important to him than any other of his spots that he isn't occupying. She's really important to Nadine, too, and the two of them will sleep next to each other, head to head, on Gail's spot on the couch when Gail isn't home.

Meanwhile, back at my chair and hassock, those are cat spots and the dogs we've had have all respected that whether I'm occupying those places or not. Cats go there, not dogs. Nonetheless, if Yoko, the lowest animal in the hierarchy, is sleeping on the hassock, spot number two, Nadine might poke her with her nose. Yoko, who defers to everyone, including Nadine in most situations, will respond violently when that happens. Nadine, though generally not a participant in cat politics, yet perceives a number of these power spots, especially if they relate to Gail. If the Cheese, who generally ignored Nadine, decided to sleep on Gail's dining chair, Nadine might poke at him and he'd respond with hisses and strikes, eventually moving to Marlena's chair. If he's on my dining chair, Nadine leaves him alone. Nor does Nadine bother anyone who's in my reading chair. This pluralectic develops due to Nadine's deep attachment to Gail, her perception of my alliance with the cats, and the fact that my attention is not as important to her.

Animals don't pet each other. Of course, we have hands. That's what they're for. Their relationship with our hands, perceived by all domestic animals as the source of affection and food, is natural enough (horses will check your hands for food and even your pockets), is a cultural relationship peculiar to their relationships with us, not each other.

If you have more than one animal, they compete for your presence, your space, your attention. Horses do it with each other, though for the most part seem to ignore other animals, like dogs, though the first time I brought HD, a very dominant female dog, to the ranch where I kept Jackie O, HD, perceiving all the attention I was giving to this other animal, waited for me to walk away from Jackie, then stood in front of her and barked and growled. Jackie struck her with her front hoof and sent her rolling. After that they ignored each other. I don't think Nikki would ever strike a dog, however provoked, and I don't know how she'd respond to my attention to other horses, but Jackie O found my attention to any other horse intolerable. If another horse came near me, she attacked her, or him.

In that regard, I began trail riding with Nikki by always going out with other riders. Nikki always sped ahead, as well as spooked and shied, or, if following, spun and tried to run the other way. As I graduated to going out on my own I found that Nikki calmed down considerably and I began to consider that her behavior had less to do with being racy and spooky and more with her desire to be alone with me, or at least away from the other people and horses. Admittedly, that's pretty speculative.

Jealousy, I suppose, is more raw than love, less complex, but in humans, like love, it's perpetuated by our ability to think about our beloved object, usually another man or woman, in their absence, e.g. my bout of jealousy when Gail had dinner with the Nobel Laureate. Nadine isn't possessive of Gail and aggressive toward Romeo when Gail isn't present, though Romeo is likely to lie in one of his Gail domination spots when Gail isn't around, or sleep on her discarded newspaper or clothes. There's more precise behavior, too. Any cat might try to get between you and the book you're reading. But if Gail is reading the newspaper and not permitting him to sit on her lap, then Romeo will sit on a part of the newspaper she isn't reading, generalizing from the material in her hand, a newspaper, to the similar material. He does the same with books, magazines, letters, bills, etc. If Gail puts it in front of her eyes, Romeo will sit on it or something like it. It's possible that the first connection made by Romeo was immediate and visceral, i.e. the lap, but a transition was made to the things and kinds of things looked at, this eventually including the TV some distance away, something that was never on Gail's lap.

Nadine, (and probably your dog, too) is irrevocably intolerant of any other dog who enters our yard, even the dogs of friends or relatives. She might whine and cry, but most likely she growls and attacks them. As anyone might say, any of us folk psychologists anyway, she's jealous, and angry, too.

A Moment: I'm sitting in my chair with Romeo asleep at my feet on the hassock. Yoko Dodo has leapt onto the coffee table and sits now on its edge. My lap is open, but Romeo covers the hassock. Older now, Yoko won't make the leap over him to my lap. For a few minutes she looks at Romeo, then my lap, then at Romeo, then my lap. Now she scans the width of Romeo and the hassock, back and forth. Then, finally, she steps on the edge of the hassock near Romeo's tail.

She moves very slowly, pausing with each step like the cat stepping over the flower pot in the William Carlos Williams' poem. She crosses the hassock to my shins, then walks into my lap. She *wanted* to sit on my lap. She had to *choose* a route.

SYMPATHY

Back in college I had an English professor, a novelist, who hated the word *empathy*. Back then, as he pointed out, it wasn't even in the dictionary. Well now it is. In fact, its use has become so prevalent that people seldom use the word sympathy anymore. We're all empathizing now. Sympathy is something almost completely reserved for condolences. And, in fact, sympathy and empathy are very different things.

My Oxford American Dictionary defines *empathy* as "capacity to identify with a person or object." *Sympathy* like this: "1, a state of being simultaneously affected with the same feeling as another. b capacity for this. 2, compassion or commiseration; condolences. 3, agreement in opinion or desire." The line here is between *identifying with someone's feelings*, empathy, and being *simultaneously affected by the same feeling*, sympathy. But it's an important line. In current cognitive ethology, the line between animals and humans is now called Theory of Mind or ToM, which requires that an individual realizes that another individual's mental states can be different from their own, thus the capacity to self-consciously empathize with another being constitutes understanding what they are feeling. You are sad, I recognize your sadness, because your head is bowed and you are weeping. I understand it by remembering my own times of sadness and respond to you by comforting you.

Of course, as soon as we employ the criterion of self-consciousness, the game is up for the brutes. ToM is Cartesianism with a shift in rhetoric, once again demanding language and self-consciousness as the criteria of cognition and emotion. In fact, animals pretty blatantly lack ToM. When Romeo tries to sleep on top of me at night, I might have to knock him off of me a dozen times and hold him down with my free arm to get him to lie next to me and stay put, until he wakes up and gets back on top of me. Cats are notorious examples of, colloquially, not giving a shit what we think. When I take Nadine for a ride in my truck on the way for our walk, she licks my ear and my neck, she licks my hand, she paws my wrist, she puts her head in my lap; when I guard the shifting console, she puts her paw on my hand. Four years of yelling "No!" and pushing her away hasn't put a stop to it. She has no idea or care about what *I want*. Interestingly, I can't play the radio either, because if I touch it, she paws it, changing the channel and if I change it back, she hits it again. If I don't turn on the radio, she doesn't paw it. This is following behavior (not imitation). More importantly, though Nadine can't empathize with me, i.e. understand that I'm driving or more so put herself in my place and understand that I don't want her attention, we are in a very real sense in sympathy with each other, both anticipating our run in the hills and, together, happy about it.

Nadine has come to understand the cues of "getting ready." She sits and waits in her seat after we've stopped, not jumping up to go until I turn off the engine. If Gail is out of the house and Nadine has come down to my office to be with me, when I turn off my computer she jumps up and runs out the door. As well, if I don't turn off the computer, but simply get up with my cup (to get more coffee or tea from inside the house), she remains on the floor and waits for my return. However mechanical those responses might be, however rote the learning, she has had to pay attention and differentiate between my leaving the office behavior and my behavior that indicates I'm going to return.

What prohibitions my domestic animals have are the development of continued and repetitious reinforcement, though as we all know, cats can only be trained to stay off the table when we're around and dogs to not steal food from the counter in front of our faces. To recognize the difference between my presence and my absence is a semiotic act. As well, the context changes the behavior. You might, if you hide, notice your dog look around to check that you aren't there before she makes her move for the food. Sneaking behavior is a close corollary, derivative of hunting behavior. Piccolo would crouch and creep into the cat room to snatch cat feces from the litter, something he'd be scolded for if caught. A cat will move silently and extremely slowly to avoid detection, though they might attempt it right in front of your face. You might want to say, well that's just stupid, but if you own cats, then you know they can sometimes quite effectively sneak onto your lap or right up to your plate if you're distracted by conversation or the TV.

Back to empathy and sympathy. Indeed, empathy requires ToM, but sympathy does not. In the same way that my animals recognize that I'm angry (sometimes even before I do), they see my expressions, my violent, quick movement, and they run away whether they've done anything wrong or not. As well, they recognize affectionate behavior toward them; I make gentle sounds, I put my hand out or even sit on the floor. In this case our feelings, our mutual affection, are shared.

Certainly, that could be rote behavior, acquired after many repetitions, although I never strike them; my angry behavior does not have physical consequences for them. It might simply scare them. Nonetheless, they must distinguish among angry behavior, friendly behavior, neutral behavior. In this behavior recognition lies the fundament of sympathetic action.

If you're sad or depressed or hurt, your dog will likely come to you and lie down next to you. She won't try to get you to play, but will likely behave as you are behaving, moping, say. This is sympathetic behavior. It's behavior *like* mine, based on my behavior. I mope, she mopes. She doesn't need to perceive why I'm moping, yet she does share it, and it develops out of the intimacy of her constant observation of my behavior. The semiotics is visceral. Anecdotally, on several occasions, when I have been extremely sad, ill, or hurt, Nadine brought me her pig ear and laid it next to me, then she lay down. The day Mucha Plata was killed, I couldn't face burying her right away and wrapped her in a towel, leaving her on the picnic table on our deck. That night, her son, the Cheese, who had never sat on my lap before, came in the window from the deck, walked across the room to me and, without purring, silently lay down on my lap.

Sympathy grows out of the acute perception of our behavior, behavior that is very important to gratifying their needs, the impulse to follow, and the conversation of gestures, similar to the joyous behavior displayed by dogs, and cats, too, and even me, when I return home. We're happy to see each other and we jump and pet and hug and bark and mew and prance together. It's shared emotion that doesn't require the self-conscious act of perceiving my emotion, internalizing it, than acting in concert with it. It's simultaneous shared feeling.

Confusing sympathy and empathy creates problems even in scientific research. On Tuesday, July 4, 2006 an article appeared in the *New York Times* entitled "Message From Mouse to Mouse: I Feel Your Pain" saying that scientists studying mice had "found strong evidence of empathy in those who saw fellow creatures suffering."

> In a series of experiments, reported in the journal *Science* neuroscientists demonstrated that mice suffered significantly more distress when they saw a familiar mouse suffering than when they saw the same kind of pain in a stranger.
>
> Researchers call this shared suffering "emotional contagion" and consider it a primitive and necessary precursor to human empathy.

They then allude to similar observations in orangutans, chimps, dolphins and elephants. Though praised by primatologist Frans B. M. de Waal, who speculates that human morality has its roots in the social mores of the higher primates, the article yet fails to address the difference between sympathy and empathy or suggest that the capacity for sympathy is the precursor to empathy; without the tools of semiotic cognitive-emotional gesturing the researchers are reduced to the mysterious and seemingly inexplicable "emotional contagion" as a biological seed of empathy.

The sympathetic behavior of the mice occurred between animals who were intimate with each other, shared space and feeding, possibly grooming, followed each other in their cage, their sympathy an impulse of following and sharing and the conversation of gestures, developed, like a lot of social behavior because it's mutually gratifying.

In this garden of sympathy lies the seeds of other emotions, like appreciation and gratitude, or that odd accretion in the arc of horse training when your animal seems to take pride in her performance. Social emotions do not require self-consciousness. In fact, without it, they aren't articulated as definitively, but, as I have argued, they are behaviors, not things, not things possessed by minds, but observable behaviors accompanied by cognitive-emotional processes.

It's difficult to find your footing in the arena of proto-social emotion. It's more complex than anger, fear, excitement (joy), gratification from pleasure, and others, though these are aroused in social contexts, too. Social emotions land in the philosophical area where cognitive ethologists like David Bekoff and Franz de Waal wish to see animal behavior as an evolutionary continuum toward human behavior. For de Waal, in the social impulses of primates lie the harbingers of human moral and political behavior and culture, for Bekoff, the emotions that spur animal interaction go deeper still, into the basic mammalian emotional matrices. Bekoff's most resilient example is play behavior in his Ridgebacks, where the exchange of pouncing, yipping, and even nipping is regulated in response to the behavior of the dog's playmate, whether animal or human, a conversation of gestures, though he does not use the term. Whether Nadine has made a choice to not harm me when we play and yet will attempt to harm another dog who enters the house is less relevant than the distinction between the behaviors themselves. My cats, who brought in up to a rodent a day, were willing to sit on my lap while Ratsky shared drinks on my shoulder. The context might govern the behavior, but it doesn't refute the distinctly different behaviors, behavior nurtured in persistent social culture of domesticity, behavior we would not observe outside domestic situations.

CONCLUSION

THIS HAS BEEN A PHENOMENOLOGICAL analysis of the domestic animals I have known. Though I've offered plenty of anecdotes, I have, as well, sought to analyze elemental, paradigmatic domestic animal behavior that anyone can observe every day. I've tried to demonstrate how semiotics explains a number of these behaviors. All behavior, human and animal, find its sources in biology and circumstance, but not all behavior is reducible to one or the other or both. In fact, the attempt to reduce behavior to these spheres is as inadequate and mysterious as speculating as to what goes on in animal brains.

Semiotics explains how animals recognize images, smells, and sounds, and manipulate them to their advantage, how they figure things out, moving from one sensory image to the next. Migrating whales might sing their way across the oceans the way aboriginals sing their way across the outback, birds likely use maps and images to migrate and find stored food.

Most human action, including thought, needs neither mind, Theory of Mind, nor language to be explained, nor is it thoroughly explained by any of them. I hope to have shown that the question of self-determination in issues of cognition and abstraction is moot. Behavior, no matter how determined, can nonetheless contain cognitive processes, likely cognitive-emotional ones. Most human behaviors and animal behaviors are cognitive-emotional. Much animal behavior, as well as human behavior, demonstrates sequences of icon cognition.

The mind-body distinction and other dualisms such as languaging vs. non-languaging sentience have fed numerous misconceptions in both human and animal behavior and created paradigms that make it impossible to perceive the obvious, that behavior itself is cognitive-emotional and all sentience demonstrates this. The spider waiting on her web, the eel waiting in his cave, are waiting for prey. If there is a difference between the behavior of animals and machines, it is that the animal, in the process of desiring an effect, imposes its expectations on the environment and expects a specific response. If a machine does that as well, then it's high time we start talking about machine cognition, too.

ACKNOWLEDGMENTS

THE IDEA FOR THIS BOOK BEGAN in 1975 when as a Ph.D. candidate at the State University of New York, Buffalo I became fascinated with Jane Goodall's field work in Africa with chimpanzees as she recorded it in *In the Shadow of Man*. Previously I'd followed the Gardener's work teaching Washoe sign language (ASL) in *Psychology Today*. I was commuting to Buffalo then and living in a farmhouse outside Erie, Pennsylvania with lots of cats and dogs. I walked to a dairy farm down the road where I got my milk, very fresh, and in the winter became fascinated by the interaction of the cows and barn cats, two species that one wouldn't expect to have much interaction with each other, though, as you've read here, in a cow barn in the winter, they have reason to engage. Though I was a pretty strict behaviorist back then, I became fascinated with, well, the reasons.

As an undergrad at Allegheny College, I'd read most of *The Collected Papers of Charles Sanders Peirce* and even went so far as to construct, for my thesis, a theory of the symbolic construction of human selfhood based on Peirce's phenomenological categories and his semiotics. This interest in the socially constructed self led me to William James' *Psychology* and his theory of "The *I* and the *me*" which postulated an essential, immediate self, the *I*, and a self developed conceptually through various social interactions, the *me*. Research led me to another person who used those terms, borrowed from James, the early social psychologist George Herbert Mead, in particular *Mind, Self, and Society*. To these thinkers I'm obviously indebted.

On my way to SUNY Buffalo I spent two years studying philosophy and sociological theory at Bowling Green State University in Ohio. There I was enrolled in a yearlong course in the history of philosophy taught by a team of professors, each covering their specialty, which examined the Pre-Socratics through Hegel. The reading was almost all primary source. I learned a lot and I'm thankful to each of these teachers, but for the purposes of this book the most important encounter for me was Immanuel Kant and *The Critique of Pure Reason*. I studied Buddhism at Bowling Green in my second year, particularly the sixth century Indian philosopher Nargajuna's critique of causality, and though it didn't make me an advocate of free will (in spite of reading a lot of Sartre), my adherence to strict behavioral psychology began to erode. It might sound like I read a lot in just two years, but I did, I took courses all summer as well as during the school year and graduated with double the amount of credit hours I needed for my degree, in fact enough for degrees in both philosophy and sociology.

So, in 1975, I thought I was ready to research and write about a theory of cognition in non-human animals. My dissertation committee did not agree. They said it wasn't philosophy. I was young, tough, and immortal. I quit the program and decided to become a novelist. Ten years later, writing every day, I became a published one.

Years passed. After spending time in the work-a-day world, I returned to the academy. I earned an M.A. in literature at the University of California, Davis, then a Ph.D. at the University of Utah. I still had a fascination with the theory of language and at Utah studied Derrida and Post-Structuralism. I became a college professor. I've published sixteen books. I teach to this day, mostly fiction writing. I've had lots of domestic animals around me for almost fifty years. I began riding horses in 1995 and acquired my first horse, Jackie O, then. She was a fascinating animal, furious, fractious, and powerful. Training her, taming her, everyday, got me interested in the ways she behaved, because there were times, moments, when her behavior meant my life. She could be dangerous.

I had a wonderful trainer, Paddy Korb Warner, to whom I am deeply indebted, who sometimes looked at me when I was atop my difficult mare and said, "I wonder what she's thinking." I began to wonder, too.

Among the books I read in that sojourn, besides detailed training books, were Henry Blake's *Thinking With Horses*; Don Blazer's *Natural Western Riding*; Stephen Budiansky's *The Nature of Horses*; Sharon Camarillo's *Barrel Racing*; Ray Hunt's *Thinking Harmony With Horses*; John Lyons' *Communicating With Cues: The Rider's Guide to Training and Problem Solving (Parts I, II, and III)*, *Private Lessons*, and *Perfectly Practical Advice on Western Horsemanship*; Pat Parelli's *Western Horsemanship* (which taught me a ton about ground work); McK.Camp II's *Horses and Horsemanship in the Athenian Agora*; Monty Roberts' *The Man*

Who Listens to Horses; Michael J. Rosen's (ed.) *Horse People*; W Dayton Sumner's *Breaking Your Horse's Bad Habits*; and Xenophon's *The Art of Horsemanship*. Most of these books introduced me to the new "Soft Training" techniques that emphasized understanding the animal instead of inflicting discipline, i.e. understanding how horses think.

I'd now entered the world of presumed animal cognition and I was combining my notes and developing what forms that might take. On my way I looked at a lot of research in the field of cognitive ethology, as well as philosophical discussions, some of which I've cited in the text. Though much has been done in recent years, I found that no one had yet offered a theory of animal cognition. I found the books in the following Selected Bibliography interesting and I'm grateful to these researchers and writers for their work.

Deep personal thanks Molly Bendall, Daniel Tiffany, Marlena Dali, Gail Wronsky, and all the animals who have enriched my life.

SELECTED BIBLIOGRAPHY

Abram, David. 1996. *The Spell of the Sensuous.* New York: Pantheon.

Agamben, Giorgio. *The Open: Man and Animal.* 2002. Stanford, California: Stanford University Press. Translated from the Italian by Kevin Attell, 2004.

Augustine. *The Confessions.*

Bailley, Jean-Christophe. 2011. *The Animal Side.* New York: Fordham University Press. Translated from the French by Catherine Porter.

Bekoff, Marc; Allen, Colin; Burghardt, Gordon M., eds. 2002. *The Cognitive Animal.* Cambridge, MA: The MIT Press.

Bekoff, Marc. 2002. *Minding Animals.* New York: Oxford University Press.

———. 2007. *The Emotional Lives of Animals.* Novato, CA: New World Library.

Bright, Michael. 1997. *Intelligence in Animals.* London: The Reader's Digest Association.

Buchler, Justus, ed. 1955. *Philosophical Writings of Peirce.* New York: Dover.

Cheney, Dorothy L. and Seyfarth, Robert M. 1990. *How Monkeys See the World.* Chicago: The University of Chicago Press.

———. 2007. *Baboon Metaphysics.* Chicago. The University of Chicago Press.

Darwin, Charles. 1982 (1871). *The Descent of Man, and selection in Relation to Sex.* Princeton: Princeton University Press.

DeGrazia, 2002. *Animal Rights.* Oxford: Oxford University Press.

Derrida, Jacques. *The Animal That Therefore I Am.* 2006. New York: Fordham University Press. Translated from the French by David Wills, 2008.

De Wall, Franz. 2006. *Primates and Philosophers.* Princeton: Princeton University Press.

Dreary, Ian. 2001. *Intelligence.* Oxford: Oxford University Press.

Fragaszy, Dorothy M. and Pery, Susan, eds. 2003. *The Biology of Traditions.* Cambridge, UK: Cambridge University Press.

Friend, Tim. 2004. *Animal Talk.* New York: Free Press.

Fudge, Erica, *Animal*, 2002, London, Reaction Books, Ltd.

Godfrey-Smith, 2016, *Other Minds / The Octopus, The Sea, and The Deep Origins of Consciousness*, New York: Farrar, Straus, Giroux

Goodall, Jane. 1971. *In the Shadow of Man*. New York: Houghton Mifflin.

————. 1990. *Through a Window, My Thirty Years with the Chimpanzees of Gombe*. New York: Houghton Mifflin.

Grandin, Temple and Johnson, Catherine. 2005. *Animals in Translation*. New York: Scribner.

Griffin, Donald R. 1992, 2001. *Animal Minds: Beyond Cognition to Consciousness*. Chicago: The University of Chicago Press.

Hearn, Vicki. 1986. *Adam's Task*. London: Billing & Sons, Ltd.

Laland, Kevin N. and Galef, Bennet G. 2009. *The Question of Animal Culture*. Cambridge, MA: Harvard University Press.

Lund, Nick. 2002. *Animal Cognition*. East Sussex, UK: Routledge

Mason, Jeffrey and McCarthy, Susan. 1995. *When Elephants Weep*. New York: Dell Publishing.

McFarland, David. 2008. *Guilty Robots, Happy Dogs*. Oxford: Oxford University Press

Mead, George Herbert. 1934. *Mind, Self, & Society*. Chicago: Chicago University Press.

Merleau-Ponty, Maurice. *Nature: Course Notes from the College de France (1956-60)*. 1995. Evanston, Illinois: Northwestern University Press. Translated from the French by Robert Vallier, 2003.

Montgomery, Sy. *Walking with the Great Apes* (Jane Goodall, Diane Fossey, Birute Galdikas). 1991. New York: Houghton Mifflin.

Narby, Jeremy. 2005. *Intelligence in Nature*. New York: Penguin Group.

Parelli, Pat. 1993. *Western Horsemanship*. Colorado Springs, CO: Western Horsemanship, Inc.

Peirce, Charles Sanders. *The Collected Papers*.

Radner, Daisie and Michael. 1996. *Animal Consciousness*. New York: Prometheus Books.

Scholes and Kelly. *The Nature of Narrative*.

Singer, Peter. *Animal Liberation*. 1975. New York: Harper Collins.

Uexküll, Jakob von. "A stroll Through the World of Animals and Men: A Picture Book of Invisible Worlds." In *Instinctive Behavior: The Development of a Modern Concept*, ed. and trans. Claire H. Schiller, 5-80. New York: International Universities Press, Inc., 1957.

Wilson, E. O. 1975. *Sociobiology*. Cambridge, MA: Harvard University Press.

Woodward, Wendy. 2001. *The Animal Gaze*. Johannesburg, South Africa: Wits University Press.

CPSIA information can be obtained
at www.ICGtesting.com
Printed in the USA
LVHW092308270620
659164LV00007B/117/J